Never Quite a Soldier

David Lemon

Having been brought up in some of the wilder parts of Africa David Lemon has a special relationship with the continent. Uncomfortable in towns, he has rowed a tiny dinghy the length of Kariba and back again, cycled from Nairobi to Cape Town and spent months alone in the Zambezi Valley. Outside his police career, he has been a salesman, legal clerk, school bursar, cricket coach, charter skipper, lecturer and gardener. He has eight books to his name and his passion in life is elephants. Between adventures he runs two small businesses in the English Cotswolds with his wife Lace.

Never Quite a Soldier

*A Rhodesian Policeman's War
1971 - 1982*

David Lemon

GALAGO

GALAGO BOOKS

Galago books are published by Galago Publishing (1999) (Pty) Ltd
PO Box 404, Alberton, 1450, Republic South Africa
Web address: www.galago.co.za

Galago Books are distributed by Lemur Books (Pty) Ltd
PO Box 1645, Alberton, 1450, Republic South Africa
Tel: (Int + 2711— local 011) 907-2029. Fax 869-0890
Email: lemur@mweb.co.za

This edition published by Galago, August 2006 as
Never Quite a Soldier: A Rhodesian Policeman's War 1971-1982
by David Lemon
© David Lemon
ISBN 1-919854-21-5
Map © Madelain Davies
First published by Albida Books, Stroud, UK, 2000
David Lemon has asserted his moral right
to be identified as the author of this work.

No part of this publication may be reproduced, stored in
or introduced into any information or retrieval system, or
transmitted in any form or by any means (electronic, mechanical,
photocopying, recording or otherwise) with the prior
permission in writing of the publishers. Any person who does
any unauthorised act in relation to this publication renders
themselves liable to criminal prosecution and a claim
for civil damages.

Typeset by Galago in 11 point Times New Roman

Colour and black and white photographs reproduced
by Rapid Repro Parkhurst, Johannesburg

Printed and bound by CTP Book Printers, Cape

Front cover design and colour corrections by Justyn and Madelain Davies

Cover photograph: (the late) Detective Chief Inspector Henry Wolhuter
Depicts a Security Force patrol picking up spoor after
a kraal head and his family had been burnt alive in their huts by ZANLA

For Missy,
who gave me her love as well as her unstinting support
and showed great courage throughout.

And

For all Black Boots wherever they are,
but particularly for those who died in the fight.

Books by David Lemon

Ivory Madness
Africa's Inland Sea
Kariba Adventure
Rhino
Man Eater
Hobo rows Kariba
Killer Cat
Never Quite a Soldier

Acknowledgements

My thanks are due to the late David (or was it George?) Morgan for his help in editing the manuscript, Barry Woan (another Charlie Nine) for putting me straight on a number of matters and Lace for listening and coping with my tears.

Others helped in various ways and to them I will always be grateful.

Picture credits
Photographs between pages 97-112 and 177-192

The following are credited for the use of photographs: The publishers of *Breaking the Silence*, Brick Bryson, BSAP (CID Photographic Section), the late Andy Gray, Paddy Hartdegan, Hoffie Hofmeister, the late Don Hollingworth, David Lemon collection, Clive Mocke, Ministry of Information (Rhodesian), Bruce Rooken Smith, Peter Stiff collection, Barry Woan and the late Henry Wolhuter. The copyright holders of some photographs remain unacknowledged although the publishers have made every effort to establish authorship, which has been lost in the mists of time or blown away by the winds of war. However, the publishers will gladly amend or add credits in subsequent editions and make the necessary arrangements with those photographers who were not known at the time of going to press, or who had not been traced.

Author's Note

This is a purely personal account of a nasty piece of southern African history and all the sometimes jaundiced opinions expressed about personalities and events are my own. I have changed the names of a few characters to avoid embarrassment and in some cases to protect them from a still paranoid authority. As a former copper I know that memory can be selective, but I kept a journal through much of the period described and I have had two decades to ponder on this story.

I have tried to stick to the unvarnished truth exactly as I remember it.

Contents

Chapter		Page
	Acknowledgements	6
	Credits for photographs and illustrations	7
	Author's note	7
	Foreword	10
	Name changes since Zimbabwe's independence	11
	Map of Rhodesia/Zimbabwe	12
	Prologue	13
1	Cat in a tall tree	15
2	Surprises in Salisbury	20
3	Early days in Marandellas	25
4	Racism and promotion	34
5	Politics and the Pearce Commission	42
6	Reluctant soldier	46
7	Sunshine and sadness	58
8	Real live admiral	65
9	Race relations and VIPs	73
10	Member in Charge	79
11	Royal Visit Farm and the District Nurse	83

12	Horror at Royal Visit Farm	95
13	First photographic section	97-112
13	A man of war	122
14	And of peace	130
15	Missionaries and murder	134
16	Violence and fear in the Mangwende	149
17	Charlie Nine	162
18	War in the Wiltshire	171
	Second photographic section	177-192
19	Cease-fire	205
20	Soldiers of the Bishop	210
21	Bitterness and boredom	214
22	All change for peace	219
23	Travelling cop	224
24	Horror at Entumbane	230
25	Back to Bulawayo	242
26	The end of the road	250
27	Never quite a soldier	253
	Glossary	258
	Index	259

Foreword

The author was a District Branch policeman in the elite British South Africa Police of Rhodesia during the Bush War days. His first serious involvement with the war came when he was member-in-charge of Macheke Police Station. Groups of infiltrating ZANLA guerrillas moved into the area and embarked on a murderous campaign that targeted both black and white civilians. The war throughout the country escalated and indiscriminate acts of terror like the bomb detonated in the Manica Road branch of Woolworth's that killed 12 black shoppers and wounded 76 more, the June 1978 massacre by ZANLA of nine white missionaries and four children — one a three week old baby, the shooting down of a Viscount airliner and the subsequent massacre of survivors and countless other terrible incidents decided him to join the Support Unit of the BSAP, generally known as the Black Boots. This elite unit of 12 companies and a half company of mounted men was made up of fighting policemen, most of them black.

The Black Boots, as smart or smarter than the Brigade of Guards on parade, and as fighting men who matched or surpassed any elite fighting unit around the world, were never exposed to the same glamorous publicity as was given to their military comrades-in-arms. But this is not unusual because it is the culture of policemen everywhere in the Western world to get on with the job without seeking publicity. And that is exactly what the author, as commander of Charlie Company, and all the other companies of Black Boots did.

Lemon fought through numerous engagements and contacts until the war ended with the elections in 1980 that saw Robert Mugabe come to power in a country that became the new state of Zimbabwe.

For him the fighting was far from over and in November 1980 Charlie Company along with the Rhodesian African Rifles were engaged in serious fighting attempting to keep ZIPRA and ZANLA guerrillas away from each others throats in Bulawayo. This occurred when both factions were being integrated into the new regular army. Fighting again broke out in February 1981 when ZIPRA forces failed to capture Bulawayo from government forces.

Meanwhile, Mugabe had formed his 5-Brigade — comprising ex-ZANLA guerrillas trained by the North Koreans — which embarked on a campaign of terrorism and genocide against Ndebele civilians in Matabeleland. They murdered their way through the province killing an estimated 15 000 to 30 000 people.

The author had no accurate idea what was going on because of a veil of secrecy drawn by the government, but rumours abounded. Massacre survivors said openly 'it was the soldiers'. This decided him to leave the unit and resume his career as a duty policeman. He found to his consternation that standards had plummeted. Most new recruits were either ex-ZANLA or ZIPRA cadres lacking in educational standards. Some boasted of having passed police courses in the Soviet Union, but that was nothing to boast about. Then a black sergeant was fast-tracked to chief superintendent to become his new commander — and as a chief inspector he was instructed to train him!

This was the last straw and he resigned from what was once a proud force and left the country.

Name changes since Zimbabwe's independence in 1980

Old Name	New Name
Chipinga	Chipinge
Chibi	Chivi
Enkeldoorn	Chivu
Essexvale	Isigodini
Fort Victoria	Masvingo
Gwelo	Gweru
Hartley	Chegutu
Mashaba	Mashava
Marandellas	Marondera
Nuanetsi	Mwenezi
Salisbury	Harare
Shabani	Zvishavani
Sinoia	Chinhoyi
Sipolilo	Guruve
Umtali	Mutare
Vila Salazar	Sango
Wankie	Hwange

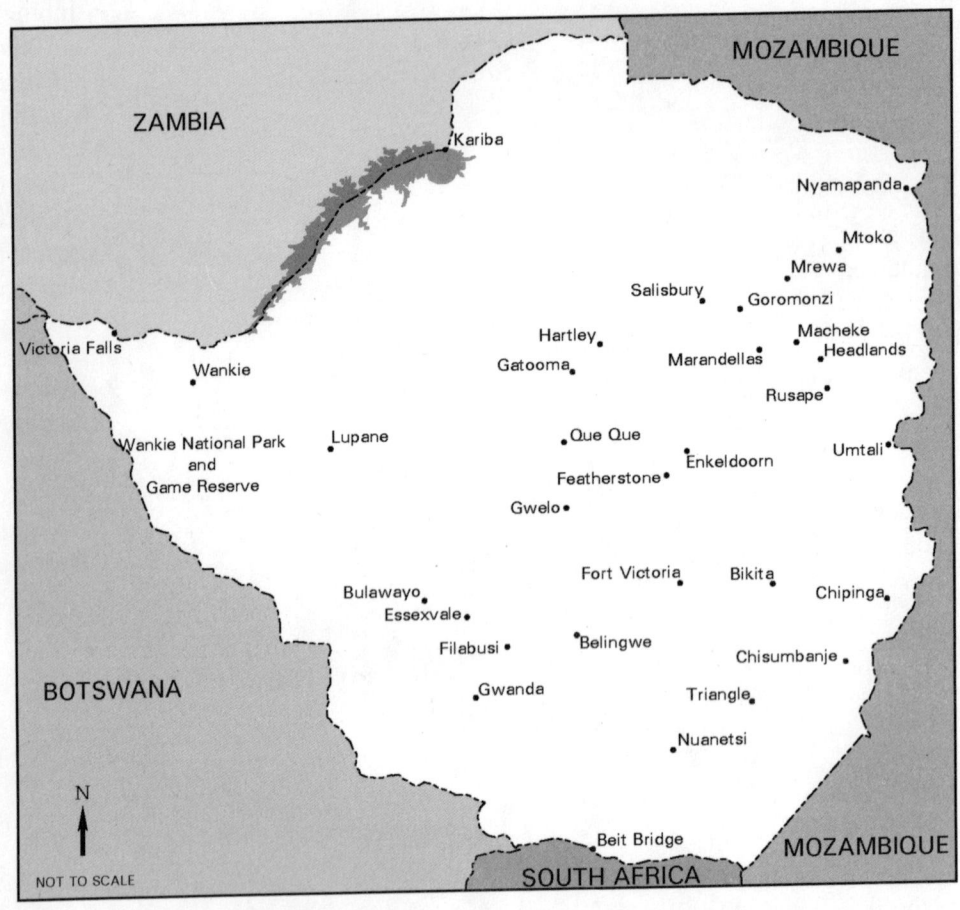

Map of Rhodesia showing centres mentioned in book.
Name changes after Zimbabwe's independence are shown on previous page.

Prologue

Fighting Cop

The parade square was nothing more than a patch of flattened waste ground between two fields of half grown maize. My starched shirt felt uncomfortably soggy against my back and I could feel a big lump of nervous uncertainty in my stomach. Morning parade was an essential part of company routine among Black Boots and one 116 fighting troopers were lined up for my inspection. Suddenly the war was real.

This was no longer a question of wearing fancy camouflage, moving coloured pins on a map board or listening in on distant reports of action. Whether I liked the idea or not I was a company commander in the British South Africa Police Support Unit. We were based deep in the operational area and my future decisions might well mean life or death to many of the hard-bitten fighting men on that dusty parade ground.

At that moment, they were all looking at me with thinly disguised contempt, no doubt taking in my spectacles, my thinning hair and the newness of my camouflage uniform. I was a uniformed copper who had been put in charge of their destiny and they were waiting for me to prove that I was good enough to lead them in a combat situation.

Company Sergeant Major Lazarus — a lumbering giant of a man — crashed to a dusty halt in front of me, saluted and roared his greeting.

'Charlie Company all present and ready for your inspection, Sah.'

Startled doves rocketed in panic from nearby trees.

'Carry on, Sar'nt Major.'

A distant rooster crowed derisively at the puny nature of my reply. Trying to keep the sweat off my glasses and look like a hardened soldier, I followed the CSM and stopped before the first man in the front rank. Built like the side of a mountain, the trooper towered above my own hundred and eighty-centimetre frame and I wondered what to say. It was the first time in my life I had been on the authoritative side of a military parade and this raw-boned giant was hardly what my fluttering confidence needed. The creases on his trousers could have been used to carve virgin rock and his shirt had been ironed to perfection. His boots gleamed a deep, glossy black beneath their dusty patina and his eyes were fixed on a point in far horizons. I gulped as I took it all in.

'Name?' I rasped, trying to sound more confident than I felt.

'Constable 19776 Totohwiyo, Sah.'

The words look pretty innocuous here but they were bawled into the air above my head and I flinched at the onslaught to my eardrums. A few more doves fled for distant safety and I still had another 115 of these trained killers to inspect. My heart quailed at the prospect.

Steeling myself to remain cool, calm and collected, I reached up to flick imaginary dust from Constable 19776 Totohwiyo's cap and his muddy brown eyes dropped to regard me with amused contempt. He knew that I was finding fault for the sake of it, but then — I had come from the Uniform Branch and knew nothing about Support Unit ways. I was a mere 'Brown Boot' and had to be allowed my bit of fun.

'Where are you from Totohwiyo?' I asked quietly, determined not to let the big man intimidate me.

'Charlie Company, Sah.'

He chose to deliberately misunderstand me.

'Always been with Charlie Company, Sah.'

The explosion of sound from the final syllable cut the raucous rooster off in mid crow and I moved hurriedly along to the next man in line. I had to keep my nervousness under control or I was likely to make a complete fool of myself. If all the fighting men of Charlie Company were half as intimidating as Constable 19776 Totohwiyo, I was in for a difficult time.

Fortunately perhaps, they were not. Augustine Totohwiyo was a giant, even among Black Boots and I think it highly likely that Lazarus had placed him first in line for inspection in order to see what I was made of. The rest of the Company seemed somehow less than awe inspiring after that clamorous introduction, but I had studied their records and knew that they were a battle-hardened group of fighting coppers. They had that wary look about them that came from months of bush warfare, while many of them bore scars of combat or carried extra medal ribbons on their shirt to attest to their experience. As a brand new company commander, they would provide me with a considerable challenge.

My own experience was confined to cleaning up the aftermath of combat and making those administrative decisions that are scoffed at by fighting men on the ground. I might have worn a fancy hat and carried a swagger stick under one arm, but to these uniformed ruffians I was a mere administrator and would need to earn their respect for myself.

As I finished off that initial inspection, I prayed for the chance to prove that I was up to the task. Over the previous eight years, I had progressed with alarming rapidity from Bobby to Black Boot, from family man to fighting man but I was less than well trained and probably emotionally unsuited for the role into which I had been placed. I only hoped I could cope.

1

Cat in a tall tree

I can't say I particularly wanted to be a policeman. Arriving in England as a youthful Rhodesian in 1963, I had my sights set on becoming a teacher of maths and Latin, but nothing worked out as planned and on 16 December 1964 I joined the Gloucestershire Constabulary as a probationer constable.

There I might have stayed had it not been for a fateful speech made by Ian Douglas Smith on 11 November 1965. Just after noon, I listened to the radio while Smithy declared my country unilaterally independent. I knew nothing of politics and had not been following the arguments that led up to the UDI declaration, but for me it was a sobering moment. This was the first rebellion against British sovereignty since the American revolution of 1776 and by choosing Armistice Day, Smith was reminding the world that Rhodesia had a proud record of support for Britain in two world wars. National pride mingled with an uneasy feeling in my heart.

'There can be no happiness in this country', Smith told the world, 'while the absurd situation continues to exist where people such as ourselves, who have ruled themselves with an impeccable record for over 40 years are denied what is freely granted to other countries who have ruled themselves — in some cases — for less than a year.

'The decision we have taken today', he went on in a flat monotone that was to become so familiar, 'is a refusal by Rhodesians to sell their birthright and even if we were to surrender, does anyone believe that Rhodesia would be the last target of the communists and the Afro-Asian block?'

With those words, Smith effectively spelled out the guidelines on which the battle for Rhodesian sovereignty was to be fought. Rhodesia's fight wasn't against her own black citizens, but against communism and those African leaders who were striving to bring the country into line with their own Marxist policies. At the time, communism was a dirty word in the Western world and I felt a surge of pride that my little country was to lead the fight against it. I was very naive in those days.

The British Prime Minister was sorely affronted by Smith's declaration and forecast somewhat fatuously that the rebellion would be over in weeks rather than months. Smith made the similarly untenable boast that 'never in a thousand years' would he hand Rhodesia over to rule by a black government. Both men were horribly wrong, but many innocent men and women were to die violently before this was finally admitted by their respective followers.

For a young Rhodesian exile, Smithy's declaration was an immediate call to the flag. I was 21-years-old, somewhat innocent in the ways of the world and terribly idealistic. Patriotic pride beat strongly in my chest and although the word 'treason' was disturbing, an expensive private education had inculcated traditional values in my soul and I knew where my duty lay.

Colonialism had become a dirty word in Britain, but I had no doubt as to the rectitude of my forebears' ideals and I didn't care what the rest of the world thought. Men like Rhodes, Beit, Dr Jameson and Allan Wilson had dedicated their endeavours to England, a free and easy life and the colonial ideal. The desire to emulate their adventurous deeds beat strongly in my heart. Like most young men of my generation, I had been brought up to abhor bullying and UDI seemed to typify the fight of the little man against the bullying British. I didn't share the English susceptibility for collective guilt over Empire and media attempts to belittle my countrymen roused me to anger. After all, hadn't Smith pointed out that Rhodesians were in the front line of the battle against communism?

In truth I knew little about it, but this was an ideal focal point for my restless nature. It was barely two years since I had arrived in England and although things had not worked out as planned, I was building myself a steady career as a constable. With my new wife and a police house, I was happy to live as an Englishman, but that UDI speech upset all my dreams of domesticity. Married a year and with a baby on the way, I had immediate ideas of flying back to the rescue of my beleaguered country. My eminently sensible wife put a stop to that nonsense.

'What happens if you get killed?' Missy demanded. 'You will soon have a family to think about, remember.'

'I won't be killed.' The idea was ridiculous. 'I will be going out as a copper, not a ruddy soldier.'

She pointed out that an inexperienced 'Bobby' was hardly what Rhodesia needed and we eventually agreed that I would get a few more years service under my belt before offering my services to the British South Africa Police should the situation still warrant that action. My country could probably cope without me till then.

Brian — inevitably his second name is Douglas — was born less than a month after UDI and Graeme followed 15 months later. With a young family to support, plans for emigration were shelved and I settled down to building my career as a British policeman. I was appointed captain of the Gloucestershire Constabulary cricket team and led them to unexpected success. I also ran a boxing club for youngsters and was eventually posted to a village police station where I had responsibility for five country communities.

It wasn't a taxing life and everything seemed to be working out for the best, but I was becoming ever more restless. Events in Rhodesia were simmering and policemen had been killed in engagements with armed infiltrators from Zambia. Smith had twice been involved in talks with British Prime Minister Harold Wilson. No agreement was reached on either occasion and although I personally blamed Wilson, the reality was that the two men were just too different in background and personality to agree on anything.

My 'parishioners' seemed to support the Rhodesian cause although I was occasionally subject to ribald mockery for my colonial origins. Even the politicians seemed divided on the issue. Many of them made fact-finding visits to Africa and returned full of praise for the stand being taken by the Rhodesian people. They were invariably dismissed as radicals but every time it happened, my heart seethed with angry envy. Why should they be enjoying the sunshine and smiles of my country while I was stuck in their grey and soggy little island?

In those days police work was a secure career but it wasn't well paid. Missy scrimped and saved to bring up our sons and there was no spare cash for luxuries. We couldn't afford holidays and this constant state of penury added to my sense of frustration. I enjoyed England but my heart was in Africa. In my dreams I saw elephants, lions and the herds of wildlife that are part of my African heritage. I longed to be back home and missed the beaming smiles and friendly hospitality that are so basic a part of Rhodesian culture. Coming down stairs on a wintry morning (police houses in those days didn't have central heating) I would clean out the grate and start the coal fire burning while I longed for a 'house boy' to do the job for me. This domestic drudgery surely wasn't living.

Like all young colonials, I had been brought up with servants and could see nothing wrong with the system. If one can afford it, why not have someone else do the hard work. Having spent my boyhood in remote areas, I don't think I was particularly racist and merely looked upon black and white as different breeds of the same animal. In politically correct Britain, this was heresy yet there was more overt racism in England than ever I remembered from my own country, where the difference between races was recognised and accepted.

Enoch Powell's famous 'rivers of blood' speech was often quoted at length. 'Paki bashing' was all the rage in university towns and ethnic unrest was simmering in inner city areas. Words like 'coon', 'darkie' and spade were in vogue among my colleagues and I often wondered why Harold Wilson expended so much futile energy on my countrymen while his own were so blatantly racist.

But the main problem in my life wasn't the rights and wrongs of British racial policy. Nor was it the escalating tension in Rhodesia. It was the general boredom of my daily existence. I had joined the police service for adventure and excitement but they were in very short supply. I had seen myself waging war on dangerous criminals, facing down bank robbers with the force of my personality and — in front of an adoring family — having an array of medals pinned to my manly chest. Things didn't turn out quite like that. In my first six years as a copper, the only unusual case I dealt with was the arrest of a young man for being drunk in charge of a pram — complete with squalling infant. Apart from that, I directed traffic, issued the occasional parking ticket and played cricket whenever I could. Two events in 1971 brought my problems to a head. The first occurred a long way from Gloucestershire.

Brought up on stories of derring-do, I had been fiercely proud of the British police record of never having backed down before an armed criminal. A number of brave bobbies had given their lives for this ideal and it stirred the pride of young men like myself. In 1971 that pride was sorely dented. In a northern city, a constable stood back and let bank robbers escape rather than be gunned down himself. I felt as though my personal reputation had been besmirched, although Missy pointed out that the PC concerned probably had a wife and family to consider.

For me, that didn't matter. He was a copper and I was old fashioned enough to believe that he should have given his all for the brave traditions of his uniform. The incident left me unsettled for weeks, even though it didn't concern me directly.

Matters came to a head one windy day in early summer. I found myself 12 metres up a wildly swaying conifer in pursuit of a scrawny kitten and wondering just what I was trying to prove. The cat didn't want my assistance. It arched its back and spat furiously at my approach, while the old lady who had telephoned the police station called anxious encouragement from below.

Breathless from the climb, terrified by the insecurity of my perch and drenched in sweat, I called that 'moggie' a series of names as I stuffed it into my shirt. Tiny talons dug agonisingly into my flesh, but at last I was safely back on the ground. With a sigh of relief I handed the wretched little animal over to the old lady, but she recoiled as though the kitten was about to bite her.

'It isn't mine, officer', she told me sweetly. 'It looked so uncomfortable up there that I just had to call you.'

I was polite but my thoughts were unrepeatable. Carefully, I placed the cat on the pavement, from where it spat disagreeably before making a determined dash for the tree from which I had so unfortunately 'rescued' it. Seconds later it disappeared and the old lady and I shrugged at each other in mutual wonderment at the vagaries of animal behaviour.

That unhappy little incident was the last straw. If rescuing kittens was all I was good for, I had had enough. That evening I announced to my startled family that we were going home. I told them about the blue skies and dusty horizons of my homeland, but I don't think they were overly impressed. Missy was pregnant again, Brian had just started school and Graeme was looking forward to joining him the following year.

However, my mind was made up. I wrote to Police General Headquarters in Salisbury and received a pile of application forms by return. With the formalities under way, Missy began to get into the spirit of the move and before we quite knew what was happening, our furniture was sold and adventure in the sunshine was almost upon us.

A fortnight before my departure (I was to leave first and the family would follow) I was summoned to Headquarters for an interview with the Chief Constable. Mr Blake-White was a keen supporter of the Force cricket team, but on this occasion my prowess on the sports field wasn't the matter at issue.

The boss read me the riot act.

'Did I know', he thundered, 'that UDI had been a deliberate act of rebellion against the Crown — that same Crown I had sworn an oath to support?'

I did, but that made no difference.

'If I continued with my ridiculous plans for emigration', Chalky told me angrily, 'I would be as treasonable as Ian Smith and his lackeys. I would put myself beyond redemption in the eyes of the law and furthermore, I would never get another job in a British police force.'

He was a fine Chief Constable, Chalky White but he didn't like Rhodesians. I left Headquarters in chastened mood but my desire to return home was undiminished. On 9th October 1971 I handed my kit in at Headquarters and four days later, arrived in Salisbury, sweaty unshaven and tired after a 24 four hour flight. The October sun battered my flagging senses, the landscape looked parched and dry and there was nobody there to meet me. For a few long and lonely moments, I almost wished I had stayed in England.

2

Surprises in Salisbury

Transport eventually arrived to bring me in from the airport and on 13 October 1971 after an incredibly friendly interview with a Board of Officers I swore an oath of loyalty to the State, feeling distinctly uncomfortable as I remembered Chalky White's comments on my previous oath. After that I was driven to Morris Training Depot where I was allocated a batman and met up with Bob Hitch.

The batman was a pleasant surprise. Much of my initial training course in Dorset had been taken up with ironing my kit and 'bulling' my boots. Here it was to be done for me at the cost of a few dollars a month. I couldn't help a wry smile at the thought of a Cotswold Bobby having his own batman. My former colleagues would have been flabbergasted.

At this stage in my narrative, perhaps I should explain how the civil police of Rhodesia came to be known as the British South Africa Police. When Cecil Rhodes decided to open up Southern Africa, he did it on a commercial basis. His idea was to develop a rail route through the spine of the continent, thereby facilitating trade, which would benefit Britain and in the process make Rhodes himself even richer than he already was. To achieve this, he formed the British South Africa Company with a mandate to explore and develop the sparsely inhabited area that lay between the Limpopo and Zambezi rivers.

At the time, this land was occupied by the Matabele people — an offshoot of the Zulus who had moved up from Zululand less than a hundred years previously — and the Shona who drifted down from the north shortly before that. Minerals, wildlife and rich pasture were plentiful throughout the area so there was no shortage of volunteers for the expedition.

The Pioneers formed their own cavalry police to protect them in their endeavours and this force of armed adventurers were known as the BSA Company Police. Once the new country was established and named after Rhodes, they took over civil policing of the administration. 'Company' was dropped from the name and the British South Africa Police continued to be a considerable force for law and order in fledgling Rhodesia. Proudly proclaiming themselves 'a Force in the Great Tradition', they stuck to their cavalry format and it wasn't until the late 1940s that District Branch troopers came to be known as constables and then — in a retrograde step that highlighted the difference between black and white policemen — constables became patrol officers.

The Force bore the brunt of fighting in the Shona and Matabele rebellions and as a result, police duties were heavily oriented toward the military. However, the law of the land was upheld to such a degree of efficiency that the BSAP was held in high esteem among policemen all over the world. Recruits were required to remain single throughout their initial three-year contract, but after UDI, demands on manpower ensured that the rule was waived to allow in married men, provided they had previous police experience.

As junior Patrol Officer 8693, I felt very proud to be a member.

Rhodesia in 1971 provided a considerable culture shock for a Cotswold Bobby. On my first evening in Salisbury I tucked into a massive T-bone steak in a pavement café and looked around me with interest.

This was hardly the beleaguered society I had been led to expect by British media reports. Beset by sanctions and threatened with armed uprising they might have been, but Rhodesians were obviously still a cheerful bunch. Black and white citizens thronged the pavements and laughter could be heard in every direction. It was a far cry from the cold October misery I had left behind and I felt immeasurably better about my move.

The cost of my excellent meal was one Rhodesian dollar — 50 British pence at the exchange rate of the time. In England, meat had been desperately expensive and although I had taken a salary cut by joining the BSAP, I had the comfortable feeling that the Lemons would be living very well indeed.

One comment of that first day lives on in my mind and was to prove ever more ironic as years went by. A uniformed inspector, Brian Cullingworth, finally arrived to collect me from the airport. As we drove towards Salisbury, he jerked his chin at a military barracks on the edge of town.

'That is where most of our problems come from', he snorted. 'It seems that every loafer who can't find a job ends up in the RLI and half of them go from there to Chikurubi Prison. They really are a waste of white skin.'

His unconscious racism was discomforting but a few years later, the Rhodesian Light Infantry became known as 'The Incredibles' and their exploits provided inspiration to Rhodesians in every corner of the land. It is amazing how values change in times of war.

My training course bordered on farce. The BSAP was a paramilitary force and training normally lasted six months, particular emphasis being laid on foot drill, equitation, weapon training and counter-insurgency procedures — all matters about which I knew absolutely nothing. This tendency toward matters military wasn't due to the prospect of imminent conflict — that still seemed unthinkable to most Rhodesians — but lay in the history of the BSAP as a cavalry regiment.

Personally I had no intention of riding horses or preparing myself for war. Although I still craved excitement, I had mellowed since the heady days of my youth and soldiering wasn't part of my plans. I was a copper by inclination and as far as I was concerned, war games were for the military and they could keep them to themselves.

One of my worries before leaving Britain was how I would react to being armed in the general course of my duties, but the situation didn't arise. British television usually showed Rhodesian policemen with rifles or sub-machine guns to hand and many of them appeared with pistols stuck on their belts. I wasn't unduly concerned with the ethics of armed policing, but one of the arguments for not arming the British police had been the danger of innocent bystanders being hurt. Besides, I didn't want to be in a position where I might have to kill anyone.

In the event it wasn't like that. Patrol officers and above were issued with personal rifles, but these were kept in station armouries and firearm issues were only for specific circumstances. In their normal routine, policemen went unarmed and the BSAP also had a proud tradition of bravery when confronted with armed criminals. In time I would carry a weapon every moment of the day, but my immediate fears of being armed were quickly mollified and I started off in Morris Depot feeling very pleased with my decision to join the BSAP.

Due to a series of quite remarkable coincidences, my training lasted less than four weeks. Those in authority called it a 'shortened course' but to be that short seemed ridiculous, even to me. Bob Hitch was a former Metropolitan Bobby who had come out a few weeks before me and officially we were part of recruit course 7/71. In practice we spent most of our time in amiable discussion with the Law and Police instructor John Hill. These daily 'lessons' were devoted almost exclusively to question and answer sessions on such vital aspects of law as the best places to buy second hand furniture and whether it was preferable to be posted to a Town or District Branch station when we graduated.

The only strenuous aspect of the course was morning PT with our fellow recruits. I had just completed a long cricket season and almost managed to keep up with energetic 18-year-olds, but poor old Bob was overweight and a couple of years older than my own venerable 27, so he really struggled. I would look at his grey face as he struggled off the assault course and marvel at the willpower that kept him going and even brought the occasional spluttered joke from his cyanosing lips.

In addition to the enthusiasm of their age, the recruits possessed the sharply defined prejudices of 18-year-olds anywhere. Few had travelled further afield than the beaches of Durban or Beira and they had the insular outlook on life that typified Rhodesian youth in those days. It was their collective view on matters of race that disturbed both Bob and myself. He was very English and I was a local, but I had travelled extensively so tended to view matters with a more cosmopolitan attitude than my young countrymen. This led to some fierce arguments between ourselves and the rest of the squad.

The main bone of contention was the fact that the BSAP had two entry levels and although these were nominally based on educational qualifications, they meant that blacks joined as constables and whites were immediately granted patrol officer status. The system ensured an officer class that highlighted the difference between the races. I felt that it was criminal for an 18-year-old to be in a position of authority over grizzled veterans with 25 years service, no matter what colour they happened to be. Proficiency in police work comes only with experience and if Rhodesia was ever to become a truly multi racial society, the rank structure had to be modified or trouble was bound to ensue.

Bob agreed with me, but we were outnumbered and outvoted in most squad discussions.

The white man would always give the orders, we were told. The black man just wasn't good enough. I eventually buried my misgivings in the enjoyment of my new job, but Bob was never able to reconcile himself to what he saw as blatant racism. He bought himself out and returned to Britain before his initial three-year contract had expired, which seemed to me a waste of a good man. The saddest part of the whole affair was that Bob Hitch was regarded as a radical merely because he was unafraid to speak his mind.

Our kit issue on joining the Force was impressive. We had six different uniforms (including jodhpurs, spurs and riding boots!) three kitbags, an instruction manual and miscellaneous items of footwear and everyday equipment. I couldn't help wondering whether it was all necessary, particularly when Rhodesia was supposed to be financially crippled.

We were also issued with personal FN rifles and mine was number 1787 — a heavy, snub-snouted brute with an air of gleaming lethality about it that terrified me. I had once owned a .22 rifle and Bob had done a desk job with the Royal Marines, but neither of us was comfortable with these modern instruments of warfare. I spent hours staring at the gleaming, brass rounds and imagining the damage those wickedly pointed missiles could inflict on a human body. For me, they were the epitome of violent death and just holding a bullet gave me a creepy feeling in my stomach. It all seemed a long way from the soft green fields of rural Gloucestershire.

The FN (*Fabrique Nationale* are the Belgian manufacturers) is a semi-automatic weapon that fires a round of 7.62 millimetres in diameter. It has horrendous striking power, but although we carried our rifles at all times nobody seemed in any way anxious to instruct us in their usage. As we came closer to the end of our depot course, Bob and I grew ever more worried about our own capabilities.

'Do you think anyone wants to teach us how to use these things?' was the question we put to John Hill.

He laughed off our worries but eventually packed us off to the depot armoury with strict instructions that we were not to return until we were qualified marksmen.

Musketry Instructor Ian Chalk laughed at our anxious faces.

'Listen fellows', he offered, 'we are up to our eyes at the moment and nobody has time to instruct just two of you. You are both experienced men so I will issue you with Uzis, pistols and a shotgun for the afternoon. You can use my office to teach yourself from the manual.

'It isn't difficult', Chalky must have noticed our concern. 'Follow the steps laid down in the manual and strip and assemble the weapons until you feel comfortable with them. I will take you out on the range in a day or so.'

And that was our musketry instruction. For three hours, Bob and I fumbled our way through the manual, taking weapons apart and laboriously putting them together again. We loaded and reloaded magazines with live rounds and brought weapons up into the aiming position without having the slightest idea whether we were doing things properly.

The following day we blazed away on the range for half an hour. I managed to gash my cheek on a viciously kicking rifle butt and that was it. We were licensed gunmen.

Many years later, I was instructing a group of new police reservists on the intricacies of the FN rifle when the irony of the situation struck me and I burst into semi hysterical laughter. My pupils looked bewildered but I didn't dare enlighten them as to the cause of my mirth. They might have lost their already diminishing faith in the system and the manpower situation in Rhodesia at the time was far too critical to allow for mass desertion.

But at last my course was over and in spite of knowing little about musketry, even less about foot drill and nothing at all about horses, Bob and I were 'trained' patrol officers. We were members of a Force in the Great Tradition and our colonel was the Queen Mum. I didn't even know the words to our marching song, *Kum a Kye* and most of the traditions were a total mystery.

It was the easiest course I had ever been through but it left me vaguely apprehensive about my ability to cope with any major problems that might crop up. However, I banished my doubts and after a suitably raucous passing out party for Bob and myself, we bade farewell to the rest of squad 7/71 and went our separate ways.

My first posting was to Marandellas and on 29th November 1971, Missy, the boys and brand new daughter Deborah flew out from England to join me in our fresh start. I met them in pouring rain at Salisbury Airport and felt my heart lift when I saw the familiar figures emerging from the aircraft. The boys were wide-eyed at their first glimpse of Africa and Missy gestured helplessly at the rain.

'Where is that sunshine you promised us?' She giggled and I couldn't help roaring with laughter. Life was good and I had the feeling that it was going to prove infinitely more exciting that it had as a British Bobby.

3

Early days in Marandellas

Marandellas was a small farming town, only 76 kilometres east of the capital. It combined the features of rural and urban Rhodesia and this was reflected in the police station, which incorporated the District Headquarters. The Officer Commanding the Marandellas District worked from one end of the long building. I quickly discovered that senior officers in the BSAP were known by their radio call signs. The OC District was Dispol, the Commissioner Compol and the OC Province was Propol. For a while I debated calling myself Lempol but fortunately perhaps, discretion kept me from making a fool of myself. Senior servicemen are seldom noted for their humour and it was too early in my career to rock the proverbial boat.

The Marandellas district covered an area about six times the size of Gloucestershire and included five other police stations. Macheke was a white farming area; Wedza and Marandellas had a couple of tribal trust lands in addition to their farms, while Mrewa, Mtoko and Nyamapanda were almost entirely TTL or State land. For me, it was amazing to see the difference between farming and tribal areas.

Soil throughout the area was very rich and the farms were lushly covered with grass and trees, but the TTLs were starkly arid, vegetation grazed away and massive erosion plain to see. Whether this was — as the white farmers claimed — due to black incompetence or — as the black nationalists claimed — part of the government's plan to subjugate blacks by giving them the worst of the land was too difficult a question for me to answer. I had the feeling that there was justification for both theories although I couldn't help wondering whether the problem actually had its roots in African culture.

The tribal people of Africa have always been pastoralists. In ages past they would move into an area, graze it flat and then move on, which would allow the land to recover. This was fine when all Africa was theirs, but with the imposition of tribal boundaries, they were no longer able to move on and the result was ecological devastation. The Land Apportionment Act was a major bone of contention among the nationalists, who claimed that blacks had been granted inferior land for settlement, but my own view was that traditional farming methods would have to change before the situation could possibly be resolved.

Fortunately perhaps I was too wrapped up in my new job to worry about the unfair distribution of land. I was a Rhodesian copper now and although I was a little piqued that in Marandellas, we wore 'town' uniform of tunic, boots and cumbersome leather leggings, rather than the comfortable grey shirts favoured by true district men, I found my new environment absolutely fascinating.

There were two strict, but distinct hierarchies in the police station. The senior ranks (patrol officer and above) were led by Chief Inspector Weare, who had command of the station, but fell under Dispol's ultimate control. Under him were two inspectors, four section officers (equivalent to British sergeants) and a gaggle of we lowly patrol officers. Some P/Os wore two bars on each shoulder to show that they had completed three years service and could regard themselves as senior to one-bar novices like myself.

Leading the African police was Sergeant Major Chenjeke, a fat and fearsome Shona who exerted enormous authority over his flock of 'AP.' Under his control were eight sergeants and 45 constables so the station was extremely well staffed by British standards. I enjoyed my dealing with the AP. They were a cheerful bunch and their turn out wouldn't have looked out of place in the smartest of Guards' regiments. Chenjeke paraded them in front of the station at eight o clock each morning and if anyone wasn't up to scratch, the sergeant major's roars of disapproval could have been heard on the other side of town.

Discipline throughout the station was formal but friendly and it was the ideal environment to work in. Assigned to the Enquiry Section, I shared a roomy office with Dave Farrington, a former Liverpool cadet as well as a human skull known only as Fred. The skull's origins were uncertain but 'he' grinned toothily down from a shelf and nobody seemed to view his presence as anything out of the ordinary. Knowing just what trouble it would cause in Britain, I was taken aback at first, but I soon grew accustomed to the grisly exhibit and in time I hardly knew that Fred was there.

The station armoury was a frightening experience for a copper straight out from England. A long, narrow room behind a heavy steel door, it contained racked rows of rifles, shotguns and riot weapons, as well as pistols and Uzi sub-machine guns along the length of one entire wall. Boxes of ammunition, flares and grenades were stacked in various corners and the place had an aroma of cold metal and gun oil. We could probably have started our own minor world war from that room and there was even an old fashioned, wind-up siren to warn of impending air raids. I tried a couple of turns on the handle one afternoon and the din was terrifying.

But I was to learn an early lesson from that armoury. Having deposited my rifle therein, I forgot all about it, only to be called before the Boss a few weeks later. When I entered his office, my trusty weapon was lying conspicuously across his desk.

'Is this yours?' He asked icily.

'Yes, sir.'

'When did you last clean it?'

'Ummm . . .'

In truth I hadn't touched the damned thing since coming out of Depot and when Mr Weare stripped it down in front of me that was abundantly obvious. Rust pitted the working parts and even to my untutored eye, the rifle was a disgrace. Fortunately my ignorance and 'Pommie' origins were taken into account and I wasn't put on a charge, but the lesson was learned.

'One day your life might depend on the efficiency of that weapon', the chief inspector pointed out and although I didn't take that terribly seriously at the time, from then on I made sure that rifle number 1787 was kept in a gleaming state of readiness.

As befits any cavalry regiment, our working day began at first light with 'stables' — an opportunity to get our steeds fed, watered and cleaned up for the day ahead. Horses had long since given way to Land-Rovers and motor cycles, but washing motor vehicles in the icy atmosphere of a Highland dawn was an enervating experience. For the first time I found myself thinking back to my easy routine in Gloucestershire with considerable nostalgia.

The Land-Rovers were long-wheel-based models, painted in battleship grey and I enjoyed driving these lumbering vehicles, particularly with the riot screens in place. It gave me a feeling of being in the thick of things to prowl around town, peering through the forward grille while the big engine rumbled beneath me and the constable at my side silently wondered at the crazy 'English' patrol officer.

Fortunately, the novelty soon wore off and by the time I really needed to use specially adapted vehicles, the focus of defence had changed. Flying rocks and beer bottles had given way to tracer bullets, rifle grenades and the impartial horror of landmines.

But that is jumping ahead of my story.

Marandellas was very English, even to the extent of having a park in the centre of town, known as 'The Green.' The streets were well laid out, while the town was kept spotlessly clean by a team of municipal 'policemen', augmented on occasion by work parties from the local prison.

The suburbs were exclusively white, while black residents lived in Dombo Tombo — a township set well away from the centre of town. I liked Dombo Tombo. It had a friendly atmosphere about it and I spent a great deal of my time driving around the narrow streets. The houses were smaller and more cramped than their counterparts on an English council estate, but they were clean and most had well tended gardens and garages, many of them housing more than one vehicle. There was a shopping centre, complete with beer hall, cinema and the Mushandire Pamwe Hotel, while on Sunday afternoons, a boxing tournament was always held outside the magnificent Rudhaka football stadium. I enjoyed the fights and was occasionally invited to join in, but the thought of being knocked on to a concrete floor effectively deterred me from having a go.

The residents of Dombo Tombo were hardly the downtrodden, potential rioters that I might have expected from British media reports. Black and white seemed to get on well and whenever I drove in to the township, local people greeted me with easy familiarity. Children would run gleefully behind the Land-Rover and whenever I paused for a chat, groups of them would gather round, giggling up at me from behind their hands or fingering my leather belt in cheerful wonderment. If there were any stirrings of agitation or discontent with the political situation, I wasn't aware of them. All the people I spoke to seemed relatively content with their lot.

There was another police camp in Dombo Tombo with houses for the AP and black civilian staff. They had a bar and club of their own, together with a dusty football field that was nearly always in use. Sergeant Major Chenjeke was in charge here too and I enjoyed the occasional cold beer as his guest in the 'wet canteen.' It was all very agreeable and my initial doubts about the future began to disperse in the general enjoyment of my daily routine.

Out of town, life wasn't quite as serene. Farmers are notoriously pragmatic people and Rhodesian farmers had suffered more than most with sanctions and the resultant scarcity of essential equipment. Tobacco prices had dropped to rock bottom over the years since UDI and most farmers had been forced to diversify, just to keep themselves going.

This state of affairs led to considerable bitterness within the farming community and I was occasionally subjected to an anti-British tirade when I arrived at a homestead. It seemed ironic that in England, my accent had marked me out as a foreigner, while here in Rhodesia, that same accent — softened by seven years in Gloucestershire — was regarded as being very English. My protests that I was as Rhodesian as any of them were initially greeted with scepticism but I eventually came to be accepted for myself rather than my imagined origins. Although they often made life difficult for me, most of those farmers eventually became family friends and we spent many an enjoyable weekend on farms well away from the restrictions of town.

Labour relations on the farms were a curious mixture of paternalism, genuine friendship and crass brutality. Most farmers employed at least 20 men and although they paid them a pittance, they supplied housing, food, medicine and anything else that might be needed for their families. Many farms boasted schools or clinics and at busy times of the growing season, wives, children and assorted relatives were called in to assist the men folk and be paid for their efforts.

Each farm compound was a community in its own right and most of them were cheerful places. Beer was shipped in over weekends and if there was any racial animosity towards their employers, it was well hidden and contained. There was the occasional exception of course and some farms were to become simmering cauldrons of resentment, but in those early days, these were merely noted by ground coverage patrols as possible focal points for future trouble.

On two occasions I prosecuted farmers for assaulting their labour and although the cases didn't win me any friends, I stuck by my principles and was given excellent support by my superiors. In both cases, the culprits were heavily fined.

A minor road accident one afternoon led to acrimonious discussion with an Afrikaans farmer who didn't want to be prosecuted. I felt that he had been guilty of careless driving and proceeded accordingly. After I had taken a statement after caution, he produced tea — Rhodesian hospitality has never depended on circumstances — and looked somewhat quizzically at me.

'Young man', he enquired with a touch of exasperation in his voice, 'do you know who I am?'

In truth I didn't. I had recorded his name but my knowledge of political personalities was sketchy at best and it meant nothing to me. He carefully explained that he was a very senior member of the ruling Rhodesian Front party and I had the impression that he was an extremely important person. Dispol asked for explanations when I returned to the station but the gentleman in question still paid a deposit fine for the offence.

But that was my first real contact with the political clout of Rhodesia's farming community and perhaps I should have been warned.

There had been a number of incidents whereby weaponry was smuggled into the country and road blocks formed a large part of our routine duties. I found myself continually amazed at how many people could cram themselves into a small space.

Admittedly, black Rhodesians have always been a tactile lot. Their handshakes are complicated with much circling of thumbs and to see men walking hand in hand does not mean they have homosexual inclinations. If two people sit beside each other, they will sit with their bodies touching and a crowd usually takes on the aspects of a solid block of humanity.

On one occasion I walked into the Dombo Tombo beer hall to find mine the only white face in a seething mass of black ones. There must have been 500 men in a room designed for 50 and there seemed no way to pass among them, but they somehow moved to one side or the other in order to let me through. I turned down numerous offers to share foaming buckets of Chibuku — a traditional beer that is more like sour-tasting gruel than a drink — mainly because attempting to drink from two-litre buckets was asking to spill the stuff all over my uniform and that could take come explaining.

But it was on the road that the African herding instinct made itself most apparent. Buses were licensed to carry 72 passengers, but it was commonplace to find a 120 or more, sitting three to a seat and apparently quite comfortable. They seemed to enjoy this cramped proximity but after seven years in crowded England, I found it difficult to get my head around it. It also made the searching of buses a labourious affair for all concerned, but the passengers seemed to accept the need for long delays and would find the nearest patch of shade to sit or sleep until the bus was ready to resume the journey. In the light of later developments, I have often wondered how much of that overcrowding was a deliberate ploy and how many items of weaponry I might have overlooked in the general tedium of bus searches.

Rhodesian law was very similar to the law I had learned as a bobby, but procedures and degrees of responsibility were vastly different. One aspect of policing that was more convenient but disturbed me with its implications was the power of detention. In England it had been a serious matter to lock a man up and all sorts of formalities had to be completed before a miscreant was safely put away. In Rhodesia the powers of arrest and detention were taken quite lightly. A suspect could be detained without charge for up to 48 hours and after that, a warrant for further detention merely required a signature from Dispol in his capacity as a Justice of the Peace. Dispol rarely disputed the facts laid out by the investigating officer with the result that investigation of a crime was considerably easier than I had known it previously. For all that, the procedure left me vaguely uncomfortable. I could imagine what the civil liberties lobby in England would have said and in many ways I would have agreed with them.

Another difficulty for me was the implementation of the pass laws. Every black male over the age of eighteen was bound by law to carry a registration certificate or *situpa*. This listed his name, family and district of origin, theoretically making it easier to keep track of him and levy the necessary taxes. There was an automatic power of arrest if the *situpa* wasn't carried and although I could see the logic behind this legislation, it seemed unfair that it applied only to blacks.

The law itself was often ignored and whenever a policeman was in trouble for not working hard enough, he could be certain of picking up a handful of 'no RC or pass' cases to impress a superior. As the certificates spent a great deal of time in trouser pockets, many of them were illegible anyway and magistrates usually granted offenders a conditional discharge or fined them a princely 50 cents, so they obviously didn't take this blatantly racist piece of legislation seriously. When I mentioned my concerns to the boss, he scoffed at my 'English outlook' and told me to get on with my job.

Mind you, Chief Inspector Raymond Weare (known to all and sundry as 'Waymond', for an unfortunate speech defect), didn't have a high opinion of the English or their policing methods. In general I got on extremely well with him, but his routine mockery of the British police did tend to get under my skin at times.

'They do everything by the book', was one of his favourite themes. 'Put a Pommie inspector at a serious crime scene and he screams for help. In this country every single officer is expected to use his initiative.'

As if to prove his point, my first experience of serious crime occurred when I was called out one night to deal with a murder. I had only a sergeant to assist, but he was very experienced and although I was nervous at first, we had the whole case sorted out by daybreak.

Mind you, it was hardly a genuine murder. An angry husband had taken a swing at his wife and hit the baby, hitched on to her hip. Unfortunately he fractured the little mite's skull but with the assistance of the government medical officer, we had him arraigned before the court and put away for two years within 24 hours. That couldn't have happened in England!

That first experience of homicide was certainly an exceptional case but it cured me of any nervousness for the future. During my initial two years in Marandellas, I dealt with further killings, rapes, robberies and arson. I regularly gave evidence in Court and spent six happy weeks, poring over company accounts in search of a bakery fraudster. This was real police work.

As in most parts of the world, Saturday nights were the time for heavy drinking and a consequent increase in violent crime. Two particular murders stand out in my memory from that time although the second had nothing to do with strong drink. A new suburb was in the process of construction on the edge of town and on one plot, two drunken night watchmen came to blows. The stronger of the two, a man called Bizare Snake flattened his friend and on finding him unconscious, piled firewood over his body and set him alight. The impromptu bonfire was helped along with a liberal dollop of paraffin.

The dead man was an awful mess and his killer wasn't difficult to find. I attended the scene with Detective Constable Govati Mhora and we arrested Bizare Snake later in the day. He was duly brought before the High Court and in spite of having several convictions for violence, got away with a seven-year prison term.

Some years later, English friends of mine bought the house in question and although I never told them about its gory history, I couldn't help feeling vaguely uncomfortable when sipping cold beer on the very spot where Bizare Snake had so effectively ended the argument with his fellow watchman.

The second murder was purely domestic and infinitely more horrific. It occurred in the Chiota TTL and once again I attended the scene with Govati Mhora.

Divorce is not common in African tribal society but on this occasion a marriage had been dissolved and custody of five very young children, given to the father. One dark Saturday night, the banished and embittered mother returned to the kraal, tied a strong rope around the hut in which the children slept and set the flimsy building on fire. All five youngsters burned to death and I wasn't the only policeman in tears when we shifted those painfully charred little bodies the following morning.

That lady took a little longer to find than Bizare Snake and when we picked her up, she denied all knowledge of the crime. Detective Section Officer Ray Ritson took over the investigation and on the evening of the arrest, the pair of us were silent spectators in the CID office as Mhora and his hard-eyed colleagues questioned the accused mother. The interrogation had been going on for over five hours without getting anywhere when Mhora took Ray and I aside.

'Why don't you leave us to it, sir', he asked Ray gently. 'Go down to the pub and have a beer while we do things our way.'

This seemed to go against all the ethics of policing and I was horrified but after a momentary hesitation, Ray nodded grimly.

'Come on', he instructed: 'these chaps have far more chance of getting the truth out of her if we aren't present. Don't worry', he added on spotting the concern on my face, 'they won't beat her up.'

I wasn't convinced but did as I was told and an hour later, Mhora called us back in to hear the woman's confession. She didn't seem in any way upset or frightened, nor did she show any signs of rough treatment, but she freely admitted her role in the murder. Many years later, I asked Govati Mhora how he had done it but he merely smiled.

'Black Africans understand black Africans far better than you whites will ever understand us', he told me quietly. 'We know how to go about these matters.'

My duties in Marandellas were not always interesting or enjoyable however. The town was on the main road to Umtali and Rhodesian roads were wide, well cambered and extremely fast. I dealt with a number of fatal road accidents and that was one aspect of the job that I never enjoyed.

In England, a 'fatal' required the presence of an inspector and a specialised accident investigation team, but in Rhodesia we were on our own. Plans, statements and summaries of evidence still had to be prepared to a standard that would have brought praise from the strictest of British judges and it was all excellent experience, but any road accident makes one realise how insignificant the human body really is.

There was one terrible week in which I attended five 'fatals in seven days. The first victim was a patrol officer from Wedza whom I knew quite well and the last was one of Rhodesia's top fashion models — a beautiful Jewish girl whose death really knocked me back on my heels. At the end of that week I was a trembling wreck and found myself in tears far more often than was proper for a big, bad uniformed cop. All the same, fatal accidents are part of a policeman's job and I had no choice but to get on with it.

Language and custom were other aspects of Rhodesian policing that took some getting used to. The front office of the police station — and sometimes the station itself — was known as the 'charge office' and all case files were 'dockets' while my lack of expertise in local languages was a real handicap.

Marandellas was in the heart of Mashonaland and I made early resolutions to improve my very basic knowledge of Chishona. Statements were taken in the vernacular and in court there was always an official interpreter. I found it frustrating to listen while interpreter and witness held a lengthy conversation only for the translation to be condensed into a couple of English words.

African customs could be more unsettling than the language problem Female witnesses often breast fed their babies while being interviewed and there was a complete lack of self-consciousness about bodily functions. Handkerchiefs were non existent, so runny noses were cleared through the fingers, the resultant mess casually flicked away. Men and women would urinate in public without embarrassment — it was a crime in England — and bodies didn't possess the same mystique that they did in Western society. Sex was regarded as being perfectly natural and although prostitution was illegal, it was a fact in most sectors of society. Many cases that were reported to us as rape turned out to be 'non payment of wages' and this caused endless frustration for those of us involved in the legal process.

All these customs caused amusement among whites and were regarded as proof positive of inferiority but this was hardly fair. In tribal culture they were looked upon as normal and my own opinion was that we should make more effort to understand.

For me it was all part of an exciting learning curve and I was enjoying my life as a cop in the sunshine.

In fact life for the Lemons in 1972 was pretty good. We had a government house not far from the police station, Missy had a job with Internal Affairs and a large garden to enjoy when she wasn't at work. The boys attended school in the town and were doing well. We employed a 'house boy' for the heavy work and a nanny to look after Deborah. I was enjoying my job and couldn't help wondering why it had taken me so long to come home.

To add to my advantages at work was the fact that apart from the boss and his two inspectors, I had more police experience than anyone else on the station and thus enjoyed a certain amount of privilege with my superiors and respect among my colleagues. I started a police cricket team and a boxing club in Dombo Tombo, both ventures adding to my street cred, while Lemon's Luck (something in which I have always had faith) sorted out the only department of my life that was causing concern.

Setting up a new home is always an expensive business. We had disposed of everything before leaving the UK and starting again from scratch meant buying furniture, a car, and clothing, even before worrying about food. All these things cost money and although I have a lifelong abhorrence of credit, we had incurred considerable debt merely starting a new life as a family. It wasn't a happy situation and I spent many sleepless nights wondering how we could get out of the financial mire. Missy scrimped and saved as carefully as she had in England but at times I despaired of ever clearing our debts. An unexpected win on the National Lottery sorted out the problem.

'The prize only amounted to $700 but it was enough to pay off our creditors, buy a round of drinks in the police pub and enable us to start afresh without money worries. Our *nom de plume* on the ticket had been 'Lemon's Luck' and it had done us proud. Suddenly we were free of debt and living in the sunshine with an acre or more of garden for the kids to grow up in. We had plenty of friends, I enjoyed my job and life was generally wonderful.

At times I couldn't help feeling that it was all just too good to last.

4

Racism and promotion

While overseas visitors were generally given a generous welcome, white Rhodesians tended to view the British with hostile suspicion. Most felt betrayed by the mother nation and in my first few months at Marandellas, I took a great deal of flak for my supposedly English origins. Colleagues mocked my experience as a Bobby while members of the public often made pointed remarks about 'know it all Poms' when I was within earshot. It took some time before I could shrug off the carping and by then, most folk had come to accept me for myself rather than any imagined national shortcomings.

Social life in the town revolved around the country club and the police pub, both of which sold cheap beer and made enormous profits. There was also the Three Monkeys Inn, but that was more expensive so we only went there on special occasions. The clientele at all these places was exclusively white and I often wondered what the black barmen thought about their allegedly superior countrymen behaving like stupid children when in their cups. For all the booze that was consumed, I can remember only one incident wherein a white man was charged with alcohol related offences. Occasionally a black reveller was 'done' for being drunk and disorderly in Dombo Tombo, but in general all Rhodesians seemed to drink a great deal and play very hard. At times it seemed almost frenetic and much as I enjoyed the festivities, I occasionally wondered just what it was all about.

Police relations with the general public in Marandellas were excellent and a good time was had by all. This was the British concept of community policing carried out to an extravagant degree and I have to admit that I enjoyed it immensely.

In those early days it was hard to believe that Rhodesia was the same threatened country I had read so much about in the British press. By English standards, the shops were not lavishly stocked, but in general black and white citizens lived very well. I noticed few signs of racial tension and the only overt racism I encountered was from a few farmers or people relatively new to the country.

White Rhodesians had always been firmly convinced that man for man, a white was worth two blacks, while any Rhodesian — black or white — was worth at least three citizens from any other country. Black Rhodesians might not have entirely agreed, but black and white mingled in easy familiarity and there was seldom any overt friction.

Expatriates on the other hand were often blatantly racist. Many came from vastly inferior social conditions to those they encountered in Rhodesia and finding themselves with servants and positions of unaccustomed authority, they tended to go over the top. Whereas white Rhodesians took leadership for granted and usually handled it with dignity, many expats seemed to delight in making life difficult for their black subordinates.

One example of this was a patrol officer called Wallace who arrived in Marandellas a few months after I did. He was another former bobby, but he bragged and bullied his way around the station, making himself unpopular among black and white colleagues alike. This led to a certain amount of ostracism for the lad and I don't think anyone was surprised or upset when he deserted before his time was up, presumably leaving for friendlier climes. Wallace and a few other ex-bobbies who didn't last their initial three years brought additional problems to my life. All too often I was identified with them and some of my colleagues took oblique satisfaction in goading me about my service with 'the bloody Poms'.

But in most cases, black and white, Rhodesian and expat, we all co existed in harmony. In any police force there is little room for dissension so colleagues are forced to get on. For my own part, I enjoyed having men under my command but there was nothing racist about my attitude. I was that sort of man and enjoyed giving orders.

In time, command was handed to me on a plate. I was summoned to Waymond's office one day and shown the latest circular from PGHQ. Promotion examinations had heretofore been restricted to those who had completed four years service in the BSAP but this particular missive directed that 'previous experience in a recognised police force would henceforth count toward qualification for promotion.' Immediate prospects of power began to gnaw at my vitals.

I hadn't done any studying but that seemed a minor matter, so my name was submitted and in due course I found myself looking down at a question paper in a room full of other candidates. Once again Lemon's Luck was working overtime and in spite of much informed guesswork on my part, a sufficient number of answers were 'ticked' for me to pass — if not with flying colours, at least with my self confidence high.

The next hurdle was a three-day extended interview at Morris Depot and that was more of a challenge. I was the only junior P/O among the candidates and I was also the only one without training in subjects that matter to paramilitary policemen. I was still reasonably fit and just about coped with the physical side of the interview, but other parts of it were truly disastrous. During the first two days, I managed to march my drill squad into a chain-link fence, halted another squad on the wrong foot and got my group hopelessly lost on a map reading exercise. I coped with the first aid, but made my stint as range officer into a farce — hilarious to everyone involved except scarlet-faced me. I gave a five-minute lecture on the Uzi sub-machine gun and that taxed my aptitude for imaginative fiction to the limit, but when it came to firing the damned thing, my colleagues were in far more danger than the cardboard targets.

Be that as it may, I came into my own with the 'in basket' test. This was a practical exercise wherein candidates sat at a desk with telephone, diary and wire basket overflowing with incomplete files, incident reports and the morning miscellany that confronts the officer in charge of any busy police station in the world.

I had run my own small station in England and during my ten months with the BSAP, had attended to most types of enquiry. Setting to with a will, I readily assumed the mantle of command. My pen flew across the paper and forms went from 'in' to 'out' tray with curt notes and cryptic instructions appended thereon. The telephone rang continuously throughout the exercise and most of the calls were infuriatingly trivial. I had authority now so I dismissed all but the most urgent requests for immediate action with an airy frivolity that probably cost me marks and led to numerous threats to report me to my officer commanding, the commissioner and even the prime minister himself. It is surprising how many people claim to play golf in exalted company when they want to browbeat a policeman.

I ploughed through the two-hour test with considerable aplomb and when it was over, there was just one more step to be negotiated. That was an interview with the promotion board and once again, everything went well. We spent time marvelling over my lottery win ('I've bought tickets for 30 bloody years and never won a cent', grumbled a gloomy chief superintendent) and I felt that I was answering with exactly the right mixture of deference and confidence that they must approve of.

'That will be all, Patrol Officer Lemon', the Board President said at last. 'You may go.'

Murmuring my thanks, I rose to my feet, jammed my cap on to my head and saluted smartly. Stiffened fingers caught the cap peak and sent it spinning across the room. I felt blood rush to my face, muttered a despairing profanity and made a dive for the still rolling headgear. Jamming it over my ears, I fled in ignominious disorder, not daring to look at my inquisitors.

It was hardly the ideal end to my interview, but when the list of successful candidates came out, my name was there. Not very high up the list it is true, but that hardly mattered. I was a *Mambo* — a leader in my own right. I could give orders to white officers as well as black and I felt pretty damned pleased with myself.

With black advancement in the force, there have been many far more spectacular promotions since then of course, but as far as I know I was the first junior patrol officer to go up to section officer without doing the obligatory 12 months as a senior P/O.

Violent death was a fact of life for members of the BSAP and it often occurred in the most unlikely circumstances.

After a long winter in 1972, the rains came with a vengeance in mid-November and I drove into a kraal in the Chiota TTL, my blood curdling to the terrible ululating that is the death sound of Africa. Men and women sat around in watery sunshine, their faces blank with grief while the victim of a lightning strike lay in her hut. She looked perfectly peaceful and might have been asleep, but the pulse was long gone and her body was cold. The only mark I could find was a small burn on one ankle and I marvelled at the random cruelty of nature.

There had been seven people sitting in the hut while the storm raged around them, yet the lightning had taken this one woman and left the rest unharmed. Even the hut had escaped damage. It was terribly sad for the family, but she wouldn't have felt a thing and for me it was an awesome demonstration of the natural violence that is Africa.

While I was enjoying my coppering, the security situation in Rhodesia was far from stable and we carried out riot drills and musketry practice on a regular basis. I still found it difficult to take such things seriously and on one occasion, baby Deborah wasn't amused when I grabbed my gas mask from her sticky little fingers. It had been her favourite toy for weeks.

The mask was needed too as riot drills included the handling of tear gas as well as CS or 'puke' gas, the effects of both being pretty horrible. A little to my surprise, I rather enjoyed these practice sessions. I also amazed myself by shooting remarkably well, but I was always pleased to get back into my office and become a copper once more.

One night, Jack Parker, Constable Wafawanaka and I were instructed to carry out a station attack drill. Shortly before midnight, we crept through the grounds, Jack and I wearing camouflage cream on our faces and Wafa gleefully brandishing a P1 pistol. I carried an Uzi that I wasn't sure how to use and Jack was the chief terrorist. He led us stealthily through the trees and although the front of the station was well lit, this created pools of shadow that were ideal for prospective attackers. We crept to within a few metres of the charge office door and I confess that in spite of my antipathy towards all things military, I rather enjoyed being a 'terrorist.' The darkness felt comforting rather than dangerous and the snub-nosed machine gun in my hands was solidly reassuring.

Our plan was simple and worked to perfection. Tucking his pistol out of sight, Wafa wandered casually inside to make conversation with the staff on duty. While they were chatting, Jack and I poured petrol over the front steps and set fire to it. When the night sergeant burst out of the door with two wide-eyed constables in tow, they were confronted by Jack and myself, looking suitably menacing. Diving back inside the charge office, the grey-faced sergeant came face to face with Constable Wafa, brandishing his pistol and grinning like a man who was enjoying himself.

Jack explained the situation to the shift and Wafa's grin grew ever broader as he herded his abashed colleagues into a cell and turned the heavy key. Those already in residence also enjoyed the situation and much ribald advice was given to the sergeant and his men.

But our job wasn't finished. With Wafa hidden in the car park, Jack and I climbed on to the station roof and fired a number of shots into the night sky. Pandemonium ensued from the house that the single men used as a mess. S/Os, P/Os and their batmen arrived at a sleep-sodden run, trousers unbuttoned and unloaded rifles waving in futile confusion. Within moments, our cheerful colleague had emerged from the car park and rounded up the newcomers while Jack and I covered the driveways to dispose of reinforcements.

The exercise proved an overwhelming success from our point of view and both Jack and Waymond were sarcastically scathing when a debrief with the entire station staff was held the following day. I was glad I had been part of the attacking party, but for all my doubts about the prospect of war, that evening opened my eyes to what could be achieved by a determined enemy. The lessons learned were to be remembered for a very long time.

Shortly after that exercise I was called in by the boss with a proposition that didn't appeal in the slightest.

'I intend to start a PATU stick of regular members from this station', he told me happily. 'You are a section officer now so you'll be the ideal bloke to lead it.'

PATU stood for police anti terrorist unit and was one aspect of Rhodesian policing I wanted no part of. I loved my job and didn't want to give it up in order to play at being a soldier. Besides, I wasn't at all sure how I would react to being shot at for real and didn't want the opportunity to find out. PATU sticks were generally made up of police reservists, particularly those qualified by their professions or lifestyle for the rigours of bush warfare. Farmers, game rangers and others who spent their lives on the land were ideal candidates, while many sticks were confined to unmarried men. For my part, I had no intention of chasing terrorists unless they robbed a bank, parked without lights or committed lewd and licentious acts in a public place. I was a policeman dammit!

'Isn't PATU supposed to be voluntary, sir?' I ventured and Waymond nodded briskly.

'Of course it is but I know you will volunteer.'

'I won't you know.'

There was a long silence and the boss looked distinctly bewildered so I tried to explain my apparently unpatriotic attitude.

'I am a copper, sir, and I reckon I do a damned good job in this station. I don't want to be a soldier. Without wishing to be awkward, I reckon the army should be left to do their own thing and we should only step in when our assistance is actually called for. Coppers are trained to uphold the law and we should stick to that until there isn't any alternative.'

It was a long speech for me and such sentiments did little for my general popularity, but I believed in what I said and was determined to stick to my principles. The BSAP was the senior service in Rhodesia and 'the Great Tradition' included campaigns in the Shona and Matabele rebellions of the 1890s. Like everything else, warfare had advanced since then but in the 1970s, policemen were still running military operations while the army was used as back-up for police actions.

Nor were the enemy spear-wielding warriors any longer. They were well-trained guerrilla fighters with weaponry that matched or was even better than our own. I didn't feel that fighting against them as a police action could possibly work, particularly with the rest of the world against us. However, I had already said enough, so tried to keep my opinions to myself, even with Waymond who tolerated my apparent eccentricities.

It is all a long time ago now and it was politics rather than tactics that lost us that war, but I still feel that the carnage might have been less had the army taken control a little earlier and left the BSAP to uphold the law of the land.

However, tradition makes a powerful opponent and in 1972 I was both junior and inexperienced. Besides, my 'Englishness' made me suspect and a number of my colleagues had already labelled me as a dangerous liberal. My refusal to take part in PATU operations enhanced that view and for a while both Missy and I felt uncomfortable in our dealings with colleagues or their families.

Rogers Makamure was a farm foreman. Money had been stolen from the homestead and he was the prime suspect. It was raining hard when I arrived at the compound and I interviewed Rogers in his hut. It was small, dark and smoky, the fumes stinging my eyes as I squinted at the black man. He squatted comfortably on his heels as only an African can, his back against the pole and dagga wall. My constable interpreter sat on a cushion while — as befitted my exalted status — I was given a wooden stool. Nevertheless I felt far less comfortable than my companions looked and that made me irritable. Neither of them seemed to notice.

Rogers laughed scornfully when I queried his knowledge of the homestead.

'I have never been inside', the constable interpreted. 'It is so big that I would be lost.' He shook his head violently.

'I do not want to go inside. The Baas has his home; I have mine. Why should I want to see where he sleeps?'

This was probably the first time I really noticed the yawning gulf between black and white lifestyles in one place. The farmer's house was indeed very large. A sprawling mansion that had been added to whenever the family had money to spare, it was surrounded by well-tended gardens and had both swimming pool and tennis court for the family to use. The farmer doubtless ate three good meals a day, owned two cars, (one of them the obligatory Mercedes) a pick-up, three tractors and a three-tonner for deliveries, yet he claimed to be a poor man.

Rogers Makamure on the other hand lived in a cramped, smoky hut, ate only *sadza* with vegetable relish and rode a rickety bicycle without brakes. By Western standards he was virtually destitute, yet he was a 'bossboy' and relatively affluent among his fellow workers. I couldn't help thinking that if black rule ever did come to Rhodesia, men like Rogers would be totally confused. How would he adapt to living in the style of the white man? Would he move into a big house and be 'lost?' Would he eat bacon and eggs for breakfast? Would he forsake his own cultural traditions of extended families and tribal law for the stricter controls of Western society? Somehow I doubted it, yet folk like Rogers would need to aspire to that sort of lifestyle if Rhodesia was ever to compete with the rest of the world.

It was an intriguing problem, made even more curious when Rogers' wife ducked her head beneath the eaves to serve us tea. I drank mine from a chipped mug and it tasted smoky and very herbal. Later I went up to the homestead and drank more tea. It was South African *rooibos* and tasted smoky and very herbal, even if it did come from a delicate china cup.

I left that enquiry with my thoughts on the future more confused than ever.

If the boss was upset by my refusal to take part in matters military, he gave no overt sign of it, but it was perhaps significant that I was sent out on patrol a few days after our discussion. Patrolling was one of the joys of district coppering and was usually designed to show the flag in the farming community. This one was to be somewhat different.

'Whether you like the idea or not, security problems are going to hit this area very soon', Jack Parker had obviously heard about my refusal to get involved with PATU. 'I want you to thoroughly explore the southern section of the district.' He pointed it out on the map and I quailed inwardly at the size of the area. 'Take as much time as you like but get to know every cave, watercourse and possible hiding place. Explore river lines and look for likely escape or infiltration routes. Plot the location of kraals that might prove suspect and learn where local *ngangas* or spirit mediums can be found. Ask the farmers for help and explain what you are doing.'

He must have seen the query on my face.

'When our problems start', he told me gently. 'I am going to use you as our resident expert on that area. I want to be able to call you in on any incident and hear exactly where the opposition could be holed up or which way they will go in any given circumstances.

'Don't worry; you will enjoy it.'

He was right — I did. Two days later, Constable Dzorwa and I left Marandellas on a motor cycle and headed south. There were few farms in that area measuring less than 700 hectares and the patrol would give me a chance to appreciate the countryside, camp out at night and get to know the farmers. In my innocence, the prospect of war seemed very remote and much as I admired Jack Parker, I felt that he was being unduly alarmist. For all that, I was determined to follow his instructions to the letter. After all, I had been ordered to enjoy myself.

Over the next three and a half weeks, Dzorwa and I had a wonderful time. We explored caves, rivers, hills and ruins. We stayed with farmers (Dzorwa stayed in the compounds but didn't seem to mind) and enjoyed lavish hospitality wherever we went. We wandered though open pastures and climbed rocky kopjes to get a view of the landscape. We crawled into ancient burial grounds and on one farm, discovered an entire village from centuries past. We spent a couple of nights beneath glorious night skies and Dzorwa told me traditional Shona tales as we gazed into a fire.

On Ponderosa Farm, John Pattison mentioned a leopard that had been worrying stock and later in the day I climbed a nearby kopje to check out a cave. Spreadeagled on a rock face, I was easing my way up when a crackling snarl cut through the air above my head. That was one cave that remained unexplored.

Other minor adventures befell us on that memorable patrol and after 24 days in the farmlands, we returned, dusty and saddle-sore to Marandellas. I completed a patrol report then spent hours annotating maps with Jack Parker and answering a barrage of questions as best I could.

Jack ran the station intelligence scheme, known as 'ground coverage' — a scheme that was to prove its worth throughout the country in the hard years that lay ahead. By the time we had finished the debrief on my patrol, he was a happy man. In time I was to run a ground coverage scheme of my own, but by the time I took over the job, conditions in the country no longer allowed the sort of gentle wandering enjoyed by Dzorwa and myself. It had been a magical experience and I wouldn't have missed it for the world.

Those were happy days in Marandellas — days I will always remember. We were like old time troopers, swaggering about in our smart uniforms and shiny leather leggings. We got on well with all sectors of society and the public loved us. I enjoyed my job, played plenty of sport and banished doubts about the future to the back of my mind. The life I had left behind in Gloucestershire seemed part of a separate existence and I wasn't going back.

Missy also enjoyed the life, the boys were doing well at school and the future seemed assured. I was glad to be back home in Rhodesia, but my misgivings were not entirely unfounded. Even as we enjoyed ourselves, storm clouds were brewing.

5

Politics and the Pearce Commission

Even though my life in Rhodesia was extremely enjoyable, worries about the future were an ever-present burden on my mind. We were an isolated community in a hostile world and Chalky White's words on treason often came back to burn holes in my mind.

Rhodesian newspapers were heavily censored and made their readers feel that we were doing incredibly well on all fronts, but most of us listened to the BBC World Service and this painted a different picture. Rhodesia had few friends in the community of nations and in spite of our pride in our own achievements, statesmen everywhere condemned us as little more than a racist rabble who had not only subjugated our own black citizens, but had deserted and betrayed our Queen as well. The fact that these condemnations were blatantly unfair did nothing to make our situation any easier to cope with.

Black leaders to the north of us were particularly vociferous in their condemnation of all things Rhodesian and loudest of all were Presidents Nyerere and Kaunda of Tanzania and Zambia respectively. What made me angry was that their own economies were bankrupt and there was mass starvation in both countries, yet they claimed that we were ill-treating our citizens, all of whom were well fed and reasonably well paid.

I had always tried to remain apolitical, feeling that policemen should serve whichever government happens to be in power, but politics was thrust upon me from the start. A few weeks after my arrival at Marandellas — 18 January 1972 to be precise — former Rhodesian premier Sir Garfield Todd was arrested along with his daughter Judith for offences against the Law and Order (Maintenance) Act. She was to be kept in Marandellas Prison and — probably because of my accent — I was detailed to drive her there.

The prison at Marandellas was situated ten kilometres out of town and being an open establishment, was surrounded by acres of carefully tended vegetables and crops. In fact it looked more like a prosperous farm than a place of detention. It was my first visit to the place and as I only had the vaguest idea of my involuntary passenger's identity, I was more interested in the prison layout than in Ms Todd's angrily vituperative opinion of all things Rhodesian. Her most vulgarly descriptive phrases were reserved for the BSAP in general and one very junior patrol officer in particular. She didn't know my name but that didn't prevent the good lady from pouring scorn on my ancestry, my moral integrity and my manly attributes. I tried to remain detached, but I was young enough to be badly shaken by her unwarranted attack.

Judith Todd wasn't good company and her language might well have upset the average naval stoker. I was thankful to leave her and her escort at the prison and driving away, I wondered what had happened to old-fashioned concepts of femininity. Occupied with my thoughts, I rounded a corner and drove straight into a pack of journalists and photographers. Forced to stop by the throng, I sat there with my mouth open and my mind in neutral as microphones were thrust into my face and unanswerable questions came from every direction. Eventually I managed to drive on, but that was my first experience of the international media and I didn't enjoy it.

Fortunately perhaps I didn't see the results but was later told that I made a fleeting appearance on the British evening news. If so, it must have reinforced the image of Rhodesian policemen as mindless thugs, not even certain of the cause they were espousing.

I never saw Judith Todd again and I can't say I was sorry about that.

I had a far more enjoyable encounter on my first patrol in the Chiota TTL. Chief Mudzimurema was a rheumy-eyed old boy who must have been well into his eighties. Dressed in tattered khaki and wrapped in a threadbare blanket, he had an air of natural dignity about him that was impressive. Squatting on my heels in the dust before him, I looked around with interest.

Most tribal chiefs lived in modern, brick-built houses but Mudzimurema seemed content with a mud hut, albeit one that was considerably larger than the normal tribal dwelling. He wore no evidence of his authority, but there were a number of people waiting to see him and he obviously carried on with his chiefly duties.

The old chief spoke in a high, wheezing voice and although I spent less than 15 minutes in his presence, I was fascinated by his stories. He told me that in his youth he had seen Cecil Rhodes when the *Nkosi Mukulu* visited the area. His description of Rhodes tallied with the history books and I felt a sense of awe that this old man had lived through the entire chronicle of my country.

I could have spent hours with Chief Mudzimurema but the time of a chief is valuable and I was soon sent on my way. I think the efforts to remember had probably tired him but I resolved that the Mudzimurema kraal would be my first port of call when next I visited Chiota.

But it was not to be. By the time I was next in the area, Chief Mudzimurema was dead, murdered by *tsotsis* for being a 'sell out'. Although it was treated as an ordinary civil murder and the chief was given a traditional funeral, that killing was almost certainly the first act of political terrorism to occur in the Marandellas area.

Any murder is tragic but the death of Chief Mudzimurema hit me particularly hard. What wonderful stories that grand old man could have told.

Early in 1972 the Pearce Commission arrived in the country to canvas black Rhodesians on the settlement terms agreed between Ian Smith and Sir Alec Douglas Home, the British Foreign Secretary. White Rhodesians were cheerfully confident that the exercise would mark the end of our troubles and the prospect of international recognition brought smiles to many normally dour faces. For all their natural enjoyment of life, my compatriots had endured too much and gone without for too long. The strain was beginning to tell and Lord Pearce and his delegation brought a feeling of hope to our beleaguered country.

In spite of my own predilection for peaceful pursuits, I was one of those detailed to supervise three of the meetings and I set off with a cheerful — and entirely misplaced — optimism that Rhodesia's troubles were over and the future of my family in this wonderful country was at last assured. Even if the political mess wasn't sorted out, the meetings would at least give me the chance to ride behind riot screens and cut a fine dash as a rifle-toting, paramilitary bobby.

The meetings at Goromonzi, Mrewa and Mtoko attracted large crowds but left me with the feeling that everything wasn't as rosy as we were being led to believe. There was an undercurrent of tension very apparent in the packed audiences and although the commissioners did their best to explain that a settlement would benefit all Rhodesians, irrespective of colour, it was obvious that many people didn't believe them. At Mrewa I was watching and listening from the edge of the throng when I became aware of youths in jeans and sunglasses mingling with spectators and haranguing those who were trying to listen to what was being said. These thuggish young men seemed oblivious to our presence, even though we were in full uniform and well armed. In my ignorance, I asked a grizzled section officer what was going on. Alan Ferguson laughed at my naivety.

'They are making sure the vote goes the way they want it to go', he told me. 'They have put their point of view in the townships and now they are assuring the doubters that if they vote 'yes' they will be beaten, burnt out or even killed.'

I was aghast.

'But surely we should do something about it? After all, these blokes are quite blatant and it wouldn't be difficult to prove.'

Fergie laughed again and there was a note of bitterness to his mirth.

'Don't be daft, Man. This is Africa and any vote here hinges on threats and intimidation. If we took these thugs to court, nobody would give evidence against them and they would end up with more clout in the community than they had before. Their leaders have decreed that the vote will be 'no' and all we can do is ensure that there is a minimum of violence.'

It was my first lesson in the realities of African politics and it left me angrily frustrated. In time the settlement proposals were indeed rejected by the populace and war became inevitable. In later years I spoke to many sincere black people who told me that they would have voted in favour of the proposals had they been allowed to do so. What misery might have been avoided if they had. To the Western mind this attitude to politics is difficult to understand but Africa is a violent continent and intimidation is a basic part of African culture. Eventually I almost came to accept it as the norm.

However, the meetings went off peacefully enough although the same couldn't be said for other parts of the country. There were riots in Salisbury, Gwelo and Umtali where police were forced to open fire on the rioters. In other centres, noisy crowds were on hand to greet the commissioners, their messages of hate leaving a nasty taste in the mouth. Nationalist leaders were thrown into detention and tension built throughout the country. Fourteen people were killed by police and among the single coppers in Marandellas, there was an atmosphere of excitement that I found disturbing.

These were pleasant young men, popular in the community and good at their jobs. Nevertheless, a league table of kills was gleefully drawn up in the mess and there was much earnest talk as to how they could get Marandellas to the top. How much of it was mere bravado on the part of fit and active young men I wasn't sure but it certainly made me nervous. If war were to erupt in the country, what would I do about my family? Had I been right to risk their futures and even their lives in a land so at odds with the world? I didn't know and it worried me intensely.

For all that, the visit of Lord Pearce's commission gave me the opportunity to see more of the country I had been brought up in. How I loved the stark landscape of Mrewa — great rocky kopjes and mile upon mile of sandy scrub stretching into dusty horizons. How I loved the painted caves of Mtoko and how I loved the rolling grasslands of Goromonzi. This was home. This was the Africa of my dreams. I was to wander all those places in time and get to know them far more intimately than most Rhodesians but those early visits with Lord Pearce were not particularly happy ones.

6

Reluctant soldier

Every member of the BSAP was required to undergo an annual counter-insurgency (COIN) course and this usually culminated in a day on the range where members shot for their musketry classification. Somewhat to my surprise, I enjoyed my first four-day course, held in the wilds of Macheke. I managed a respectable 'first class' classification with the rifle and revelled in the physical challenge of working in rough countryside. I even enjoyed the thunderous confusion of range work, the seeping dust and the smell of burnt cordite. I didn't think I would need any of it and all the training made me no whit keener to get involved with PATU, but I did get a basic idea of what might one day be required of me and it was fun.

After the Pearce Commission had returned to Britain with their strident 'No' verdict, we were all confused and apprehensive. The cost of living was increasing by the day and monthly emigration figures were rocketing. These figures were read with as much interest as cricket and rugby scores, a strange situation for sport-mad Rhodesians.

On 21st December 1972, Altena Farm in the north-east of the country came under terrorist attack. It was a short and fairly harmless affair, but it was the first really aggressive incident since the late sixties. Marc de Borchgrave who farmed Altena, moved his family to Whistlefield Farm next door and this came under heavy fire two nights later. De Borchgrave and his daughter were both badly wounded on this occasion and an army landrover coming in to assist, went up on a landmine. A Corporal Moore died in the blast and suddenly the situation became real to Rhodesians.

The terrorists were no longer a faceless threat, occasionally mentioned in Special Branch memos. They were real, they were with us and they intended to kill. A Joint Operational Command centre was set up at Mount Darwin and the daily situation reports from JOC *Hurricane* as it was known were read with avid interest by policemen, soldiers and authorised civilians all over the country.

Marandellas was no exception and I was one of those who listened eagerly every morning when Waymond read out the sitrep for the previous 24 hours. Afterwards, those of us in the enquiry section would repair to Jack Parker's office and discuss the latest incidents. Unlike me, Jack was a born soldier and after carefully analysing each incident, he discussed the strategy and counter-strategy of the factions involved. I listened with the rest but it still seemed somehow unreal. I was a copper dammit! This spate of murder and mayhem had nothing to do with me. It wasn't until some years later that the benefit of those early morning tactical discussions really made itself felt.

Nor was the action confined to the north-east. Before any of us were really aware that the war had started in earnest, we had our own messy little incident to deal with and I had my first taste of very violent death.

Andries Joubert was a young farmer in the Wedza area. His property bordered on South Marandellas and I had called there on patrol, although I didn't know Andries particularly well.

Ishe Gorumatanga was a political commissar for FROLIZI and had come into the country to show the flag for his party and hopefully recruit a few more fighting men to the liberation cause. Ishe's band originally consisted of six men, but two coloured members had been killed along the way and in their flight from the security forces, Ishe and his three remaining colleagues had stopped off in Wedza. Like all guerrillas, they lived rough when in the field but in this case their camping arrangements went tragically wrong.

On 3rd March 1973, Joubert's workers reported the presence of strangers in an outlying maize field and without any inkling of trouble, the farmer wandered down to send them packing. He wore a pistol in his belt but the weapon was still unfired many hours later. By that time Andries Joubert was dead. I didn't really know the circumstances of his death but I could picture them in my mind.

> The burly young farmer climbs from his motor cycle and approaches the maize plants, probably squinting against harsh sunlight as he tries to make out the strangers, resting among serried stalks. The men panic, there is a sudden crackling rattle of automatic fire and a cloud of swirling dust as Joubert falls to the ground. The insurgents — probably aghast at what they have done — make off at the high port.

We will never know exactly how it went, but that is how it appeared to me at the time. District Headquarters received the report as 'the shooting of a farmer at Wedza.' There was no indication as to how or why he had been shot, nor as to who had done the shooting. In view of the security situation elsewhere however, it was deemed prudent to despatch as many men as were available to the scene in case the incident was anything other than domestic.

It was Saturday afternoon and the call-out meant my missing an important cricket match so I went through the ritual protests that I was a copper not a soldier, but Waymond was unsympathetic and there was nothing I could do about it. The exigencies of the service came well before cricket, even when a league title was at stake, so I reluctantly changed into camouflage uniform and withdrew my rifle from the armoury.

It was my first visit to the little whitewashed police station in the lee of Wedza

Mountain and I immediately fell in love with the place. It was an old-fashioned bush station that brought to mind bugles at dusk and belted troopers retiring to the mess veranda for sundowners as the flag was lowered. Wedza was a relic of Kipling's empire and everything that such an outpost ought to be.

But when we arrived that Saturday afternoon, the entire police camp was in a state of chaos. Andries Joubert's murder had been decreed an act of terrorism and the member in charge worked like a beaver to issue rifles, shotguns and anything else from his armoury to worried farmers and police reservists. The car park overflowed with dusty pick-ups and Mercedes Benzes, while the airfield next door had gaily coloured aircraft lined up in rows for refuelling.

For my sins, I was ordered to accompany fellow Patrol Officer Roy Barnard and collect the body of Andries Joubert. With five years service under his belt, Roy was waiting for promotion while I had only just sat my examination so I deferred to him in most things. We were both edgy on our way out to the Joubert farm where the scene that greeted us was worthy of a Gilbert and Sullivan extravaganza.

In the centre of a dusty farm road, two figures in civilian clothing were having a right royal row. One of them was Angus Ross — a hulking detective superintendent, built on the lines of a battle cruiser — and the other was Andries Joubert's father.

The farmer was so small that he barely reached the superintendent's chest but his anger more than made up for his lack of bulk. He carried a rifle as large as himself in one hand and the other was waving furiously beneath the policeman's nose.

'Driesie was my son, Mr Ross', he thundered. 'He has been murdered by the blerry kaffirs and we are going to form a commando and kill them ourselves.'

Hard-faced, bearded young men in shorts, veldskoens and wide-brimmed hats nodded in silent agreement. They were ranged behind Joubert and every one of them carried a rifle in his hands and an assortment of lethal looking hardware draped about his person. They looked a formidably terrifying bunch but Angus Ross was an experienced copper and appeared unmoved by the situation.

'You are not going to do anything without my say so', he rumbled in a Scottish brogue that contrasted strangely with the little farmer's guttural Afrikaner tones. 'Army trackers will run these men down and then they will be sorted out by the Security Forces.'

'Bah!'

Joubert spat forcefully into the dust. He was obviously unimpressed. Before he could say more however, the arrival of an open Land-Rover, full of lean and fit young men in camouflage shorts and little else eased the tension. Their leader saluted the superintendent and they moved away to speak in low tones.

I watched in silent bemusement as my first experience of war on the ground unfolded. The newcomers were a tracker combat unit and after a few moments with Ross, they moved off across the fields, long legs eating up the ground and FN rifles swinging easily in their hands. They looked awfully tough to me and I wasn't sure which bunch I would prefer to have on my side — the army trackers or the silent commando of Afrikaans farmers.

The Wedza patrol officer, Chris Aitken was on the scene and he told us what had happened. Adrenalin was obviously running high in Chris and his excitement was curiously infectious. This was the sort of action that district coppers craved and the fact that friends had to die to provide it was neither here nor there. I was fascinated but wondered a little sourly why I couldn't share the general enthusiasm. After all I had wanted excitement.

The body of Andries Joubert lay on the edge of a maize field, his arms thrown out to the sides and his scalp neatly removed by the path of a bullet. I learned later that the first shot of a sustained burst had killed him, the rest of the rounds flying high into distant trees. There was a slightly surprised expression on the young farmer's face but I couldn't get over the way his head had been opened up — just as though someone had taken the top off a breakfast egg.

It was the first time I had seen what a bullet could do to the human body and it was worse than all my imaginings. The memory of Joubert's head would haunt me for months. Every time I was in any situation where shots might be fired, I would feel the skin of my scalp tighten with fearful anticipation.

There was nothing that Roy or I could do for the dead man. Chris had taken the necessary photographs and the experts were in control, so we loaded him gently into the body box and headed back to camp.

That was my only participation in the hunt for the killers of Andries Joubert, but it was my first experience of warfare and its horrors. A young man had been gunned down, purely because he was in the wrong place at the wrong time. He was a husband and father of very young children, but such factors count for nothing when it comes to war.

Two of the men who killed Joubert were cornered on the slopes of Wedza Mountain and one was eventually hanged. Soon after the Wedza incident, Ishe Gorumatanga was spotted on a bus by an alert constable from Enkeldoorn and shortly afterwards he died under a storm of Security Force gunfire.

I don't think the fourth cadre was ever accounted for and it is likely that his bones rest in some corner of Zimbabwean countryside — unremembered and unmourned by any but his immediate family. There are many hundreds of men resting like that and although for many years I hated them with considerable passion, I have mellowed now and find it ineffably sad that it should be so.

Even the basest of men deserves a grave.

I had never really thought on the difference between insurgents, guerrillas and terrorists so I usually listed those armed infiltrators to the north-eastern border area under the first category. This led to stern correction from a few of my more militant colleagues. It was the death of Section Officer Duncan Mackay that brought home the fact that we were up against cold-blooded terrorism. To refer to our steadily accumulating enemy in any other terms was to grant them a status they didn't deserve.

Duncan was a quiet spoken lad, a couple of years younger than I was. He was stationed at Marandellas when I arrived, but moved on soon afterwards so I didn't know him long.

What I did know, I liked as he was an efficient, fair policeman with a quiet sense of humour and an eagerness to help anyone in need. We gave him a grand farewell party and I don't think there was anyone at the station who wasn't sorry to see him leave. However, once Duncan had gone, I forgot all about him until the day his name appeared on the morning sitrep.

Duncan Mackay had been driving a police Land-Rover in the Eastern Highlands when he came across a black man lying apparently comatose in the road. This is not an unusual sight in rural Africa and being the kindly fellow he was, Duncan stopped the truck and alighted to assist the 'drunk' from the road. As he moved away from the vehicle, AK rifles opened up on him from all sides and Duncan Mackay died as he had lived — in the act of helping somebody else. Duncan's concern for his fellow man had been the direct cause of his murder and if that is not terrorism, I really don't know what is.

The news of Duncan's killing caused a great deal of tight-lipped anger in Marandellas and from that day onwards, I never thought of our opposition as anything other than terrorists, terrs, gooks or some of the other more colourfully colloquial names that were used by Rhodesians in those terrible days.

I also spent many a contemplative hour wondering what I would have done in the situation that Duncan found himself in on that dusty highland road. With hindsight, I would have driven over the man, but Duncan had done what was right. I liked to think that I would have acted just as honourably, but I knew that if I had I would also have died.

It was an uncomfortable thought.

A liaison visit to Mrewa in the depths of winter added to my sense of disquiet. I was driving alone through the Mangwende TTL and all around me, a barren landscape stretched into hazy infinity. The Mangwende was one of the largest TTLs in the country and for a white man alone, it was a forbidding place indeed — miles and miles of bleak, sandy countryside with tiny kraals huddled beneath giant rocks. Towering euphorbia cacti between the rocks provided the only greenery on view and the absence of young men was very noticeable. In those kraals that were obviously inhabited, women and the very old watched my passing with dusty inscrutability and the lack of emotion in their stares made me nervous. *Picannins* drove scrawny cattle through the landscape. I should have been enjoying myself for this was old-time Africa. But there was a sullen acceptance about the landscape that made my blood run cold.

In one field an old man prepared the ground for planting only 20 metres from the road. His back was bowed, his hair was a sparse collection of grey peppercorns and he had no modern machinery to make his work easier. His plough was the implement of ages past — a curved wooden tine that bit through the crumbling earth and was powered by the sagging steps of an old ox, ribs starkly outlined in the afternoon sunshine.

I waved to the old man but he didn't return the gesture. His eyes were blank when he looked across at me and there was no sign of reaction in the seams of his face. He had that look about him which has puzzled and frustrated the white man since the first Christian settlers arrived in Africa — a look that appears sullen but is merely a form of self-protection, a cutting off of society and its problems. The old man had raised an invisible barrier between himself and the outside world, of which I was all too obvious a part. I don't think it was just because I was white. I happened to be there and he didn't want to know me.

The road to Mrewa was a chasm of thick, soft sand. Dust billowed in a rolling yellow cloud behind me as I drove on. I felt sad at the innate hostility of the old man, but tried hard to understand. He was part of a timeless Africa that will endure long after the white race — and myself with it — have abandoned the continent to its own devices. His appearance, his plough, his ox and his blank, sullen look remained with me for a very long time. They were the real Africa and they terrified me.

In fact, I was probably justified in feeling afraid. After my meeting at Mrewa, I mentioned my feelings about the Mangwende to a Special Branch officer who laughed in cynical derision.

'The old bastard probably had a group of gooks hidden away in his kraal', was his comment. 'If you had gone any closer, you would have been shot.'

Perhaps he was right. Later events in the Mangwende certainly supported his observation, but to me, the old man had merely been part of Africa.

War in those early days of what modern historians like to term 'the armed struggle' wasn't all blood and excitement for we dashing troopers of the BSAP. There were occasions when it was almost fun.

For some time, Special Branch sources had reported a 'presence' in the Ngarwe TTL north of Mrewa and this necessitated a major operation in Chief Nyakasoro's area. It was here that my next lesson in military routine took place.

Once again I was the only officer available and found myself driving into wild countryside, filled with gaunt baobab trees and dusty tracks. Kudu bulls watched incuriously as I trundled past and I couldn't help reflecting that this was the kind of landscape I had dreamed about during my years of exile. The base at Nyakasoro dam was equally idyllic.

Throughout Africa's colonial history, District Commissioners have been particularly important people and their rest camps were always sited in the most picturesque places. This one was no exception. The house was big and sprawling, with gauze over the windows and a long veranda overlooking the water. On a clear day, the dusty blue mountains of Inyanga could be seen on the horizon and the landscape around camp was dotted with mighty baobabs. The veranda faced the sunset of course, otherwise the old-time DCs wouldn't have been able to appreciate the sunsets with their evening sundowner beers.

The police presence at Nyakasoro consisted of a Special Branch section officer, a couple of PATU sticks and a number of GC constables. My job was to arrange our daily menu. Hardly inspiring and unlikely to put me in line for any medal awards, but I was still viewed with a certain amount of suspicion by my hard-bitten colleagues. I had cheerfully confessed my lack of training to the D/S/O in charge and he wasn't going to risk me in

51

the field so I became the 'scoffboss.'

We had a regular issue of military ration packs at the base, but these were shared out among the junior ranks and often used to bribe locals into giving information. Those of us who slept in the house and ate in the palatial dining room expected finer cuisine than mere ration packs, or ratpaks as they were commonly called. The dam was well stocked with bream, we had a pot licence for one kudu a month and guinea fowl, francolin and wild duck were plentiful so menu planning wasn't difficult.

I spent much of my time hunting or fishing and we ate very well indeed. Venison, fresh fish and wild fowl make a marvellous staple diet and this was occasionally varied with the gift of a goat or scrawny cow from Chief Nyakasoro. A visit from Jack Parker elicited the comment that he had not eaten as well when on a recent holiday in Durban.

If this was war, it wasn't quite what I had expected. I passed my days in idyllic contemplation of rural Africa and my life was hardly at risk. The opposition were certainly in the area and we had regular reports of their presence to keep us on our toes, but of sightings or contacts, there were none.

I didn't mind. I certainly wasn't bored.

A Support Unit section visited Nyakasoro for a few days and this was the first time I had seen the notorious Black Boots in action. They were the military arm of the Force and had a reputation for being inveterate thieves and very wild men indeed. Working in small sections, they foraged the remoter areas for news of the enemy and built up an ever-increasing standing as formidable jungle fighters.

The nickname 'Black Boots' came from the colour of their leatherwear. Members of the Duty Uniform Branch wore brown boots, brown belts and brown cap straps. Our leggings were brown too, but the Unit had all these items in black — probably to spare the rest of us from being associated with their excesses. They were also entitled to wear medal ribbons on their shirts and their martial eagle emblem was prominently displayed on their left sleeves. Most of them spent weeks at a time in the bush, which accounted for a certain amount of hooliganism when they were allowed back into civilisation. At the time of their visit to Nyakasoro, the entire 240-strong Support Unit was banned from every police pub in the country.

The group we had with us at Nyakasoro certainly lived up to Unit traditions. They were hard, watchful men and we had a number of thefts reported during their stay. I lost a favourite hunting knife, although this was eventually returned to me by the Unit section officer with stern instructions to 'look after your kit, hey.'

One cold early morning I found myself huddled in the front seat of a sawn-off Land-Rover with Section Officer Duncan Beveridge driving and three of his hardened cut throats arrayed in the back. We were on our way to investigate a terrorist sighting and I have never been so scared in my life. It wasn't the possibility of imminent action that terrified me, but the speed at which we travelled. The road was a narrow defile between tall trees, it wasn't yet full daylight and the lights didn't work. In spite of these minor handicaps, we hurtled along at 65 kilometres an hour and didn't slow down for anything. Bends were taken on two wheels and other obstructions went unnoticed. Had any living creature ventured across our path, it would assuredly have died, but there was nothing living about at that hour and we eventually arrived at our destination in one piece. As I prised my fingers from the dashboard, my companion must have noticed my set features and fluttering nerves.

'We have to travel at speed', he said off-handedly. 'It makes us less of a target for ambush and if we hit a landmine — well we wouldn't know anything about it anyway.'

Hardly reassuring from my point of view but it was this casual attitude to death and destruction that set the Black Boots apart from we lesser mortals. Staggering from the truck, I thanked my lucky stars that I was but an ordinary copper.

Fortunately perhaps, that sighting came to nothing and I resumed my carefree existence at Nyakasoro, my opinion of the Support Unit as a bunch of unruly hooligans decidedly reinforced.

My only previous contact with Black Boots had been at Tomlinson Depot where black recruits to the Force were trained. Quite what I was doing there I cannot remember, but I stopped beside the parade square to watch a group of Support Unit recruits being put through their paces by a solidly built section officer.

To me they looked frighteningly smart but the instructor was obviously unimpressed with one man's performance. Having brought the entire squad to a shuddering halt, he screamed abuse at the luckless detail and ended his tirade with a smack across the face that visibly rocked the man back on his heels. Sickened by this evidence of racist barbarity, I waited for the lesson to end.

When that S/O came off the square, I told him exactly what I thought of his behaviour and after he had recovered from his surprise at my unexpected attack, his mustachioed lip curled in contempt. His eyes rested momentarily on the single bar adorning my shoulders and I distinctly saw big hands curling themselves into fists.

'You bloody Englishmen', he told me slowly, 'come out here and think you know it all. You apply your own lily-livered standards to the problems of Rhodesia and cannot adapt your thinking to the African way of life. When you've been in this job for five years, Sonny — if you last that long — your views will change, I can promise you.'

I never did meet up with that section officer again, not did I discover who he was, but as years went by I often reflected on that little incident and had to agree that he was largely correct in his thinking. Like so many allegedly civilised folk, I had been guilty of applying Western standards to a situation that was purely African. To a certain extent I was wrong and although I still can't condone that section officer's handling of the situation, I can at least understand.

My escort on hunting trips around Nyakasoro was Constable Kwande from Nyamapanda. An experienced ground coverage detail, Kwande had obviously appointed himself my bodyguard and one evening was a splutteringly mute witness to my greatest embarrassment since joining the BSAP.

On the evening hunt I missed five successive guinea fowl in half an hour, all within a kilometre of camp. Kwande's grin grew broader with each thundering shot and occasionally he shook his head in mock sorrow. I could only imagine the stories he would tell in the African police mess that night but for the life of me and no matter what, I couldn't shoot straight. I was using an automatic shotgun and the final straw came when I expended three rounds of SSG on one particularly scornful bird. The guinea merely fluttered its wings as lead pellets hummed about it, then made off with a derisory cackle. No longer making any attempt to conceal his mirth, Kwande was doubled up with laughter. On the other hand, I was not amused.

Empty handed and disgusted with myself, I wasn't enjoying the walk back to camp when a duiker jinked frantically away from almost beneath my feet. In one instinctive movement, I slammed the shotgun shut, brought it up to my shoulder and fired. It was probably more luck then judgement, but for once my aim was true and the unfortunate duiker rolled over with a soggy thump 20 metres away. Kwande was grinning all over his face when he turned to congratulate me on my shooting.

'You would have been known forever as Bwana Shitshot', he told me happily. 'However, Bwana Shitshot has now become Bwana Goodshot so you have been spared.'

I was so pleased with my own shooting that I couldn't be cross with Kwande for his insubordination. After dinner that evening I relaxed with a pipe on the veranda, admired the night sky and murmured to one of my colleagues.

'If this is war then I take back all my reservations on the matter.'

Rain was falling in solid sheets of warm water and the ground was a swirling mass of sticky red mud. The Land-Rover slid alarmingly along the rough track and forward progress was minimal. I was delivering mail to the police camp at Nyamapanda and although I left Nyakasoro at first light, conditions were so appalling that I didn't complete the 30-kilometre journey till well into the afternoon.

Nyamapanda was a border station and apart from the police camp and a customs post, there was nothing there. On the Mozambique side there was a ramshackle customs shed and George's Store — the only emporium within many hundreds of square kilometres.

Ken Ward who had served with me at Marandellas had recently transferred to this little Outpost of the Empire and my motivation in volunteering for the mail run was to see what he had got himself into. He greeted me outside the charge office.

'It's a bloody marvellous place', he enthused over tea. 'Nothing to do except bush patrols and a spot of hunting. I only wish I had come here sooner.

'You are staying for the Ball of course?'

In modern times my expression would probably have been described as 'gobsmacked.' A 'Ball' out here? There wasn't a white woman within 200 kilometres and the only source of music was probably tribal drums dammit! Ken hastened to explain. The date was November 11th and in common with major centres throughout the country, Nyamapanda was staging an Independence Day Ball.

'All the Porks are coming from across the border', Ken went on. 'Food has already been prepared and there will be gallons of grog. We've set up a record player and even have a couple of dolly birds imported from Bulawayo.'

In my bedraggled camouflage I was hardly dressed for any sort of function, but I had been away from home for three weeks and the prospect of convivial company (and cold beer) was difficult to turn down. Having borrowed a safari suit from Ken's wardrobe, I radioed Nyakasoro that conditions were too bad for an immediate return and made myself available for the festivities.

Over the years I have attended many grand functions. Balls, investitures, ceremonial dinners and a host of formal, celebratory occasions. I have worn dinner jacket, lounge suit or dress uniform and usually managed to enjoy the proceedings without looking too out of place. I can safely say, however, that the UDI Ball at Nyamapanda in 1972 was the most unusual and enjoyable celebration of its kind, I am ever likely to attend.

All the senior staff of the station were in attendance, most of them dressed to the nines. Miniature medals glimmered and chinked, while white-jacketed waiters flitted silently among the revellers. Background music came from scratchy Mantovani and a radiogram, powered off the station generator. The main table was a glittering array of cutlery, glassware and immaculately pressed white linen, while the food and drink on display would have brought gasps of admiration in the finest of European hotels.

The evening began slowly but once the Portuguese contingent arrived, the proceedings began to lose a bit of their solemnity. These men had been in the bush for a long time and obviously welcomed the chance to let their hair down. Mantovani gave way to the Beatles and Rolling Stones while beers disappeared at an ever more frenetic rate.

The 'dolly birds' were teachers from Bulawayo and they entered into the swing of things with a will. Pretty girls both, their virtue might have been considered at considerable risk among all those love-starved bush men, but by eight o'clock, every man present (including myself I regret to say) was in such a state of inebriation that their continued chastity couldn't be in any possible doubt.

Toasts were ceremoniously drunk — to Ian Smith and to Rhodesia: to Mozambique, Portugal and the continued excellent relationship between the countries. Further toasts — not quite the correct word in the circumstances — were knocked back to the everlasting ill health of a number of British politicians and then the games began.

After a fairly lengthy spell of alcoholic abstinence, I was soon feeling the pace but volunteered to represent my country in a boat race. This was one of those silly games where pints of beer are consumed at a tremendous rate, two teams lining up to drink 'against' each other in an alcoholic relay.

Three months previously I had boxed for a Rhodesian team at the South West African championships, so after my visit to Nyamapanda, I suppose I could claim to be a double sporting international. The end result of both my representative appearances however was a severe headache and a feeling that all wasn't right with my world.

But what an evening that was! The Ball proceeded apace and all thoughts of war or political chicanery were forgotten. Beer, wine, prawns and crayfish were consumed in quantity, while the decibel count rose by the moment. It is all a very long time ago, but I can still see the laughing faces, remember the creaking music and taste in retrospect the divine flavour of Mozambican seafood at a time when such things were in desperately short supply in my own beleaguered country.

My return to Nyakasoro the following morning was carried out in an atmosphere of acute alcoholic remorse. My head pounded in time to the bumps in the road and my teeth itched to distraction. For some reason, I still wore Ken's muddied safari suit beneath my camouflage and an almost empty bottle of Borges Port wobbled on the floor between my feet. I let the unlicensed but enthusiastic Kwande do the driving as I wasn't sure that I could see the road. When we finally arrived at Nyakasoro, the boss took one look at my bloodshot eyes and sent me out again with instructions to replenish the larder.

He knew full well what I had been up to and obviously felt that a walk in the hot sun would do wonders for my hangover. It didn't, but my first visit to Nyamapanda had certainly been a memorable one.

Back in Marandellas the parties continued. Missy and I were forever dressing up to attend one 'do' or another and if there wasn't a party arranged, we would end up at someone's house. Beer was good and cheap so the drinking was enthusiastic, but in my somewhat cynical frame of mind, I couldn't help wondering how much of the frenetic social activity was due to the ever-increasing tension of our situation.

Prospects of a settlement with Britain were becoming ever more remote and terrorist attacks in the north-east were an almost daily occurrence. Policemen and their families had been killed and in one horrifying sitrep, it was estimated that there were more than 200 armed terrorists already in the country. None of us knew how we could possibly cope with that many and even my normally placid wife was beginning to worry.

In time we were to cope with 20, 30, 40 times that number, but fortunately for my own peace of mind, I had no inkling of the horrors to come and concentrated on dulling my vague misgivings with beer.

It must have been well into 1973 when Dispol called me in to his office. 'Yogi' Blair always had the welfare of the troops at heart and he was in benevolent mood.

'You are a section officer now', he told me. 'You are also overdue for a move so you need to get in first with a transfer application. If you don't, you could well end up in some hell hole like Zaka. Have you any idea which stations you might prefer?'

An immediate transfer wasn't part of my plans. I liked Marandellas and my family was settled so the thought of moving didn't appeal. I tried to explain this but the OC was unconvinced.

'It is Force policy', he said firmly. 'As an S/O you are in a position of command over your mates and that could lead to difficulties, so you will be moved whether you like the idea or not.'

I could see his point but asked for time to consult with Missy. The OC agreed but advised me not to take too much time over my decision.

'Zaka is not the nicest place to spend a summer', he warned broodingly and I was dismissed. Missy didn't seem at all upset by the prospect of an imminent move, which surprised me a little, but then she had been reading the sitreps at Internal Affairs and worried about the situation even more than I did.

'I want to go to Kariba', she decided immediately.

I laughed a little hollowly. Kariba was the dream station for everyone. Boats, wildlife, water sports and a holiday lifestyle — there would be a queue of section officers trying to get themselves to Kariba. We discussed a few alternatives but Missy had that determined air about her that I had come to recognise. She wanted Kariba and nowhere else would do. We had enjoyed an unofficial honeymoon there and she was determined to return.

A few days later Yogi Blair cornered me in the corridor. I started to explain that we hadn't quite made up our minds when he took the wind out of my sails.

'How would you like a posting to Kariba?'

I wondered whether I was dreaming.

'There is an immediate vacancy if you want it.'

'Great, sir', I spluttered. 'When can we go?'

Once again, Lemon's Luck was moving along in top gear and less than a month later we were on our way to the great lake of Kariba. I was to be second in command at the station and it seemed that the world was at my feet. As we passed our first wild elephant past Makuti on the Kariba road, my doubts were forgotten and life in rural Gloucestershire seemed like part of another world.

7

Sunshine and sadness

1974 was a bad year for Rhodesians. On 6 March, Harold Wilson returned to power in Britain and on 30 September, the Portuguese premier Marcello Caetano was ousted in a left-wing coup.

The Portuguese coup led to immediate independence for Mozambique, bringing FRELIMO to unelected power and opening up a 1 100 kilometre border for us to guard against terrorist incursions. This meant that we now had over 3 000 kilometres of unfriendly border and only 200 of common boundary with South Africa, who most of us believed were our only friends in the world.

In November, a meeting was held among nationalist inmates of Que Que prison. Ndabaningi Sithole, who had blotted his copybook by publicly denouncing the armed struggle in 1969, was suspended from his position as leader of ZANU. Robert Mugabe was secretary-general at the time but he abstained from voting on the grounds that without a quorum, the meeting was unconstitutional.

Mugabe's doubts didn't prevent him from accepting the leadership a few months later however and for most of us, he was to become the real bogeyman. Fanciful tales were told in Rhodesian pubs about his intelligence, (estimates of his university degrees varied between three and eight) his cruelty and his hatred for whites. None of us really knew what we were talking about, but it gave us a focus for our nervousness about the terrorist threat.

More disturbing was the fact that outsiders were deciding our future. That at least was how it appeared. Talks were held in Lusaka between President Kaunda, Prime Minister Vorster of South Africa and Lonrho executives. A detente exercise and subsequent cease-fire was announced but it had disturbing implications. I couldn't help wondering why a business corporation should have a major say in the fate of my country, but I suppose I was being naive again. Lonrho possessed vast holdings throughout Africa and consequently demanded and was granted considerable influence in the future of individual countries. That is the way of African politics. I have no doubt that it goes on everywhere, but in other parts of the world financiers are covert in their string pulling. In Africa, political connivance with the moneymen is far more blatant.

More serious still was the release from custody of the detained political leaders. Mugabe and Nkomo were both freed to work their insidious damage and this was generally believed to be the direct result of South African pressure on Ian Smith. Their release was supposed to bring an end to the war, but the loudly proclaimed detente proved an unmitigated disaster. Within days of the announcement, four South African policemen were cold-bloodedly murdered by terrorists near Victoria Falls. Hailed by the killers, the SAP members — often derided by Rhodesians for their supposed lack of intellect — laid down their rifles to talk. They were immediately gunned down and that incident knocked the heart out of the cease-fire. Even the South Africans must have seen that it couldn't possibly work.

But it was Wilson's election that really depressed Rhodesians. How we hated that man!

For me 1974 was a good year. Kariba was as wonderful in fact as it had been in prospect and I took to lakeside life like a pig in the proverbial. Within days of my arrival, I had learned to handle the big, twin-engine police launches, been fully accepted into community life and enjoyed my first real bush patrol through the Matusadona National Park.

I had also taken over the station ground coverage scheme while Missy and the kids were happy as crickets in our house on the edge of Kariba Gorge. We had regular visits from leopard and baboons, while our veranda overlooked the boiling Zambezi River nearly 400 metres below. The only drawbacks to life were the searing heat and the fact that Kariba was a long way from civilisation. Shopping facilities were almost non existent and petrol rationing had been in effect for some time, but we were allowed one trip per month to Salisbury — presumably to keep us vaguely sane — and the coupons issued by Internal Affairs for this trip more than covered our needs. As for the heat — well, we grew accustomed to it in time and the surroundings more than compensated for a little discomfort.

The Kariba charge office was a single storey building in the camp itself and we were a self-contained community in our own right. We had our own pub — the Jam Jar — as well as an assortment of houses and flats for all ranks. It was an idyllic spot and if wildlife were inclined to use it as a transit road to Kariba Heights, I wasn't too upset by their presence.

One of my earliest Kariba memories is of a late night telephone call from the charge office. I have never been one of those men who is instantly awake and it took a while for the duty constable's voice to register in my groggy mind.

'There are five lions outside my window, sir', the luckless detail whispered nervously. 'What should I do?

'They are female lions', he added helpfully, but I still wasn't fully awake.

'Hold on, I will come down', I muttered and replaced the receiver. Pulling on a tracksuit, I staggered sleepily from the house. To reach the charge office necessitated a 60-metre walk through the darkness and it must have been the night air that brought me to my senses.

'Lions', the man had said. Real live African LIONS!

My head was suddenly very clear, I yelped inwardly, darted back inside and picked up the telephone.

'Just keep the window closed', I advised the nervous constable and went back to my nice warm bed.

It had been easy to see myself as a hero back in rural Britain, but I had no intention of shooing away five lions.

The following morning we marvelled at saucer-like pug marks only metres from the flimsy gauze of the charge office windows. We had been having trouble with night shift details sleeping on duty, but for some time after that everyone was very much awake.

But that was the joy of Kariba. It was old-time Africa in the 20th century. One moment a copper could find himself waiting patiently behind elephants ambling up the centre of the main road and the next, he would be streaking at 35 knots across the lake, 240 Volvo-inspired horses howling behind him. It was all incredibly exciting.

For me the main appeal of Kariba was that we were relatively untouched by the war. On the hill behind us was an army camp, complete with a resident battalion of national servicemen and ten kilometres out of town, the Rhodesian Air Force held their lethal machines in constant readiness for action. The Tracking Wing — those tough young men I had encountered so fleetingly in Wedza — did most of their training in the rough countryside around Kariba and in time they were incorporated into the newly formed Selous Scouts, led by the charismatic Major Ron Reid Daly.

The Scouts were to build up an awesome reputation among Rhodesians and a fair degree of notoriety elsewhere in the world for their exploits, but they were a truly multiracial unit. Black Rhodesians worked closely together with white Rhodesians, each one never hesitating to give his life for the other. They were easily distinguished from other members of the Security Forces by their bushy trademark beards.

As number two in the police hierarchy, I read all sitreps and attended inter service meetings. I occasionally wore camouflage and spent the odd hour in the frenetic bustle of army or air force ops rooms, where I listened entranced to messages from troops in the field. These laconic communications came from men who were actually fighting a gruesome war but it still seemed somehow remote from my daily life and for most of the time I was left to get on with being a copper.

There was no friction between services in Kariba and I mixed socially with men who were to become national heroes over the years to come. Majors Harry Harvey and Ian Bate did stints at Kariba as did Squadron Leader Rob Tasker — a quiet man who handled helicopters like extensions of his own arms. Others — including various generals and a succession of cabinet ministers — came up on official or unofficial visits. I did a great deal of saluting, but the atmosphere of the place was such that protocol seldom lasted longer than the initial introductory period. No matter how exalted they were, visitors wanted to fish or party and usually went home so relaxed or hung over that they hardly remembered who they had been talking to a few moments before.

The only permanent military residents were the Selous Scout instructors and they spent more time on active service than they did in camp. Ant White, Martinus Kok (who answered only to 'Bushpig') Alan 'Stretch' Franklin, Dale Collet, Jimmy Lafferty and

Pete Clements — their names were to become part of Rhodesian folklore, but to us they were mates from 'up the hill' and great fellows to have at a party. The contrast between cheerfully boisterous revellers in smart safari suits and their daytime alter egos in worn camouflage never ceased to amaze me and I tended to look upon them all with a certain degree of awe.

These were men who had seen action, been shot at and killed other men in the frenetic excitement of combat. They were battle-hardened veterans yet they cuddled and cooed over baby Deborah like any gentle city type. In fact, they were perfectly ordinary fellows who did an incredibly difficult job.

The Scouts did produce a few extra problems for me but they were the sort of problems I was trained to cope with. Their fighting life was a stressful one and whenever they had time off in town they went on the rampage, visiting all the pubs and becoming rowdier and more prone to fighting with every beer they downed. Inevitably many of them ended up in police custody and although I knew it was a waste of time, I would ensure that they were locked up in the cells. The end result was always the same.

First thing next morning my phone would ring and it would be Major Ron or 'Mac' McGuinness, the SB superintendent attached to the Scouts. There would follow a polite request for the miscreants to be released without charge. I would refuse and a few minutes of friendly argument would ensue. If I stuck to my guns, it wouldn't be more than ten minutes before my phone rang again, this time with some faceless desk-jockey from PGHQ on the other end.

'Release them immediately.' Would be the terse message and the felons would be allowed to go free.

In a way it was a defeat for the legal system and a gross miscarriage of justice, but it was also understandable and I tried not to let it affect my sense of humour. After all I had not let them go myself, so my conscience was relatively clear. Besides, Major Ron and Mr Mac always bought me a beer or three when they were in town.

In time I took my 'driving test' under the watchful eye of Frank Andrews, the Lake Captain and came away from that little adventure with a plastic card proclaiming to the world that I was a Launchmaster (Class 1) according to the Inland Waters Shipping Act. Now I was entitled to take the police launches out on three and four day patrols and that was a marvellous experience. Out on that vast expanse of water with the blue sky above and warm wind in my face, I felt that all my dreams had come true. Daylight hours were spent among Tonga fishermen living in isolated camps around the lake shore and at night I would curl up in the boat and let the gentle rhythm of the waves lull me to sleep. Security problems were far from my mind and although I questioned the fishermen about terrorist visits, it was routine rather than genuine interest. These fishermen were gentle, uncomplicated folk, still living in a bygone age and uninterested in war or insurrection. Nor were they interested in politics or the nationalist cause. Of all the indigenous citizens of Rhodesia, they were the most apolitical and would support anyone who could provide them with a regular supply of fishing hooks or 'twine' for their makeshift fishing rods.

In view of my exalted status, I no longer worked shifts and my weekends were usually free. Sundays would see us relaxing as a family at the Kariba Yacht Club or driving across the lake for 'liaison visits' at Bumi Hills Safari Lodge. The DC's rest camp was available to us for weekend visits and the Bumi police post was uniquely beautiful, even in a country famed for spectacular scenery.

Six hundred metres above the lake itself, the little whitewashed building perched precariously on the edge of a mountain. Far, far below was the Bumi airstrip and beyond this the magnificence of Sibilobilo Lagoon stretched into hazy infinity. I spent many a contented evening watching the sun go down beyond that magical island chain while marvelling inwardly at my luck. This was even better than coppering.

The safari lodge was the epitome of luxury and the kids would play in the swimming pool while Missy and I mingled with tourists, enjoying quantities of cold beer and wondering absently how the poor people were faring. The lodge was famous for the quality of its cuisine and we took full advantages of special discounts for servicemen. And to think I was paid for it!

Missy had taken a part-time job working for Special Branch in Kariba and she knew far more about the security situation elsewhere in the country than I did. Although we seldom talked about it, I could see that her worries were increasing and there were weeks when she wore a frown that disturbed me intensely. Hard-eyed SB men paid regular visits to Kariba and Missy spent hours listening to their talk with Ashley Collings, her immediate boss. I chatted with these chaps in the bar, but I was a uniformed cop and not allowed in on their confidences. My wife was 'one of them' so she was and it seemed to upset her more than I liked. Although she enjoyed Kariba as much as I did, the overall situation was wearing her down.

'Do you know', she said to me one evening, 'that one of the biggest bones of contention among black and white in this country is the disparity in wages?'

'Yes', I agreed hesitantly, 'but that isn't really as bad as it seems. After all…'

'Of course it is', she snapped, cutting me off in mid flow, 'why should two people get different pay for doing the same job merely because they happen to be of different colour?'

It was an argument, often brought up by critics of Rhodesia and one that was difficult to counter. Even in the police force, patrol officer recruits took home four times as much as experienced sergeants but the cost of living between communities varied to an enormous degree. I tried to explain this to my indignant wife.

'Whites live according to European cultural standards and their everyday expenses are on a totally different scale to their black counterparts. We eat, eggs, meat and fish. We pay income tax and housing rates, as well as for schooling and medical expenses, while bottled beer is infinitely more expensive than the traditional variety.'

'Trust you to bring that up', she snorted but I hadn't finished.

'Black Rhodesians on the other hand live on *sadza* and vegetable relish or '*derere*.' When they eat meat, they love the 'ration' variety, which is mainly fatty off cuts and bits of the carcass that you or I wouldn't look at. For many blacks, their greatest culinary delight consists of mopani worms, flying ants or roasted field mice. Even when they are offered European food, they invariably wrinkle their noses in disgust.

'A 20 kilogram bag of mealie meal', I was warming to my theme, 'costs less than five dollars and that is sufficient to keep the average family going for a month. Nor are they subject to income tax or housing rates; they pay nothing for hospital care and a minimum for schooling, while most of them don't need a car, as public transport is both plentiful and cheap.

'Housing in both township and TTL is simple and inexpensive to maintain. In the case of farm workers, they might not earn much but they get free housing and their wages are supplemented by food, bonuses and beer laid on by their employers.

'The average labourer lives well on a salary that would be untenable to a white man.'

Missy still looked doubtful so I went on.

'Our black coppers are among the elite in the land when it comes to financial security. They look forward to a healthy pension and many of them drive far more splendid vehicles than we do. Most of their salaries go towards buying cattle for their retirement and in spite of the differences in actual pay scales, I don't think money lies at the roots of the country's problems.'

For all my impassioned oratory however, it did seem horribly unfair that different sectors of society — classified solely by skin colour — should get different wages for doing the same job. I thought long and hard on the matter after that conversation and had to admit that as Rhodesians, we seemed intent of showing ourselves in the worst possible light where the rest of the world was concerned.

The sight of my first genuine terrorists was a considerable disappointment. I don't know what I had expected — possibly some sort of supermen, complete with fangs, horns and forked tails — but these were two very ordinary and very frightened young men. They had been captured in a contact with the army and brought in with three of their dead colleagues and a pile of spoils.

It was the Kalashnikovs that first caught my eye. I had seen them in displays of captured weaponry on COIN courses and training days, but these somehow seemed more like the real thing and ten times as nasty. The wickedly curved magazines oozed with callous menace, while rust and dirt encrusted around the working parts only made them appear all the more lethal.

The dead terrorists were laid out on the lawn in front of the police station, but they had been reduced to mere bodies and I wasted little time on them. The prisoners were another matter. Huddling beside their dead colleagues, they obviously each took comfort from the presence of the other. Terrorists were normally manacled and fitted with leg irons, but these two slouched in the shade of a marula tree, unfettered and able to flee if they dared to do so. With lions about that was an unlikely scenario. I tried hard not to be too blatant in my study of them, but this was my first look at the ogre that was ravaging my country and I was curious.

Detective Section Officer Pete Stanton — already building up a formidable reputation as a security force interrogator — was to question the captures and when he arrived, he interviewed them in the open, one at a time and on his own. Sitting together under a tree they appeared to be chatting quietly in Shona and I couldn't help admiring the Special Branch man's technique. Never once did he appear flustered, impatient or annoyed and he spent at least three hours with each man before deigning to write anything down. It was said among those who worked with him that Stanton had an encyclopaedic knowledge of ZANLA operations and knew most of the terrorist hierarchy better than they knew themselves. His results were certainly impressive and although I only saw him in action on that one occasion, I had nothing but admiration for the man.

When Stanton had finished with the captures, they were left on the grass, their faces drained from the effects of baring their souls to the quietly spoken section officer. I watched them through my office window and any awe I might have felt about the enemy we fought, quickly dissipated. These were little more than casual labourers, recruited to do a job with the tools that were available. They were victims of a cause and depending on their history, they would either be hanged, incarcerated for a long time or be used by the Selous Scouts in operations against their former colleagues.

Neither of them could have been more than 18-years-old.

'Security Force Headquarters regret to announce…'

This sombre prelude to the evening news was bound to produce a sudden hush wherever Rhodesians were gathered together. The announcement would detail the death in action of one, two or sometimes more members of the Security Forces. On many occasions, the dead were mere names to anxious listeners but all too often, they brought to mind faces from previous postings and sometimes the names were of friends. Rhodesia was a small country and there were few people who didn't lose friends or relatives in the conflict. Missy and I were no exception.

I felt particular sadness at the death of Constable Kwande, that cheerful young reprobate who had mocked my shooting prowess at Nyakasoro. We had shared some good times he and I, but fine policeman though he was, he didn't even die in battle. His death was announced as 'killed in action' but the grim sitrep told a different story. Kwande had been on ground coverage duties when he had been denounced to the opposition as a 'sell out' and had his throat cut. Violent death in any form is horrific, but Kwande was too fine a man to deserve such a fate.

Another bitter blow — this time for us both — was the death of John Walters. The son of a former district commissioner, John had been with his father's department in Marandellas and had become a friend when Missy was working there. A burly, cheerful young man, he had been great fun to have around the house and the kids had loved him to bits. We would all miss him.

There were many others we didn't know, but whenever I listened to the dread announcements, I couldn't help reflecting that somebody somewhere was feeling as I had felt for Constable Kwande (I never got to know his first name) and John Walters. When a country is at war, nobody escapes the trauma.

8

Real live admiral

When Margaret Thatcher was elected leader of the Conservative Party in Britain, many Rhodesians seemed to think it was the end of our problems. As so often happened, I was looked upon as an expert in all things English and people seemed most surprised when I said that I had never heard of the lady.

With the Portuguese out of Mozambique, we needed all the help we could get but I couldn't help feeling that Rhodesian celebrations were premature. Thatcher might be the new Tory supremo but Wilson and his henchmen were still in power so we were no better off with the change.

Ignatius Sithole was the best of my ground coverage constables. An extroverted and cheerfully ugly young man, he was a born policeman and brought in many useful snippets of information from his wanderings in the tribal lands. I was always afraid that Special Branch would poach him from under my nose, but events were to take a hand long before that could happen.

Sithole was patrolling with Sergeant Mupepe on the other side of the lake when things went wrong. Both men were in plain clothes and while visiting the kraal of Chief Mola in the Omayi TTL, they were abducted by armed terrorists. The chief and some 30 of his followers were also taken and the police post at Bumi lost its somnolent atmosphere forever.

An immediate rescue operation was mounted, but by the time news of the abductions filtered through to Kariba we were already 12 hours behind. I took a boatload of anxious coppers across to Bumi, requisitioned vehicles from Internal Affairs and mounted an extensive search of the Omayi TTL. Army trackers had already gone in on the spoor and helicopters had been called in but I felt that we had to do something and I needed to be involved. It paid off too. I was driving along a seldom used bush road when a black man staggered out on to the track ahead.

Ant Crossley, a Special Branch aide from Salisbury was with me in the Land-Rover cab and two CID constables stood in the open back. Even as I wrestled the vehicle to a dusty halt, the constables were hammering frantically on the roof. Long before the Land-Rover stopped, all three of us were sprinting toward the exhausted man, rifles and pistols forgotten in the truck behind us.

For the next few minutes there was pandemonium on that lonely road. Sergeant Mupepe — for it was he who had staggered from the bush — and I danced around in the dust while the CID men pounded our backs in the excitement of the moment. Only Ant Crossley remained unmoved. He didn't know Mupepe and besides, he was more experienced and worldly-wise than we were. Standing watchfully beside the halted Land-Rover, he kept his rifle at the ready and doubtless wondered what on earth was going on.

In later years or in other areas, such crassly irresponsible behaviour on my part would have killed us all. My only excuse now is that we knew nothing of war in Kariba and any common sense I might have possessed was overcome by my delight at the survival of at least one of my men.

When we had calmed down and Bumi had been informed of events, Mupepe told us how he, Sithole and the others had been herded at gunpoint through the bush and taken to a remote shoreline on the Sengwa Basin where rubber dinghies had been hidden. The terrorists had originally rowed across the basin — a frightening expanse of wild water that stretches for 33 kilometres across the middle of the lake. Having cached their dinghies, they travelled inland with murder and mischief in mind, only to return with a far greater prize than they might have expected. Fortunately for my sergeant, termites had been feasting on the booty left behind by the ZPRA men and the rubber dinghies were well and truly holed. While repairs were being affected, Mupepe and a few of his fellow prisoners managed to escape.

I never did see Ignatius Sithole again, nor was his body ever recovered.

The abduction of Chief Mola, his people and my ground coverage details had enormous repercussions for Kariba. The follow up operation was a massive one and I think our Lords and Masters were nervous about the incident for two reasons. Firstly because crossing the Sengwa Basin in anything but powerful motor vessels had always been considered impossible and secondly because it was the first positive proof that terrorists were entering Rhodesia from Zambia. This had always been hotly denied by President Kaunda and his government.

There had been 23 terrorists in the party that carried out the mass abduction and the forces mobilised to hunt them down were considerable. South African helicopters were called in from Chirundu. The RLI and 2-Independent Company from Kariba went in on the ground while the Air Force and Police Reserve Air Wing flew their craft into Bumi. As if that wasn't enough, almost every powerboat on Kariba that belonged to police reservists were requisitioned and brought into the fray. As is the way with matters military, the operation was given a code name and so *Operation Detonate* was launched, with its most senior protagonists basing themselves in the Bumi Hills Safari Lodge. The lodge took on the appearance of a luxurious battle camp with heavily armed men in camouflage mingling with the guests and the bar doing a roaring trade. War can be hell!

The police post on the other hand was somewhat overcrowded. The grounds were filled with rows of stretchers and the tiny kitchen overflowed with dirty pots and crates of empty beer bottles. Off duty airmen sat on the veranda, passing critical comment on every pilot bringing his craft into the tiny airstrip, 600 metres below. One unfortunate Cessna jockey managed to clout a careless impala and this roused the pilots to almost hysterical laughter, but it also ensured that we ate well for days.

The Rhodesian Light Infantry — rapidly building a reputation as awesome guerrilla fighters — were deployed in support of the local soldiers. Every time I saw one of these hard-bitten troopies, I couldn't help remembering Brian Cullingworth's scathing comments on their criminal tendencies when we were coming into town from Salisbury Airport all those centuries ago. Instinctively I regarded them with suspicion.

The boats became my problem. There were too many of them to fit comfortably into Bumi harbour or the government anchorage at Katete, so I set up camp in a protected bay on Weather Island a few kilometres to the north. It was a lovely spot but the island was in plain view from Zambia so we could be assured that the enemy were watching our comings and goings. This wasn't a comfortable thought and in any case, even that enchanted bay was too cramped for my oddly assorted armada, so we were soon on the move again.

This time I chose a small island on the edge of the Sengwa Basin. Hidden from Zambian eyes by the bulk of Photo Corner, it had a sheltered anchorage, plenty of firewood and a panoramic view of the basin where our operational duties were concentrated. I set up a tented camp and radio communications, worked out 24 hour deployments for my waterborne warriors and settled in as Rhodesia's first admiral.

Our task was to ensure that nobody crossed the Sengwa Basin without authority. To this end, I had at least three craft out at a time, each sticking to its allocated sector and patrolling for eight hours and sometimes longer. A few vessels had radar sets, which made life considerably easier, but most of my reservists had to rely on their eyesight and that put a considerable strain on individuals.

The camp itself was basic and initially there were no toilet facilities on the island. Having the crews of 30 boats confined in so small a space was a hygienist's nightmare and it wasn't long before visitors could smell the island long before arriving. On one memorable morning, a boatman who was obviously fed up with the apparent futility of a long nights work, sighed with angry resignation as his craft nosed into our makeshift harbour.

'Back to bloody Paradise Island', he muttered to his crew-mates and that little comment went down in Kariba history.

The original Paradise Island was a holiday resort — long beloved by Rhodesians — off the Mozambique coast. Now we had our own Paradise Island and the name stuck. It soon became official and modern Kariba charts all have Paradise Island inscribed thereon — a legacy of *Operation Detonate* that should last forever. In time the island was designated an official patrol base, concrete buildings and ablution blocks were set up and it lost all the cheerfully rustic charm of its primitive beginnings. Even the post of 'Admiral' was upgraded, the work being taken over by a border control superintendent operating out of Kariba.

But those days were still far ahead and in the meantime we lived well on our island in the sun. Police Reservists and their boats changed over every fortnight and in every new intake there was at least one expert cook. The basin was famous for its fishing and there was nothing to do while patrolling through the long night hours. When the boats came in at first light, cooler boxes were usually well stocked with tiger fish and bream so mealtimes provided a welcome diversion from the general tedium of off duty hours. I rationed us all to two alcoholic drinks per day but there was plenty of coke and lemonade, while tea was generally on the boil.

All we needed was action, but sadly — or perhaps fortunately for me — nobody tried to cross the Sengwa Basin while I was in charge of Paradise. We didn't think so anyway. There was one wild night when flares were seen in the basin and streams of brightly coloured tracer lit the skies towards Zambia but in spite of intensive investigation, we were never able to discover who was responsible for the pyrotechnics. The strangest part of that particular incident was the fact that neither ZANLA nor ZIPRA cadres were issued with flares. I have often wondered what nefarious deeds were being done during that particular night.

When *Operation Detonate* started, my boss Paul Rens assured me that I would be 'on the boats' for about three weeks but time went on and there was no sign of a replacement for me on the island. It was a lovely life and hardly the rigours of war, but I soon became bored to tears. Occasionally I would go out in one of the boats and on a couple of occasions, we landed in Zambia to start bush fires — an exercise that began as a joke but proved startlingly successful. On one occasion fire roared down the shoreline for days and the little Zambian town of Chipepo must have been in grave danger of disappearing beneath the flames. The problem with these little outings though was choosing the right crew to accompany. Although attested into the police reserve, they were basically civilians and every one was fiercely proud of being captain of his own vessel. My presence was accepted grudgingly and I had to be careful to suggest rather than instruct when I wanted anything done.

On occasion, I was able to hijack a larger craft from other government departments (the BSAP might have been the senior service but we felt like poor relations where equipment was concerned) and then I would tow a 'mini fleet' down to Chete Gorge to prevent any crossings in that area. This gave me a chance to control my warlike matelots like a real admiral and I enjoyed these forays if only for the change of scenery.

There were other minor diversions when SAS troops needed to be taken across to Zambia. My job was merely to act as a waterborne chauffeur but it was fascinating to see real warriors preparing for action. The soldiers would go in blackened up and heavily armed, their demeanour quietly serious and their hardware terrifyingly lethal. Deployments were made at night and as soon as I grounded the big launch on a Zambian beach, they would leap lightly over the prow and disappear into the darkness, leaving me to find my own way home. I could only marvel at the fact that these fellows actually seemed to be enjoying themselves.

When the mission was complete or an extraction was needed, the code word would come through on my radio schedules and off I would go again. Pick-ups were usually scheduled for half an hour before first light and I would be guided into the correct inlet or beach by a couple of flashes from a hand-held torch. The SAS men would be waiting, their shoulders slumped with fatigue and their eyes shining with adrenalin-charged reaction to the dramas they had been through.

It was then that the sheer professionalism of the SAS made itself manifest. Bypassing Paradise, I would take them back to Bumi or Katete where they would be debriefed in situ by the senior Special Branch officer. Thirty minutes later, those torn and weary looking troopers would be back in full uniform, their faces bright and clean, their shoes shiny and their demeanour that of first class soldiers. It was hugely impressive and in stark contrast to the Selous Scouts who revelled in their scruffy appearance.

On one memorable occasion a raiding party returned, laden down with maritime loot. There were dinghies, outboard motors and a couple of long canoes, complete with paddles and life jackets. There was also a large government craft fitted with a 16 cylinder Rolls Royce marine engine that really made my mouth water. For a long time we had been receiving snippets of information about a big Zambian craft that was very fast and these reports worried those of us who spent time in the relatively ponderous police launches. The SAS had decided that the best way to investigate this vessel was to hijack the damned thing.

I towed the makeshift flotilla around to Weather Island where under orders from above, we burnt the canoes and sank the dinghies in Honeymoon Bay. The outboards were loaded up for transfer to Bumi. The soldiers seemed very pleased with themselves but I didn't dare ask how they had managed to filch so much of Zambia's shipping industry.

Later in the day I was called in to Bumi where I was taken aside by the SB superintendent for *Operation Detonate*.

'We have no choice but to sink that boat', Dave George told me grimly and I knew he was talking about the big government craft still floating under guard in Honeymoon Bay. It was a lovely vessel and the engine alone seemed worth saving, but he was adamant.

'The world media are slating us for raids into Zambia and Mozambique', he pointed out. We justify them with the excuse of 'hot pursuit' but if they learn that we are stealing expensive equipment from a supposedly neutral government, they will crucify us. That bloody thing has to disappear.'

I knew he was right but it seemed a terrible pity. We were desperate for reliable marine engines and the thought of consigning a genuine Rolls Royce thoroughbred to the bottom of the lake didn't appeal. Nevertheless as the man with local knowledge, I was required to select a suitable spot where the vessel could be sunk unseen and never recovered. That wasn't particularly difficult but the task of sinking the big boat was to present unforeseen problems.

For obvious reasons, the operation had to remain secret and only Dave George, myself and two SAS soldiers were allowed in on the sinking. By the time we were ready to go, the weather was worsening and my launch wasn't powerful enough to haul the Zambian vessel out of Honeymoon Bay and directly into a heavy swell. I tried the Immigration boat, *MV Moira* but she almost foundered and after anxious discussion with Kariba, the

60-foot *Erica* was requisitioned from the University Research Station. In view of the required secrecy, I was given a crash course in handling the big craft and we were ready to go.

But it wasn't to be. The storm raged well into the night and when we prepared for action the following morning, the wind was still howling around our ears while massive waves rolled into the shore from the centre of the lake. In spite of her size, *Erica* struggled to tow the Zambian craft but at last we were under way and I lost no time in making for the spot I had chosen for the sinking. Once there, the heavily ballasted Zambian was packed with explosives, cut loose and blown up. I saw her stagger like a punch-drunk middleweight as the plastic blew but she then refused to sink. I cannot remember where that lovely craft had been built but wherever it was, they knew how to construct sturdy vessels.

With the Zambian wallowing unhappily in the swell, we were in serious trouble. She was badly down by the stern but showed no inkling to disappear and the swell was driving her at ever increasing speed towards a rocky lee shore. We watched in helpless anxiety as the crippled boat, slightly black around the gills from the explosives finally went ashore with a shuddering crash and lay half out of the water like a beached whale. Our secret sinking had gone horribly wrong and the stolen vessel was visible to anyone who happened to pass by. With a decent pair of binoculars, she could probably be seen from Zambia.

I was the local expert. I had chosen this particular spot to hide the evidence. It was up to me to find a solution. That at least was what my companions seemed to think and I became the unhappy focus of three decidedly hostile stares. Personally I blamed the soldiers for botching the business with the explosives but I didn't dare tell them so. They looked awfully tough and I am certainly not that brave.

Something had to be done however so I took *Erica* hesitantly inshore, though it was a dangerous and uncomfortable procedure. Waves smashed down on the rocks around us while our huge propeller must have been within centimetres of the stony lake bed. With only a single engine and that heavy swell, breaking the prop would mean inevitable disaster and I had no wish to end up beached beside the Zambian craft. Moving back to deeper water, I explained the problem and my companions frowned in obvious chagrin. I still do not know why I felt so guilty. It was hardly my fault that they had not been able to sink the Zambian.

After a long discussion, the soldiers swam ashore and attached a rope to the wrecked vessel, but we were still fighting the anger of that mighty lake and the towline parted long before our prize was back in the water. It went with a crack like a pistol shot and it was fortunate that the loose end didn't hit any of us or we would have provided another grim statistic for the evening news.

By the time we had chugged back to Katete harbour, found a suitable length of steel chain and returned to the scene of our collective embarrassment, the morning was nearly over and the swell was dying down. The lull in the weather merely increased my anxiety. It might well mean tourists and fishermen appearing on the lake and our efforts to remain clandestine would come to nothing.

This time however, that great boat did come away from the rocks. With a shriek of tortured steel and a terrible clanging sound, she bumped and bundled her way into the water and *Erica* leaped forward with the sudden release of tension. Moments later we were in deep water, badly down by the stern and on the point of sinking ourselves. Eight tons of Zambian property dangled from our rear end and *Erica*'s bow reared high above us. The towing chain was bar taut and there was no way on earth that we could release it. Trying to suppress mounting panic, I cursed the war, the Zambians, Special Branch and the SAS. I even cursed poor old *Erica* but I kept all my curses very quiet, as I didn't want to offend my companions any more than I had already.

The soldiers appeared unruffled. Muttered words were exchanged, they stripped off their uniforms, donned air tanks and disappeared over the side with a small haversack held between them. Moments later they were back, one of them fiddled casually with a couple of wires, there was a muffled thump from somewhere beneath us and *Erica* settled thankfully back on to an even keel. They had blown the chain apart and the Zambian boat sank to the bottom in 70 metres of water.

Inevitably, rumours have spread over the years and I have been asked on occasion to show people where that Rolls Royce engine is lying. To be honest, I am not sure I could find it now. Not only has the topography of Lake Kariba changed radically over the years but it all happened a very long time ago. I don't know where my companions of that momentously embarrassing day are now, but that Zambian craft went down in very deep water and probably wouldn't be worth the finding. Besides, boats are special creatures and after all she went through, that one deserves to rest in peace.

On another occasion I was called away from Paradise Island to assist with tests of a new radar system. We had been asking for a suitable set to be used on the island and this one seemed ideal. South African made, it was contained in a massive trailer, crammed with wires, screens and speakers. In a pinch, this could be towed by a Land-Rover so if it worked, might well prove the answer to all our prayers.

The smallest boat we could find for the test was my son Brian's canoe. This was a two-metre, fibreglass shell and like a fool, I offered it as the ideal craft for the purpose. We couldn't use Brian for the test, so that meant using me as nobody else could sit with any sort of safety in that unstable little contraption.

Loading it into one of the launches, Paul Rens cast us adrift off the mouth of Sanyati Gorge. As the launch burbled into the distance I felt horribly lonely in all that water. Waves slapped spitefully over the side and I paddled gingerly, hoping that if I capsized, Paul and the radar people would find me before the crocodiles did.

In the event, I didn't capsize, the crocodiles didn't get me and the radar was magnificent. They tracked my tiny lump of fibreglass at 26 kilometres and that was in the lee of the Matusadona Mountains. With three of those sets strategically placed, we could have covered the entire lake and I had the feeling that our naval difficulties were over.

It wasn't to be. In their wisdom, the powers-that-be decided that Rhodesia couldn't afford the South African sets. I don't know how much was asked for each one, but they would soon have paid for themselves. On Paradise Island we were hiring 30 boats at a time, paying the crews and using an astronomical amount of fuel. That was without the helicopters, fixed wing aircraft and ground crew used in daily patrols around the lake. Not to mention the soldiers and policemen patrolling on the ground in the TTLs.

Even when *Operation Detonate* was officially over, lake patrols from Paradise Island went on for years and the overall cost must have been horrendous. One of those big radar sets on the island could have covered the entire Sengwa Basin and obviated most of that expense.

Still, the politicians — as always — knew best and we never did get those marvellous sets. All the same, *Operation Detonate* ended up a resounding success, all but one of the original terrorist band being accounted for. In its way it had been enormous fun and for one former Cotswold Bobby, it offered the chance to be a real live admiral.

After four months on Paradise Island I came home — tanned, fit and confident in my ability to arrange the logistics of a waterborne operation. I had been to war — if only on a very limited scale — and enjoyed the experience. There had not been any shooting or bloodletting involved but the possibility had always been there and my decisions had to be formulated accordingly. I had enjoyed the responsibility, although at times I felt somewhat lonely and cut off from the real world. Things were happening out there and the only news I received was at second or third hand. For one third of a year, I had alternated between boredom and worry but being in charge on Paradise Island certainly had its compensations.

Sitting outside my tent of an evening with a beer to hand and the sun going down over the heaving vastness of Sengwa Basin, it was impossible to believe that I didn't have the best job in the world.

9

Race relations and VIPs

For all the joys of Paradise Island, it was nice to get back to being an ordinary copper again. With operational duties increasing among regular policemen, my enquiry section was often short staffed and I gave more and more docket work to the Station Sergeant Major, Nebbie Madziwa.

A tall, ascetic-looking man, Madziwa was very quiet but he was keen to do as much as he could and on one occasion, I took a risk and gave him a fatal accident docket to prepare for court. It sounds patronising I suppose but 'fatals' required a high degree of competence from the investigating detail, as they often ended up in High Court and were subject to endless wrangles and discussion between opposing attorneys. In the BSAP they were supposed to be handled by patrol officers or above. In other words by white officers.

Nebbie Madziwa didn't turn a hair at the unexpected responsibility and I couldn't help but be impressed with the result. Plans were beautifully executed, statements and reports were to a high degree of professionalism and although I picked a few holes in the overall result, I would have done that with anyone and the sergeant major took it with a smile. He knew I was nit picking.

'This is excellent work Mr Madziwa', I conceded eventually and if there was a hint of gently mocking satisfaction in his smile, I certainly didn't mind. I should not have been surprised that a policeman of 20 years standing could produce such a fine example of court preparation but I was thinking like a Rhodesian rather than a copper. Reflecting on it afterwards I had to admit that I had been surprised at Nebbie's competence because he was black and that couldn't be right. Madziwa was a fine police officer whatever his colour and I felt that if change ever did come to the BSAP, he was going to go a long way.

And so he did. After Independence, Nebbie went on to become a deputy commissioner in the Zimbabwe Republic Police, only to lose his job in a corruption scandal during the mid-eighties. I was sad at his eventual disgrace but that is another story and as far as I was concerned, Nebbie Madziwa was a hell of a nice chap and an extremely efficient cop.

White society in Kariba during the 1970s was broken down into three sectors. The services, (police, army and air force) civilians and Capco — employees of the Central African Power Corporation who ran the power station that was the sole *raison d'etre* for

Kariba town.

All three sectors of the population were different in both outlook and policies. Like servicemen everywhere, members of the security forces tended to stick together, visiting one another's messes and looking after wives and families when the man of the house was away on active duty. The civilians were generally hoteliers, hospital staff or artisans — many of them working on boats or running tourist enterprises around the lakeshore. Capco folk were usually expatriates, although a few had been in town since the dam was built.

Social life in town revolved around the country club, perched on the top of a hill and with probably the finest outlook of any such establishment in the world. The club offered excellent meals at reasonable cost, an open-air cinema and regular entertainment to its members. Dogs and children were always welcome and it was a focal point for the entire community.

In 1975 Capco had started their own transfer to majority rule and they appointed a black man as Deputy General Manager at the power station. This was an obvious move for a large corporation straddling Rhodesia and Zambia but it led to an immediate crisis in the town. In common with other heads of department, the Capco boss and his deputy had always been granted automatic club membership, but what was to happen now that one of them was black?

Meetings were held between members and their committee and eventually it was reluctantly agreed that the new man could attend the cinema with his family rather than go to the one in Mahombekombe Township. Letting him into the hallowed confines of the club was another matter and it was amazing how many people claimed that they definitely were not racist but didn't want to see standards slipping in the country club. The fact that this particular black man already occupied one of the grandest houses in Kariba, had been brought up in England and America and was a thoroughly nice fellow was conveniently forgotten.

After all, the general line of reasoning seemed to go, this bloke was probably all right but once one black member had been admitted, there would be an immediate flood and then what would happen? And of course, he might invite his friends! The furore went on and on while tempers became ever more heated and more than one long-standing friendship foundered on the argument of racial tolerance.

We tried to remain aloof from the squabbling, although Missy and I agreed that allowing the chap into the club would be a major step towards racial equality in the country and set a precedent that could only prove beneficial in the long run.

Be that as it may, I was driving a sergeant around the town one afternoon. New to Kariba, he was a confident, personable young man who obviously enjoyed his job and his rank. I already rated him on a par with Nebbie Madziwa and that was high praise indeed. As I showed him where things were in Mahombekombe Township, he set my senses into a spin by asking about tennis facilities in Kariba.

'Forget it, Sergeant', I admonished flatly. 'There are courts at the country club but for the moment at any rate — you're *not* going anywhere near that place unless it is in the course of your duties.'

He looked surprised at my outburst but I explained the nonsense that was going on about the Capco number two and he seemed to understand.

'I played a lot of tennis in Shabani', he mused, 'and we didn't have that problem there.'

Shabani was a mining and farming town with a large proportion of Afrikaans residents and I couldn't help feeling that the notoriously racist and universally hated Afrikaners could teach their fellow Rhodesians a thing or two about race relations.

Many years later, Senior Assistant Commissioner John Chademanah and I laughed about his introduction to Kariba, but I have often felt that I missed an excellent opportunity to strike my own blow for multi racialism by proposing ''Chadders' for club membership in Kariba.

On the other hand it would have probably meant an instant transfer for both of us.

If 1975 had been another bad year for white Rhodesians (South African forces had been withdrawn, constitutional conferences had failed and Mugabe had been appointed leader of ZANU) 1976 started incredibly well. On 16th March, Harold Wilson resigned as British Prime Minister and we all celebrated. Nobody was quite sure why he had gone, but as far as Rhodesians were concerned, it was a case of 'good riddance.' I often wondered whether Wilson had any inkling of how much he was hated by the citizens of one little country.

James Callaghan took Wilson's place and I had vague memories of him as the police representative in Parliament when I had been a bobby. He had done his best for us then, but I doubted whether he would prove quite as sympathetic towards white Rhodesians. If ever we needed a friend in high places it was during that fateful year. As a result of a huge escalation in ZANLA incursions, new operational areas were opened up in the Eastern Highlands, (*Operation Thrasher*) in the south-east (*Operation Repulse*) and in Matabeleland (*Operation Tangent*). That only left the Midlands and Kariba as places that were still regarded as non operational and after *Detonate* that seemed somehow farcical.

Worse was to come. In March, Samora Machel not only closed Rhodesia's border with Mozambique but declared all-out war on us. This caused much amusement among Rhodesians but economically, it was serious. It meant losing the outlet for nearly 30% of our exports as well as 2 300 precious railway wagons that remained stranded in Mozambique. What made Rhodesians particularly bitter was that Britain promptly paid over £15 million of taxpayers' money in compensation to Mozambique. It was Rhodesia who needed the money. We were the ones being sinned against but nobody cared — least of all the perfidious British.

Our Defence Minister PK van der Byl summed it up for all of us.

'It is quite unbelievable and grotesque', he drawled in his horribly plummy accent, 'that a Marxist and terrorist regime should be financed by the British government in order to destroy a section of what was part of the British Empire'.

On 18 April, four South African tourists were ambushed and three of them killed on the Beit Bridge road and this had a devastating effect on our tourist industry. Boatmen were shot at on the lake as well and Kariba virtually faded away as a holiday resort. Not that we were getting many visitors from outside the country in any case. Tourism was dying and we all knew it.

The last straw for many Rhodesians came in September when in a terse radio broadcast, Ian Smith announced to a shocked and horrified nation that we were to embark on a two year plan for black majority rule. The government was to be replaced by a Council of State which would be half black and half white, with a white chairman. They would presumably decide how a future black government would run the country.

Smithy's announcement met with mixed reactions in Kariba. Some folk cheered at prospects of any sort of settlement, others looked gum and forecast disaster. Missy and I discussed the news and decided that the country was in such a desperate state that something had to be done or absolute chaos would ensue. My own feeling was that Smith had been pressurised by the South Africans who were not proving nearly as friendly as we had thought they were.

Henry Kissinger was later given much of the credit for the new arrangements and as a result of Smith's compliance, Kenneth Kaunda released some of the ZANU leaders he had detained for the murder of Herbert Chitepo — one of their own colleagues who had actually been killed by the Rhodesian Central Intelligence Organisation. That finally shattered what few shreds of confidence remained among the white community but life had to go on and I was still a police officer. Neither Missy nor I wanted to leave the country and so we kept going, although in common with many of our friends, neither of us could see the new government being accepted and recognised by the outside world. The terrorist leaders held too much sway with Britain and America so they would have to be involved, abhorrent though the thought was to decent people. Besides, while Smith still clung to the reins of power, any new government stood little chance of recognition from Britain's Labour leaders.

It was another worrying time for us all.

One of the supposedly glamorous chores that fell repeatedly to Kariba policemen was escorting VIPs around the sights. In my three years, I had the dubious pleasure of meeting one prime minister, two presidents and sundry cabinet ministers. I also spent time with three generals, an air vice marshall, two commissioners of police and a host of slightly less important service big-wigs.

Not bad for a simple Cotswold Bobby I suppose but my initial sense of awe at being in the presence of so much authority soon wore off. Most of these visitors were anxious to get out on the lake and have a good time while I had work to do. Besides, good men were dying in other areas and I felt hot under the collar that so many of our leaders should be swanning about in the sunshine while the war was escalating elsewhere. I was undoubtedly being unreasonable, as even military leaders need relaxation but official visits soon became something to avoid rather than occasions to be enjoyed.

Of them all however, two visits stand out among the rest. One was when Senior Assistant Commissioner Ray Stenner came to Kariba with his brother — a parson from England. I showed them around, took them to Bumi Hills and ensured that they enjoyed some good fishing and a couple of magical sunsets. They were excellent company and before returning to the big city, stood Missy and I to a slap up dinner at the Cutty Sark Hotel. This was Stenner's way of thanking me for my trouble and was much appreciated. Senior officers visiting Kariba usually took such things for granted but Ray Stenner was a true gentleman.

Tipped by those who know about such things as a future commissioner, Stenner died of a heart attack a few years later and when the news came through I had a big lump in my throat and a tearful wife to contend with.

'Why is it always the good ones who go?' she sobbed but there was no answer to that.

Another gentlemanly visitor was the outgoing Rhodesian President, Clifford du Pont. His was a farewell visit to Kariba with all the military 'brass' and as I was acting member in charge at the time, I lined up with army and air force commanders to meet the presidential Dakota. When it landed the rigmarole began.

The temperature was in the upper 30s and I wore my uncomfortably heavy best uniform but when the tiny presidential figure approached, I saluted smartly and shook his hand, hoping inwardly that I wouldn't do him any permanent damage. The commissioner was next and I threw him a salute and shook his hand. Then came General Walls, the army commander. Once again I saluted and shook his hand but by now I was beginning to wilt.

Air Vice Marshall Archie Maclaren saw my discomfort and when he stopped in front of me his eyes were twinkling.

'For God's sake don't salute again Boy or your bloody arm will fall off.'

He shook my hand, patted my sweaty shoulder in encouragement and ambled away. There followed some five hours of trailing behind President du Pont while he visited all 'his boys.' We drank aperitifs at the air force base then had a boozy lunch at the Officers' Mess on the hill. From there it was on to the Sergeants' Mess and while the rest of us set the world and the war to rights in alcoholic wisdom, the outgoing president of a sovereign nation disappeared.

After ten minutes of absolute panic, we found him sitting on the step of a dormitory in the army camp. A group of troopies had gathered around and were hanging on his every word. They were not used to such exalted visitors to their living quarters and a grand time was had by all.

The president was bundled away by his abashed bodyguard and we all breathed a sigh of relief once he was firmly ensconced in his Dakota. A real man of the people was President Clifford du Pont but men of the people can be difficult to protect.

It was in 1976 that the harsh realities of war first hit the white population of Kariba. Most young men in the town were members of the police reserve and on the way back from a routine training day in Sinoia, a vehicle was ambushed near the Elephant Walk Motel. Field Reservist Dave Carey died in the gunfire and we all mourned his passing. A small, cheerful Englishman, Carey worked for Capco. Not by any means an aggressive character, he only joined the police reserve because he was ordered to do so and he died at the hands of those he wanted to help.

Carey's death dampened the party scene in Kariba for a while but we had been lucky to escape direct involvement in the war for so long. Other communities had not been so lucky and farmers everywhere were taking a pasting. From Zambia we heard that Mugabe and Nkomo had merged their fighting armies to form the Patriotic Front and it seemed that we were faced with death and destruction whichever way we turned. Rhodesia was still a lovely place to live but a pall of worried sadness hung over the entire country and many of us wondered what on earth to do.

For me, my time on the great lake had to be ending. Because of the heat, Kariba was normally a two-year posting for a married man but by the middle of 1976 I had done well over three. Missy didn't mind this situation, as she loved the hot sunshine and vigorous social life, but I was bored and anxious for something new. I had sampled all the delights on offer locally and loved the lake with a passion, but my work no longer held out any challenge.

The issue was solved by a phone call from my old friend Dave Farrington. He was the member in charge at Macheke in the Marandellas District but he too was hankering for a move. His wife wanted Kariba (where had I heard that before?) and he suggested a straight swop. It would mean having my own station and the challenge appealed, but Missy was difficult to convince. She knew more than I did about the security situation elsewhere and her inclination was to let matters ride until an official transfer came through. It was only when I pointed out that we might end up somewhere diabolical (Zaka perhaps) that she reluctantly agreed to the swop. Dave and I submitted reports on the matter and a few weeks later, approval came through from PGHQ.

I was sad to leave Kariba but the sadness was alleviated by two farewell parties — one at the Jam Jar itself and the other with my AP at their own pub, known unoriginally as the 'Mini Jam Jar. Missy and I received a magnificent silver punch bowl from the citizens of Kariba, but when I walked into my office on the last morning, I found a newspaper-wrapped parcel on my desk. It contained a wooden carving and an almost illegible note saying 'from your African Policemen.'

That carving has stayed with me through the years as one of my most reassured possessions and I often boast that it was presented by a group of coppers that included both a deputy commissioner and a senior assistant commissioner. Their glories were yet to come but that little gift meant a great deal to me and restored some of my battered faith in the future of Rhodesia.

10

Member in Charge

I made a bad start in Macheke although it was amusing at the time. The boys were at boarding school in Sinoia and as we were given three days to move in to our new home, Missy and I booked into the Macheke Hotel while our furniture was being sorted out.

Walking into the bar after dinner that first evening, I could hear rain lashing down outside. There were few people about and we were making desultory talk with landlord Matt Carson when a party of men in camouflage uniform stumbled through the door, wringing wet and swearing at the weather. A tall, grey-haired fellow who didn't seem in the best of humour slipped a dripping poncho from his shoulders.

'If this bloody fool of a new member in charge thinks I am going to do road blocks in this weather, he can bloody well think again.' He grumbled wetly. 'Give us a beer please Matt.'

Mine Host was grinning all over his face as he poured the requested drink. Sliding it across the bar he gestured toward the corner table where we were sitting.

'Meet the new member in charge, Tom', he laughed. 'I'm sure you are going to get on well together.'

That was how I came to meet Thomas Potts Kinch — like Ian Smith, a former member of 'The Few' and one of the finest men it has been my privilege to call friend. Tommy spoke with a cultured drawl, called everyone 'love' and had a heart of pure gold. He is dead now but in many ways, Tommy Kinch was typical of my police reservists in Macheke. They were rugged, individualistic and at times, hard to handle. At the same time they were fiercely loyal and generous to a fault. We bickered and fought over many things during my two years as their member in charge but by the time I moved on, I would have trusted any one of them with my life and I knew that the feeling was mutual.

Under continual harassment from terrorists operating out of Mtoko and Manicaland, the community grew ever closer together against the rest of the world and formed a frighteningly cohesive little unit that could so easily have achieved great things. The pity of it was that through a combination of horrific circumstances, Macheke ended up with a notoriety that wasn't deserved.

However, when Missy and I moved into the picturesque police camp that hot October day, we knew nothing of what was to come. At that stage, war in the area had been confined to a minor blast on the railway line and I felt that if that represented the worst the terrorists could do, I could certainly cope — reluctant warrior or not.

In fact the horrors of war were a long way from my mind that first morning. I had an area the size of Gloucestershire to control and I revelled in the challenge of such responsibility. The lack of ambition that characterised my early days as a copper had been replaced with a fierce pride in my own way of doing things and I was determined to stamp my personality on the district. I suppose most new bosses feel the same but on 13th October 1976 I felt pretty damned pleased with myself.

Five years to the day since joining the BSAP, I had 'arrived.' I even had a scrambling device on my telephone and although I wondered what was going on when Dispol first asked me to 'go across' I soon got the hang of it and used the 'secret means' for even the most innocuous phone calls.

The radio call sign used by military field commanders was 'Sunray' and this had been taken up by the police force. I was Sunray 213 — the numbers denoting Macheke — and enjoyed answering as such, military connotations or not. Sitting in my office, surrounded by maps, radios and the general paraphernalia of command, I was a proud and contented man.

'Macheke' means separation or divide in Chishona and the place was so named because it marks the spot where two provinces meet. The boundary is marked by the Macheke River and beyond it, the cattle plains of Manicaland stretch through Headlands and on to the distant purple ramparts of Inyanga.

In 1976, Macheke Town — if such it can be called — was the sort of settlement one sees in grainy sepia prints depicting the Africa of long ago. Graced by a ramshackle hotel and a railway station, the dusty shopping centre consisted of two Indian stores, a butchery and any number of itinerant hawkers selling trinkets, matches and fruit beside the road. The only other buildings in town were the District Council office, a few European houses and of course the police camp. We were set back from the main road to the Eastern Highlands and the charge office nestled in six hectares of ground. It was a small, whitewashed building with tiny windows, a wooden floor and a towering ceiling. There was one main room containing a counter, a couple of partitions for office work and an impressive array of radio equipment. This was the part seen by the average 'customer' and was very much the engine room of the station.

My own office had been tacked on to one side and there were two smaller buildings around the back, which were used as the AP *dare* (communal office) and an odds and sods room, used for interviews, staff meetings and the occasional chastisement of juveniles.

This was an aspect of Rhodesian police work that would have been frowned upon by progressive-thinking reformists in the West but was effective in practice. When a youngster was brought in for an offence and it was felt by the investigating officer that a court appearance wouldn't be in his best interests, the member in charge or his deputy would consult with the parents. These consultations often resulted in the miscreant being taken around the back of the station and lustily caned by the station sergeant.

Rough justice perhaps and evidence of the white man's brutality towards the black? I don't know but it worked and I witnessed the same system being used in Tanzania 20 years later, so there was nothing racist in it. Few of those caned ever re-offended and we had a row of cells on one side of the charge office for those that did.

Macheke police station had been built in the 1920s and those early coppers had obviously been concerned about the heat. Fir trees had been planted on either side of two long driveways and these had grown into 15 metre giants. Even on the hottest days there was ample shade to be found and this was appreciated by our customers, many of whom came from far afield. Having made their reports, they would rest in the shade or sleep a while before returning to wherever their home might be.

On either side of the charge office was the patrol officer's house for my deputy and the AP lines, a double row of small but comfortable dwellings occupied by the two sergeants and seventeen constables who made up the station complement. Their families were also in residence and the camp was always full of happy chatter or the shrill giggling of children at play.

My own house was tucked into the rear of the camp, well away from traffic noises and surrounded by a high hedge. Missy had an acre of garden to keep her happy and after our cramped Kariba pre-fab, the house seemed like a mansion. Directly behind us was an area of waste ground and a granite kopje that towered above the camp and provided an ideal vantage point for anyone who wanted to know what the local law was up to. A football field and helicopter landing pad were the only other locations that mattered.

The piece of station equipment that most interested me was the agric-alert system. I had heard about this marvellous item of community protection but this was the first time I had seen one in close up.

Every farm in the area — and there were about 70 — had its own radio set and they were all inter-connected and controlled from a panel in my charge office. When I arrived, the system was used almost exclusively for family messages and swopping recipes but this was to change as the security situation deteriorated. It wasn't long before I issued instructions that communication was to be kept to a minimum and all messages were to be channelled through the police station. This effectively cut down much of the chatter.

Each Agric-alert holder had an alarm button and when this was pressed, a klaxon would howl in the charge office, effectively drowning out every other noise in camp and the surrounding hills. This was as it should be but in the best of systems, accidents happen and my comments when alarms went off accidentally were anything but sympathetic. On Saturday mornings we held a general testing of sets and alarms, so if I didn't have an outside enquiry or meeting scheduled, I made sure that I was playing golf.

North of the main road, a smaller highway stretched between forbidding hills and disappeared into the Mangwende TTL, from where it led on to Mrewa, Mtoko and Nyamapanda. It was the road on which I had seen the hostile old man when I had still been new to the job. The Mangwende was the large, barren tribal area that had so disturbed me at the time.

Although the TTL fell inside the Mrewa police area, it bordered directly on to Macheke farms and was an obvious focal point for any racial animosity that might arise. I think I always sensed that the Mangwende was to be a major source of trouble and made an early point of meeting Chief Mangwende himself. After some initial verbal sparring, we established a relationship of semi-hostile cordiality that lasted for years, but did nothing to spare either of us from the horrors to come.

Our only other main road was a single track artery off the Mrewa highway. This led through rich tobacco lands to Virginia and Mtoko. My area extended for 60 kilometres along this narrow thoroughfare and took in the whole of the Virginia farming area — another place that was to exert a major influence upon my life and career.

As a brand new member in charge, it was essential that I came to know as many of my 'parishioners' as possible and I set about arranging this even before I established a station routine. I held a meeting with police reserve section leaders then asked for a farmers' meeting to be held at the Virginia country club a week later.

Individual farmers called in at the station, some of them to offer assistance or hospitality and others to report matters of routine police interest. We studied each other with matter of fact curiosity and Missy spent much of her time preparing tea for visitors. It was all exceedingly pleasant and civilised. I was very much the colonial copper and enjoyed the feeling but all that was about to alter. Violence and bloodshed were poised to descend upon my little fiefdom, changing all our lives forever.

11

Royal Visit Farm and the District Nurse

Now that I was a real live member in charge I was no longer looked upon as a 'Pom' but anti-British feelings ran high among Rhodesians. They felt ever more betrayed by the Mother Country and this was reflected by an escalation in media comments pouring scorn on Britain and its people. White Rhodesians were developing a laager mentality that did wonders for community relations. Personal squabbles were forgotten in the general mood of defiance against the world and those who decided to get their families away from the daily carnage of life in an operational area were mocked for their cowardice by those who stayed.

Call up periods for army and police reserve were radically extended to cope with the exigencies of war and this made the general feeling of isolation seem even worse. On 9th August 1976, the South African Foreign Minister Dr Hildegard Muller had declared that he supported majority rule in Rhodesia and his comments were another terrible blow to Rhodesian morale.

South Africa also withdrew 26 of the 40 SAAF helicopters that we were using in the north-east and the Zambezi Valley. Fifty desperately needed aircrew went with the choppers and our own Air Force was in trouble,

Shortly before my transfer from Kariba, I had been to a meeting in Sinoia with the local squadron leader. He drove us there by car and when I asked why we hadn't taken a chopper, he ruefully explained that none of our military aircraft would be allowed off the ground in any other country.

'They should all have been scrapped long ago', he told me. 'We keep them flying with homemade bits and pieces but most of them are in a hell of a mess, so we only use them for essential flights.'

We were going to miss that South African support.

Toward the end of 1976 the first Geneva Conference opened to negotiate transfer to majority rule but it folded in disagreement nine weeks later. I don't think any of us were surprised. We had heard it all before and no longer believed that a peaceful settlement was possible.

While the conference was in progress, the Right Reverend Adolf Schmidt, 70-year-old Catholic Bishop of Bulawayo was ambushed and killed by a terrorist called Charles

Ncube in Matabeleland. A nun who survived the attack accepted a farmer's offer to fly her to Geneva where she could tell the negotiating parties exactly what had happened. Inevitably perhaps, her Mother Superior refused to allow this.

I was remained of Edmund Burke's famous comment, 'All that is necessary for the triumph of evil is that good men do nothing.'

It seemed terribly apt for the times.

The year ended on another note of horror. Terrorists visited a tea estate in the Eastern Highlands and told the labour force to stop working. When they refused, 27 men were lined up and shot in front of their families. This brought the total of civilians killed by terrorists over the previous four years to 716. Only 61 of those murdered civilians were white.

According to the international media, the terrorist war was being fought on behalf of black Rhodesians yet it seemed that black Rhodesians were the ones taking most of the punishment. Nobody seemed to care.

My first meeting with the police reserve section leaders went off smoothly enough although I was immediately forced to make concessions. Official uniform for reservists was a grey shirt and long blue trousers but when they arrived, the section leaders were all in camouflage. When I mildly suggested a return to the traditional, it was angrily pointed out that we were on the very edge of the *Thrasher* operational area and also under terrorist threat from Mtoko and Mrewa. Farm attacks were increasing in frequency and severity all around us, and it was likely that we would come under fire very soon. Men on roadblock duties might be called away for something far more serious and there wouldn't be time to change their clothing. Seeing their point, I reluctantly gave way. It seemed that like it or not, I was going to be involved in the war.

They were an impressive bunch those Macheke section leaders. In general, they were older than the average although I had three PATU sticks to control and PATU was considered a young man's prerogative. One of the Macheke lot was the first all black stick in the country. I automatically christened them the Black Watch and it was a nickname they came to accept with pride. Trained by Tony du Preez — an Afrikaner who spoke with an English accent and was fluent in Chishona — they were a well-drilled unit and were to do an excellent job for the community.

The other two PATU stick leaders looked hard men indeed and I wondered whether I could handle them. James Leask was beetle-browed, bewhiskered and volatile, while Fred Platen was a big, slow-spoken Afrikaner with a ready smile and disconcertingly direct eyes. The other section leaders were Athol Brown and Keith Baisley from Virginia and they worked with Danie Krynauw and Tommy Kinch from Macheke while Ewen Farrar acted as the district sage and controlling influence over them all. Daphne du Preez (Tony's wife) ran the WFR and all of them studied me with frank curiosity.

These section leaders of mine were all responsible members of the community and I couldn't help wondering how they would feel if they knew how limited was my own experience. As member in charge, I was expected to orchestrate their training, sort out deployments to the operational area and if necessary, lead them into battle, yet I had never done anything remotely like it before. However, they looked to me for guidance and I knew I would have to muddle along somehow.

That meeting went off smoothly enough but a week later I was to face the farming community in general. By then the situation had changed and I found myself facing an angrily hostile audience. Macheke had suffered its first farm attack and although nobody on our side had been hurt, I had been put into an invidious position, been found vaguely wanting and was then left to face the flak on my own. I didn't enjoy it much.

Pieter and Violet van Aardt were an elderly Afrikaans couple, farming on Royal Visit — a sprawling tobacco farm on the eastern boundary of my area. The farm bordered directly on to the Weya TTL, itself in Manicaland and already recognised as a fertile recruiting ground for terrorists.

The Agric-alert alarm had me out of bed and running for the charge office some time before midnight. Even as Mrs van Aardt panted out her report of the attack, I could hear the rattle of gunfire amplifying her words. Fortunately the Van Aardt sons Peter and Louis were at home that evening and the attackers got back more than they must have bargained for. One was killed and the rest of the gang fled without doing any real damage.

It was my first experience of genuine warfare and I struggled to keep calm. Through Dispol at Marandellas, I asked for air support from the military. The JOC at Mtoko was only a few minutes flying time from Royal Visit and if we could get flares down and illuminate the fleeing terrorists, perhaps we could give them a real lesson and deter further attacks. My request was turned down flat on the grounds that the attack was over, nobody had been hurt and there was no point in risking a precious helicopter at night.

They were right of course, but I was indignant at the time and didn't relish passing the news on to the beleaguered family on Royal Visit. When I did, the Agric-alert was immediately blocked with offers of assistance from neighbouring farmers and James Leask rang in to say that his men were ready to go in whenever I gave the word.

I had little choice but to turn these offers down, even though they were well meant. It was far too risky to go in before daylight. Approach roads to the farm could well be mined and in those early days, nobody had mine protected vehicles. The Van Aardts were okay and had each other for moral support, so I brusquely ordered everyone to stay clear of Royal Visit.

It was hardly a popular decision and my telephone went mad for a while but I stuck to my guns. The JOC had promised a reaction team at first light and there was no point in risking lives unnecessarily. Ignoring the howls of protest, I put my point of view over the Agric-alert and advised everyone to take themselves off to bed. The fun was over for that night.

For me it wasn't so easy. My hands were trembling with reaction and I kept wondering whether I had done the right thing. Sleep was gone for the moment and I spent the rest of the night in my office, catching up on paperwork and chatting to the Van Aardts over the telephone from time to time. I had not met the couple at that stage but we built up a considerable rapport during that long night. As the sky paled in the East, I drove out to Royal Visit and without even thinking about it, took the station Renault 4 — an unprotected little tin can of a vehicle that I normally used as my 'staff car.' It was a stupid thing to do, particularly as I had forbidden others from doing much the same thing during the night, but it was to set a precedent that would lead to many an anxious moment over succeeding months.

The Van Aardt family greeted me with shy smiles, gallons of tea and a dining table heaving with eggs, bacon, boerewors and homemade rusks. They gave me graphic descriptions of how they had fought off the midnight attackers and I could only marvel at their matter of fact attitude.

'It is difficult at night, man', Pieter van Aardt waved calloused hands. 'You cannot see anything to aim at so you have to go for the flashes see.'

They showed me chips in the cement where Kalashnikov bullets had peppered the house and the broken window that was the sum total of damage sustained. Out near the tobacco barns, a young man lay sprawled in the dust and although there was no weapon with him, I had no doubt he had received his just deserts.

Even the old lady had got in on the fighting and a couple of days later, she lightened up the whole incident as far as I was concerned. Coming shyly into my office, she demanded that I issue her with a rifle from the station armoury.

'I can't do that Mrs van Aardt', I told her gently. 'FN rifles are only issued to police reservists. Besides, you did so well the other night; why on earth do you want another rifle?'

Leaning over my desk, Violet van Aardt — a sweet, gentle, old-fashioned lady — scowled fiercely into my face.

'The trouble was, Mr Lemon', she told me grimly. 'I had to use the twelve bore and do you know what? That shotty gun gets too blerry hot!'

I couldn't help laughing aloud at her vehemence and after a somewhat uncertain smile, she joined in with me. She was a very dear lady, Violet van Aardt and although she was to suffer a great deal more over the next couple of years, she never failed to provide me with a warm welcome whenever I came to Royal Visit. Her fortitude in the face of terrorist violence was to be a shining example to the entire community and I often felt that it was a pity Rhodesia's detractors saw only our political mouthpieces and not the humble folk like Violet and Pieter van Aardt.

When I stood up to address the meeting at Virginia a few days later, I knew I was in for a hard time. The country club was packed and most leading lights in the community had already been in to my office, expressing their discontent at the lack of immediate support after the Royal Visit attack. I had passed their feelings on to my OC but he shrugged them aside. The decision had been made by military minds at Mtoko and it wasn't his fault.

'Besides it was an isolated incident', he told me airily. 'Other districts have them every night but your farmers are notorious whingers. You wait 'till they really have problems.'

On that Tuesday afternoon, it was me who had the problems. Missy had accompanied me to Virginia and I was very aware of her presence as I rose to face a grimly hostile audience. Her pride in my achievements might well be dented over the next few minutes and I made a conscious effort to steady my fluttering nerves. Starting my address with a general security briefing, I emphasised that the ZANLA presence in operational areas now amounted to thousands of cadres rather than hundreds. Faces set in ever-grimmer lines and when I came to the problems affecting our own district, the meeting threatened to erupt with explosive anger.

Trying hard to sound non-committal, I read out details of farm attacks in Mtoko, Headlands and Mrewa — three of the four areas adjoining our own. I told them of terrorist murders, arson and beating in the tribal lands and I detailed Special Branch estimates of the threat facing us from those districts.

'But what is being done about it?' somebody shouted from the audience. 'Are we expected to sit back on our arses and wait for something to happen?'

'Then deal with it ourselves because nobody else is willing to do so', said somebody else sarcastically.

'Just like we did with Royal Visit', another voice chimed in and a murmur of agreement ran through my audience.

Holding up my hands for silence, I carefully explained the decision taken by JOC Mtoko and the reasons behind my own refusal to sanction an immediate reaction.

'We could have sorted it out', another voice shouted.

I reacted angrily. I have never been good under personal attack and now I was really under fire. Besides I'd had plenty of time to reflect on my actions over Royal Visit so I knew I was right.

'I'm sure you could', I told them flatly. 'But if any of you had gone up in a landmine blast on your way in, it wouldn't have helped anyone, least of all the Van Aardts. Not only that, but I would have had the task of telling your next of kin.'

Taking a deep breath, I looked around at my audience and continued my broadside.

'We are going to have further attacks in this area and I am warning you now — if anyone tries to supplant my authority and act on their own, I will ensure that they are charged under the Emergency Powers Act and locked up. In fact I will personally throw away the key.'

It was a foolish threat on my part and for a moment I thought I had overdone it. Support came from two unexpected quarters. The first was Pieter van Aardt himself. He got to his feet slowly and after telling the gathering that he understood the problems faced by Security Forces, he thanked me personally for the support I had given his family during their ordeal. It certainly calmed my critics and the next intervention did even more for my personal cause.

Tim Peech was perhaps the leading light in the community. Born and brought up in Macheke, his Salama Farm was a model of how a modern tobacco spread should be run. Tim had his own radical ideas for the future of the country. He and his Texan wife Michelea brought their children up on progressive lines, making them speak Chishona whenever possible and — unlike most white Rhodesians — encouraging them to bring black friends into the house.

In spite of these liberal tendencies, Tim was hugely respected in the community. He was a captain in the Territorial Army and a natural leader of men. Although I had not met the man until then, I knew his reputation and felt more than a little nervous when the chairman answered his request to speak.

Fortunately, Tim was on my side. Citing his army experience he told the meeting of various incidents when reacting forces had gone up on landmines.

'The member in charge is right', he went on quietly. 'Think how you would feel if you had beaten off an attack and a neighbour was killed on their way to rescue you. The Van Aardts did wonderfully well in the circumstances and hardly needed our help in any case.'

With Tim Peech on my side, I was accepted and my hard line and completely artificial attitude came to be looked upon as marking an experienced fighting man. Suddenly I had the confidence of my parishioners and even if it was misplaced, it certainly made my job easier. Violet van Aardt put the icing on the cake.

'Do you know, ' she told the meeting, 'that Mr Lemon has so much contempt for the terrs that he came to our place the next day in his dinky little Renault. That was brave hey?'

The meeting clapped and I coloured. My action hadn't been brave. It had been thoughtless and irresponsible. I glanced somewhat sheepishly at Tim Peech and he closed his eyes.

Skating over that aspect of the incident, I carried on with the meeting but when it was over, my street cred was up through the roof and I felt extremely pleased with myself. Perhaps I might make a soldier after all

My euphoria was short lived. The war was soon encroaching on my family life. We had chosen the first Sunday of the school holidays to go fishing on Tommy Kinch's dam. It proved a lovely day and we were packing up to go home when I saw the Land-Rover nosing down to call me out. Leaving Missy to finish off, I hurried back to the station.

The call was from the district nurse who had received a report that children in the Mangwende had been injured by a grenade. She was on her way to the scene. Could I provide an escort?

It was Sunday evening, the incident had occurred outside my area and I still had time to rejoin my family. On the other hand, I could get to the scene quicker than coppers from Mrewa and if the kids were badly injured, time was of the essence. There wasn't really a choice, so bundling Sergeant Nduna and a couple of rifles into my Renault, I set off for Nhowe Mission, right on the edge of the tribal area. Sister Schlachter was waiting at the mission and as we drove into the TTL both my passengers expressed doubt in the wisdom of using the flimsy little motorcar. It was too late to turn back however and there was considerable tension in the Renault as we motored deep into the Mangwende.

At the affected kraal, we were greeted by a grave-faced elder who explained that four children had been playing with a phosphorous grenade when it exploded, showering their little bodies with sticky fire. Politely asking us to follow, he made his way to one of the larger huts and gestured for me to precede him through the narrow doorway. I paused on the threshold, my senses spinning and my knees suddenly weak.

The smell in that hut was terrible. Sickly sweet, it clutched at my nostrils and seemed to kick its way down into my stomach. Gulping hard, I concentrated on not losing my lunch.

The four children were lying uncovered on rush matting and even through the gloom I could see strips of skin and charred flesh hanging from their blistered bodies. Three of them were deeply unconscious while the fourth stared mutely up at me, eyes huge in his hideously peeled face. Dragging my gaze away from that terrible stare, I felt my own eyes fill at the child's torment. So badly were all four of those children burned that I couldn't have said whether they were male or female, nor could I have guessed their age.

I don't know how long I stood rooted in the doorway, but Jenny Schlachter eventually pushed past me and moved across to kneel beside the ravaged little bodies. Swallowing the lump in my throat, I went to help but my eyes kept filling with tears and I couldn't have inspired much confidence. Waving me away, the district nurse muttered something about the gathering darkness. I called for light and a hurricane lamp was produced. This was hardly sufficient so I held my torch while a sombre villager did the same with Sergeant Nduna's.

Remembering somewhat belatedly that we were in an area dominated by the terrorists, I had sent the sergeant outside to keep watch for possible trouble. Two women sat motionless and silent in one corner of the hut and I guessed that they were the afflicted mothers.

For the next few hours Jenny Schlachter worked with tight-lipped efficiency and I couldn't help marvelling at her skill. In semi-darkness, she gently cut away scraps of ruined flesh, applied salve and bandages and set up saline drips on all four of her little patients. I watched with tears in my eyes and my stomach still curdling at the stench of burned flesh. I was no longer a stranger to violent death but this all seemed so senseless. Children will always play with strange objects and the solid shape of grenades make them fascinating to the very young. The incident had been largely accidental, but whoever had jettisoned the grenade ought to have been there to witness the awful effects of his carelessness. My gloomy musing was interrupted by the arrival of another elder who gently took the torch from my trembling hand.

'It is better for all of us that you keep watch with your sergeant outside, sir', he said quietly. 'The *vakomana* will already know of your presence and you cannot fight them from here.'

So I joined Nduna in his lonely vigil. We stood a few paces apart, each of us listening to the soft sounds of night and peering through clinging darkness with the intensity of badly frightened men. The nape of my neck crackled with nervous anticipation and at any moment I expected to be the target of automatic fire.

But the *vakomana* left us alone and after nearly three hours of exhausting work, the district nurse emerged pale and drained from the hut. Shortly afterwards an armoured ambulance arrived and the kids were taken away. Subdued villagers supplied us with sweet tea and then we went back to our respective homes and families — the scene in Mangwende seeming even more horrific for the contrast.

For me, that incident instilled a deep admiration for the courage and efficiency of our district nurse. She had put her life on the line for those children and never once shown any sign of nervousness. That admiration was to be enhanced on many more occasions. Jenny Schlachter went on to become a legend in the community for her work with victims of landmine, bullet or grenade and among black and white alike, her arrival on a scene was an enormous relief.

Three of the injured children died that night and the fourth succumbed to his injuries a few days later. For me, the greatest tragedy of all was the fact that the phosphorous grenade had almost certainly been dropped or discarded by a member of the Security Forces. The fiendish little weapons were on general issue to army and PATU patrols, but seldom seen amongst terrorist forces. In fact the opposition had done their best to rescue the situation by making no attempt to interrupt proceedings, even though the local member in charge must have made a tempting target.

With call-up periods for reservists being extended regularly, my farmers were becoming ever more restless. Their biggest bone of contention was that they often ended up guarding farms in other areas while their own families were left unprotected, merely because Macheke wasn't looked on as a fully operational area. It was a silly situation and I passed their concerns on whenever I could, but the voice of one lowly section officer — even if he was Rhodesia's first admiral — was unlikely to carry much weight with the men who co-ordinated the war effort.

And yet the war came closer by the day. Throughout the country, the situation was deteriorating and by early 1977, the Security Forces were losing on average, one man a day to the terrorists. The kill rate had dropped from ten to one down to seven to one and with the increase in white emigration, the lack of available manpower became ever more critical. The defence budget was increased and by the end of January, the war was costing a million dollars a day. That was money that beleaguered Rhodesia couldn't afford.

Compulsory national service was extended from nine months to two years and whites in the 38 to 50 age group were also called up. That didn't affect many of my farmers, almost all of whom already belonged to either police or army reserve, but when all military deferments were cancelled irrespective of economic implication, they were up in arms. Until then, farmers had been exempt from call-up at busy times of the year but that now fell away to the general need and the district was boiling for an explosion.

To make matters worse, our opposition had what seemed an inexhaustible supply of terrorist recruits. There were mass abductions of schoolchildren from Matabeleland and the north-east, many of the abductees ending up in Zambia and Mozambique where they were subjected to military training before being sent back into Rhodesia as fully-fledged guerrilla fighters.

Nor were these abductions as indefensible as they seemed. Youngsters crave adventure and when a group of parents was bussed into Botswana by the government in an effort to get their children back, all but a few of the kids refused to return. They obviously wanted to join the war effort but I couldn't help wondering if they were ever told exactly what they were getting into. Rhodesian servicemen were a frighteningly efficient bunch and after years of war, they took few prisoners.

While all this went on, settlement talks continued and the next phase included a tour around Africa by Ivor Richard, the British minister handling the settlement deal. At this stage, the idea seemed to warrant bringing in an entirely new scheme — again! — and this time it was proposed that there should be direct British involvement in an interim government for Rhodesia. The main problem with this proposal was that white Rhodesians regarded all British politicians — particularly those from the Labour party — with contemptuous mistrust. They were hardly likely to approve of those same politicians having a major say in running the country.

Richard himself was a grossly fat man, totally unprepossessing and not the sort of man to improve support from Britain among sport-mad Rhodesians. Even those who prayed every day for a political solution were put off by the man. He was obviously extremely clever, but he was also a poser with a readily apparent bad temper. On 23rd January he sneeringly demolished our top broadcaster Lawford Sutton Pryce in a radio interview and brought home to most of us that in many matters our homegrown experts were vastly inferior to their international counterparts.

But for all his intellect, Ivor Richard didn't bother to hide his dislike and contempt for all things Rhodesian and my personal opinion was that he set the settlement cause back some considerable time.

But these were national problems and my own personal problems lay with matters pertinent to Macheke and Virginia. This included murder and mayhem on all sides. Tribesmen and their families were killed in the Mangwende for being 'sell outs', while stock thieves from the Weya went on the rampage, taking animals from most of my boundary farms. Tony du Preez and his Black Watch worked almost continually on stock theft enquiries but although they did well in the circumstances, their recovery rate was minimal.

On three occasions the stick came under fire and acquitted themselves well without managing to kill any of the opposition. In spite of their ever-increasing efficiency, the farming community regarded them with deep suspicion and this definitely hampered their operations. I felt that it probably had something to do with Tony's own lack of popularity, as for some reason I could never get to the bottom of, Macheke folk disliked him intensely.

Farm attacks and vehicle ambushes on rural roads increased in Mtoko and Mrewa, while both districts lost white farmers to terrorist attack. My own farmers looked increasingly grim and became ever more hostile to Security Force discipline and government policies in general. These were strong-willed men and the area was spoiling for an explosion. Increasingly worried by the situation, I sought advice from Tim Peech.

'The only way to sort it out', he told me over a beer, 'is to get all our young men out of the army and into the police reserve. If we do that, they can be used in this area where they will be far more effective. We can form them into PATU sticks and use them for immediate reaction to local incidents. They know the area and would soon put the lid on any trouble in Macheke or Virginia.'

In theory it was an admirable scheme and we spent a few hours in working out exactly how it could be handled. I enjoyed the planning but for all his enthusiasm, I didn't think Tim had a chance of swinging it with those who really mattered. However, I had underestimated the political influence of his family connections.

'Leave it with me', he advised as I was leaving. 'I will see what I can do, but it might take time.'

It did take considerable time and meanwhile we had more trouble to contend with. Ground coverage patrols and local informers had reported terrorist visits to a number of Macheke farms and I spent a great deal of my time organising follow-up operations with my PATU sticks. I was becoming quite expert in military tactics and my initial abhorrence of war had given way to the excitement of the hunt. For me it was like a gigantic chess game played out on a map and I revelled in the organisation of patrols, logistical problems and the terrible tension that always arose when an operation was in progress.

One entire wall of my office was covered with a map of the area and I spent a lot of time studying this, while making play with coloured pins and behaving exactly like every other armchair general in the country. It might not have been war but it was fun. My lieutenants were the PATU stick leaders and they provided a fascinating contrast in appearance, background and methods.

Fred Platen was a very big man, whose gentle manner belied a grim determination to come to grips with the enemy and kill as many of them as possible. His men were all Afrikaners, experienced hunters and born to the veld. They handled their weapons like additional parts of their anatomy and all of them seemed to possess the same quietly phlegmatic attitude as their leader.

James Leask's bunch were considerable more mercurial. James himself had the reputation of a wild man when in his cups, but he was a good leader and handled his men efficiently in the field. He and I had the occasional roaring argument about his drinking habits but we remained friends and I relied on him a great deal.

The odd man out was Tony du Preez. I liked Tony and enjoyed the way his Black Watch performed, but because of the general hostility he faced, I had to keep his stick apart from the rest when it came to deployments.

Tony's wife Daphne was equally unpopular but she ran the Women's Field Reserve and ran it very well indeed. As soon as the Macheke security situation began to deteriorate, she arranged a roster of WFR ladies to man the station radio sets. In fact, before I had been in occupation five months, my little police station had taken on the air of a minor army camp with myself at the hub of things as an non-commissioned general. And I was the bloke who had refused to join PATU on the grounds that it would interfere with my police duties!

Mind you, there were interludes in the general tension that was gripping the district. With Missy's assistance, I resurrected the long-forgotten Police Ball that was often an annual event in district police stations. Missy organised the local ladies and they provided food and decorated the Farmers' Hall while Matt Carson ran an excellent bar. My reasoning for the ball was that it would give everyone the chance to let down their hair and forget their problems.

It would also provide an excellent target for any wandering terrorists but I borrowed a stick of armed APR from Marandellas. These were deployed around the Farmers' Hall and fortified with beer and food to keep them alert. Fortunately, perhaps the opposition left us alone and the ball proved a roaring success. It was amazing to see men in dinner jackets and ladies in magnificent ball gowns solemnly stacking rifles and shotguns by the door before getting down to the festivities. The police band did us proud and the sun was well above the horizon when we finally called a weary halt to proceedings.

It had been a wonderful night and one that was desperately needed in a community that was threatening to tear itself apart. Squabbles between neighbours were becoming ever more prevalent and many of these degenerated into bitterness and acrimony that was completely out of proportion to the original quarrel. Drunken punch ups and reckless gunfire in the hotel and country club caused damage that we didn't need and one or two farmers vented their frustrations on their workers. Entire labour forces deserted *en masse* and I was never sure whether they had gone over to the enemy cause or merely wandered home in disgust.

It couldn't last and I tried to explain my worries in intelligence reports to my superiors. These were ignored and when a dusk-to-dawn curfew came into effect throughout the area, it added to the simmering tension. Anyone out on foot after 6 pm could be shot without warning and although the curfew technically applied to all citizens, everyone knew that whites seldom went anywhere except in a motor vehicle.

The entire district carried on their lives in an atmosphere of ever increasing strain and my own feeling was that — although I dreaded it — the need for positive action against the enemy was becoming desperate. The farmers needed a focal point for their frustration and I hoped that when it came, our first contact would be a successful one.

It was James' stick who had the first battle with terrorists in the Macheke area. By coincidence it took place on Fred Platen's farm where a brief, but successful (from our point of view) firefight took place. Two of the opposition were killed and although they turned out to be recruits on their way for training, it was our first success as a fighting district and did wonders for community morale.

From then on the pace of events quickened. We had vehicle ambushes on both main roads, a 300% increase in stock theft and continued reports of terrorist activity. Farm stores were regularly looted and burned down and at the scene of one such incident, my own war almost came to a decidedly messy end. It was only the vigilance of Sergeant Nduna that saved me from becoming another sad statistic on the evening news bulletin.

The store was situated on the main Mrewa road and I attended the scene shortly after first light. There was little I could do other than call for Special Branch and the forensic experts so after interviewing the storekeeper, I jumped into my Renault intending to warn nearby farmers while we waited. As I was driving away, Sergeant Nduna leaped from one side of the road to stop me. Shaking visibly from excitement, he pointed out a small piece of black rubber showing through the dusty road surface a metre from my front bumper. We knew from sitreps that in some areas, terrorists covered landmines with bicycle tubing in the hope that it would fool the mine detectors and needless to say I didn't continue my journey.

Later that morning, an army bomb disposal man lifted a dull green canister from beneath the rubber. Having cheerfully informed me that it was a British Mark 4 landmine, he went on his way but on hearing about this, many of my parishioners pointed out that the Brits were still after my blood for going against the Queen. I ignored the joshing but the fact that the mine had been British made did nothing for my sense of loyalty to the Crown.

My sense of loyalty to Sergeant Nduna was another matter and I made sure that he was well supplied with beer that evening and for a fair old time afterwards.

There had been no more farm attacks in the area but it was inevitable that as the pace of the war in Macheke hotted up, so the day of our first serious casualties was drawing ever closer. Perhaps it was also inevitable that when the casualties occurred, they would take place on Royal Visit and the victims would be the Van Aardts.

12

Horror at Royal Visit Farm

In February 1977 St Paul's mission at Musami in the Mangwende TTL was attacked by a group of terrorists. Seven white missionaries were callously murdered and the attack was doubly personal for me. Not only was the mission on the edge of my area but the sole white survivor was Father Dunstan Myerscough, who had taught me Latin and gave me my first boxing lessons at school.

The terrorists had announced themselves as ZANLA, but the international media promptly pinned blame for the massacre on the Selous Scouts. By then it had become fashionable to blame the Scouts for any atrocity that took place and such was the insidious nature of this propaganda that on occasions I almost believed it myself. The Scouts were quite capable of the most barbaric acts, but in the case of Musami they couldn't have been responsible.

Ever since the accidental shooting of Andre Rabie by his own forces in the early days of the war, the Scouts had made sure that an area was 'frozen' before going in on any operation. This meant barring access to all other Security Forces in order to avoid similar 'friendly fire' accidents. I had cursed this process on occasion but at the time of what the media called 'the Musami Mission Massacre' the Mangwende TTL had not been frozen. Once again Western politicians were using the Selous Scouts as convenient scapegoats.

I passed news of the killing to Sister Placidis and the Catholic priest at Monte Cassino mission just south of Macheke, but they merely shrugged and didn't seem overly concerned. At the time I couldn't help wondering if they already knew about it or whether violent death had become an acceptable hazard in missionary work.

The British government refused Rhodesia's request for an international enquiry into the Musami killings, but this was regarded as par for the course by disillusioned Rhodesians.

In March 1977 the military finally took full control of the war effort. Combined Operations (Comops would you believe?) was set up with Lieutenant-General Peter Walls as overall commander and my old Kariba acquaintance, Air Marshall Maclaren as his deputy. Roger Hawkins was appointed Minister of Defence in place of PK Van der Byl and that was a bit of a surprise, but I personally welcomed the creation of Comops even though I was enjoying my responsibility for pursuing the war in Macheke.

Security duties now occupied most of my time and leaving routine police work to my patrol officer, I really got in on the 'general' act. I wore a camouflage jacket over my police uniform and usually carried an Uzi sub-machine gun. On occasions I even tucked a P1 pistol into my belt but gave up that practice when Missy waxed sarcastic about wearing the pistol with my 'civvies' to Salisbury airport. We were meeting my sister-in-law from England and I was accused of showing off. Me!

As member in charge I managed to avoid having my military shortcomings exposed on training days, but felt sure that it was only a matter of time before I was subjected to the ultimate test of being involved in a contact. With this eventuality in mind, I used the rifle range whenever I could, practising with various weapons and above all, learning to shoot straight. Missy had joined the WFR and she occasionally accompanied me on these impromptu training sessions, cheerfully displaying an inborn penchant for handling the heavy rifle.

I was coming to realise that there was more steel in my meek little wife than I had ever realised.

In April, the British Foreign Secretary David Owen arrived on a visit and he also demolished poor old Lawford Sutton Pryce in debate. Owen was far more personable than Ivor Richard, but he had that same veneer of thinly concealed contempt about him that seemed to typify British politicians. If he was a genuine sample of those masterminding change in Rhodesia, I wasn't at all sure I wanted change.

I was looking forward to joining a Kenya Kongonis cricket tour of Britain later in the year, however, and the anticipation helped to take my mind off our problems, but just before dawn on one fateful morning, the Agric-alert howled its warning and the real horrors had begun.

Since the original attack on Royal Visit the main house had been altered beyond recognition. Firewalls had been erected, grenade screens were fitted on all windows, massive floodlights were kept on all night and a tall security fence had been erected around the house. The beautiful, rambling old farmhouse had been converted into an easily defended fortress but it availed the Van Aardt family not a single jot.

Peter and Louis van Aardt were both army reservists and as such, subject to periodic stints in the operational area. Leaving the house at the start of one call-up, they waved cheerfully to their parents and drove away from the homestead.

The landmine had been cleverly laid. Sixty metres from the house and 15 centimetres below the road surface, it nestled in deadly anticipation some 30 centimetres off the crown of the road. The front offside wheel of Peter's car went over the mine and the weight of the vehicle triggered the firing mechanism.

The resultant blast of high explosive whipped up through the chassis on the driver's side, shredding poor Peter Van Aardt and blowing the vehicle into twisted remnants of shiny metal. The ignition key flew like a small, deadly missile and hit Louis under the chin, smashing its way through the bones of his face to lodge behind one eye. One of the most horrifying aspects of the tragedy was that Violet was still waving from the door when she saw her sons explode.

(Above) Prime Minister Ian Smith signs Rhodesia's unilateral declaration of independence on 11 November 1965.

(Left) This determines Rhodesian born David Lemon, serving as PC G881 in the Gloucestershire Constabulary, to return home to do his bit for his country.

PC Lemon becomes 8693 Patrol Officer Lemon in the British South Africa Police, Rhodesia — a Force in the Great Tradition.

(Left) A BSAP mounted escort.

(Right) The BSAP band plays on a ceremonial occasion in the Morris Depot.

(Left) A BSAP motor cycle escort.

(Right) Office work while on patrol in the bush.

(Left) The author, weary after his first Kariba patrol.

(Right) The Kariba charge office, 1974

(Above) It was thought impossible for guerrillas to infiltrate Rhodesia from Zambia across 33km of wild water in small boats. But in 1975 a guerrilla presence in the Omay TTL was discovered and for Kariba the war was on.

(Left) In the tobacco farming areas of Mashonaland, like Macheke where the author was posted, the terrorism threat escalated. While husbands were away on Army or Police Reserve call-ups, wives managed the farms but they always carried guns.

(Right) In district areas responsibility for fighting the war fell increasingly on the shoulders of Police Reservists. Here seen undergoing training.

(Left) A Police Reserve PATU unit on patrol

(Right) Women Field Reservists were increasingly called on to man radios around the clock at District police stations.

(Above) When Andries Joubert, a Wedza Farmer, was murdered by ZANLA in March 1973 men from the army's elite Tracking Combat Unit hunted down those responsible. The unit was later incorporated into the Selous Scouts.

(Right) Captured Soviet-supplied weapons.

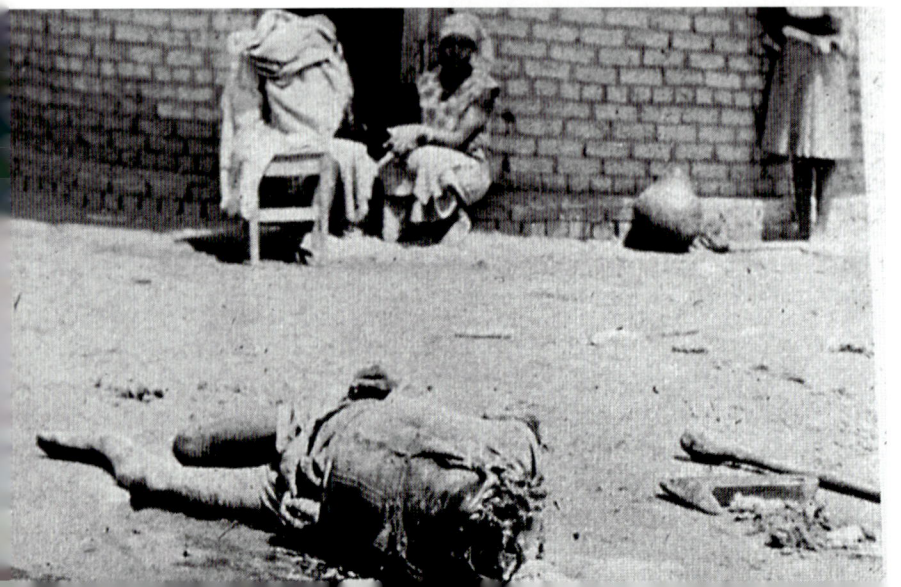

(Left) Accused of being a 'sell-out' to the government, ZANLA detonated a grenade against this tribesman's head.

(Above) Another tribesman given short shrift by ZANLA.

(Left) Here ZANLA locked all men, women and children of this village into huts and burnt them alive.

(Right) A country hotel shot up by ZANLA. Security Forces survey the damage.

(Above) ZANLA gangs hamstrung or shot cattle both on white farms and in the TTLs

(Below) No one was exempt from their murderous onslaught. Not even the Red Cross.

(Right) ZANLA laid landmines indiscriminately on country roads. This one blew up a black-owned bus killing and wounding innocent passengers.

(Left) Another ZANLA landmine detonated. A Police Reservist demonstrates the depth of the crater.

(Below) The little that is after a black-owned car detonated another ZANLA landmine. There were no survivors.

(Above and below) Bomb blast at Woolworths Manica Road. !2 Saturday morning shoppers died in the blast and another 76 injured — all of them black.

(Above) 27 black field workers mercilessly slaughtered by ZANLA. It was presumed to be a warning to others not to co-operate with the Security Forces.

(Left) Seven white missionaries and three children massacred at Elim Mission near the Mozambique border.

(Above and below) Salisbury's petrol storage sites rocketed and set ablaze by guerrillas. November 1978.

(Above) And another fuel tank erupts.

(Above) Another bomb blast in Salisbury.

(Below) Seven white missionaries were slaughtered by ZANLA at St Paul's Roman Catholic Mission at Musami.

(Above and left) On 3 September 1978 ZIPRA terrorists shot Air Rhodesia's Viscount 'Hunyani' from the sky at Kariba with a Soviet-supplied SAM-7. They followed up to the crash site and butchered some of the survivors.

(Above and left) On 12 February 1979 ZIPRA shot Air Rhodesia's Viscount Umniati from the sky using a Soviet-supplied SAM-7. 59 passengers and crew perished in the crash. There were no survivors.

I had an Agric-alert set in the house by then and was able to get straight on the air. I could feel the lump in my throat at that wonderful, strong and kind-hearted Afrikaans lady reported the fact that both her sons had been blown to smithereens.

'Peter is dead, Mr Lemon', she said matter of factly and I could sense every other person in the district listening tensely to her words. 'I am not sure about Louis, but please come, hey.'

In spite of my warnings to the rest on instant reactions, there was no way I could resist such an appeal and I ran for my Renault, not even bothering to take a constable as escort. There wasn't time.

The first thing I saw on entering the gates of Royal Visit was the engine block of the family Renault. It had been blown nearly 300 metres in the blast and the crater left in the road was enormous. Old man Van Aardt was wandering aimlessly along the side of the road and I slowed to a halt beside him. When he looked at me, his face was slack with grief and his eyes were unfocussed. Putting my hands on his shoulders, I could feel his body trembling with suppressed shock and unhappiness.

'I am looking for Peter's leg', he answered my query as to what he was doing. 'He cannot rest in peace without his leg.'

With my arm around his bowed shoulders I led the devastated old gentleman gently into the house where Violet took him off me at the door. Although her features were set and her eyes were rimmed with red, her indomitable spirit showed in the straightness of her back and her attempt at a welcoming smile.

'Louis is still alive', she told me. 'I have laid him down in a bedroom and I will get the cook to make you some tea.'

Struggling to suppress my own tears, I put my arms around her for a while before rushing outside to examine the scene. It wouldn't do for the member in charge to be seen as a cry baby.

The Renault was a tangled mass of shredded metal and I shuddered at the thought of what such a blast would do to my R4. Peter van Aardt lay on the ground nearby with a blanket spread across him. Although his face was peaceful, he had been completely gutted and one leg was indeed missing. There was nothing I could do and as I turned to go back inside a motorcycle drew up with neighbouring farmer Andrew Clark on board. Andrew smiled a little warily.

I had given strict instructions over the air for everyone to stay put, but by that stage I was only too pleased to see him. Andrew was an army medic and that was exactly what was needed.

Back in the house, Louis van Aardt was conscious and even tried to smile. His face was blackened by the blast and we had no way of knowing about the ignition key that had already claimed the sight in one eye. There was blood everywhere and I looked at Andrew while Andrew looked at me.

'You are a trained medic', I said. 'You had better patch him up.'

'You are the member in charge', he countered. 'You must be better trained than I am.'

I almost laughed aloud and would probably have disillusioned Andrew for all time with my incompetence, had not Jenny Schlachter burst into the room.

'I heard it on the Agric-alert', she muttered with a warning scowl at me. 'I got here as quickly as I could.'

Her look challenged me to do what I liked about that, but I was so relieved by her comforting presence that I could have kissed her. By the time an army helicopter arrived with a doctor on board, Jenny had Louis van Aardt securely bandaged and safe from Andrew and myself.

Never again did I attempt to keep the district nurse away from the scene of an incident, no matter how dangerous it might have been. Her competence and courage in the most horrific circumstances were an inspiration to all those who saw her in action.

Louis van Aardt lost the sight in his right eye, but otherwise made a full recovery and became a friend. His parents could no longer take the strain of living on Royal Visit and moved to Marandellas where they promptly erected a security fence around their house in the suburbs Other urban dwellers mocked them for their caution, but I certainly couldn't find it in my heart to blame them. They had taken so much as a family and deserved a bit of peace and tranquillity in their old age. Their strength and good humour through horrific circumstances was long an inspiration to me and to many other Macheke residents.

I don't think any of us who knew them will ever forget the Van Aardts of Royal Visit.

As 1977 wore on, financial curbs were beginning to affect our daily lives as much as the security situation. As a nation, Rhodesians were on the verge of bankruptcy. Fuel had long been rationed, with every vehicle owner having a monthly allocation of coupons — an annual grant of extra ones being granted for holidays. Now even the holiday ration was being taken away and people were upset.

As member in charge, I had an allocation for the station and there were usually plenty of them left over so we were not affected as a family. I had to submit the inevitable return as to how my coupons were used each month, but took full advantage of 'stranded motorists' to doctor my figures.

Police vehicles were nominally restricted in their mileage but this was an impractical situation and whenever I exceeded my allocation — which was every month — extra kilometres were written off to operational duties. Far more serious was the situation with ammunition stocks. One particularly inane circular from PGHQ self-righteously informed members in charge than a single FN round cost 29 cents and advised us to use these rounds sparingly.

My comments on reading this piece of bureaucratic garbage were unrepeatable and I heard Missy giggle from her desk in the charge office. She had taken a part-time job assisting with station paperwork and often seemed to be running the whole place herself. Perhaps it was because I was so rarely behind my desk.

The ammunition was a problem though. Fortunately I had a number of unrecorded boxes in my armoury and these never featured on monthly returns, but it seemed sad that we were forced into dishonesty in order to keep the war effort going. I often wondered whether the desk jockeys in PGHQ ever realised how much contempt they inspired amongst policemen on the ground.

That extra ammunition was certainly needed as the war got worse. Further attacks took place in Macheke and Virginia, both on farms and on the road. Ted Hodgson, Keith Baisley and Duncan Rixon came under night attack at home and Gerry Pephanis had his house burnt down. So too did Johan Mostert and that was more of a surprise. The Mostert farm was in the southern part of the district and nowhere near a TTL. In fact it was only a few kilometres from the police station, so the war was getting far too close for comfort.

Roger Britter who lived alone in a remote Virginia homestead was attacked three times, but enthusiastically resisted all attempts to drive him out. I arrived at the farm after one attack to find Roger bristling with indignation.

'The bastards shot a hole in my fish tank', he waved his rifle at me.' 'I lost all my bloody tropicals.'

The mental picture of Roger fighting a battle in the midst of wetly flapping guppies roused me to semi-hysterical mirth and when the army reaction team arrived, they were somewhat nonplussed to find the pair of us howling with laughter.

But laughter was a commodity becoming ever rarer in the community and much of my time was spent in public relations visits to farmers who had suffered in one way or another. These visits were an enormous strain and many of them ended up in long bouts of heavy drinking, accompanied by ribald comments on the cowardice of our enemy, the ineptitude of our own politicians and the craven attitude of the British. It was a recipe for personal disaster but there was worse to come.

It wasn't only the white citizens of Macheke who suffered from terrorist attacks. Farm labourers were subject to constant harassment from 'the boys' and I had continual beatings, burnings and cruel mutilations to contend with.

One middle-aged woman had her ears cut off, was raped by seven laughing terrorists and then had all ten of her fingers individually broken because her son was believed — quite erroneously — to be a member of the Security Forces. A farm foreman was crucified on a tree while his family were forced to watch and any number of innocents were brutally beaten, raped or tortured, often with burning brands stuffed into the tenderest regions of their anatomy. Children disappeared and an informer of mine was beaten to a bloody pulp and had to spend months in hospital.

There were other atrocities too horrific to describe, but most of the victims survived. Two family planning workers didn't. They hit a landmine in their unprotected truck and it was the only time I saw Jenny Schlachter give way to emotion. She had worked with the medics for years and ended up sobbing in my arms at the futility of it all.

'They were honest, dedicated folk', she said tearfully. 'All they cared about was the welfare of their own people, yet it is their own people who have killed them.'

One Saturday afternoon I was standing outside my office with a young sergeant, newly arrived at the station. We were idly discussing the latest football scores when the ground shook to a distant explosion.

'Landmine', muttered Sergeant T V Gundani. 'There is no mistaking that sound. I'll get my rifle.'

African police were also subject to COIN courses and regular weapon training by then, so we quickly armed ourselves, confirmed the approximate position of the blast and sped off in my R4. Thirty minutes later we arrived at a scene that was to disturb my sleep for many years to come.

Fifteen farm labourers had finished work for the day and were on the way home from the tobacco lands. Seated in cheerful discomfort on a flatbed trailer, they had been singing happily as a tractor towed them back to their compound and the weekend round of beer drinks. Somehow the tractor failed to detonate the hidden mine but the trailer didn't. The seated work force were totally unprotected from that awful blast and the resultant carnage was horrifying. When we arrived on the scene, torn and mangled bodies lay sprawled across the road and a severed arm had draped itself obscenely across a telephone cable. The unmistakable smell of violent death hung like a pall over the scene and the tractor driver — miraculously unharmed — sat with his head in his hands beside the road. Two other survivors walked in shaken aimlessness among the bodies and I felt the hot anger of hatred boil in my stomach.

This was surely not war. How could the slaughter of innocent farm workers be condoned as an act of liberation? This was callous, brutal, cold-blooded murder — entirely without reason or justification and aimed quite deliberately at helpless innocents. Those who had died were anything but soldiers. They had no choice in the battle that was being waged, allegedly in their name and on their behalf. Most of them had families and to keep those families fed, they had to work. Only the farm workers were likely to use that remote road and so they had died for a cause, they could never hope to understand.

Where were the politicians now? Where were the world leaders and those outspoken members of the international media who gave tacit support to the terrorist cause?

Sergeant Trevor Vitalis Gundani was a very fine young policeman. He came to Macheke with an excellent record of service and in the time he was with me, proved himself well above average in all departments of coppering. His previous station had been in an operational area so he ought to have been hardened to the horrors of war, but like me, he broke down badly on that terrible afternoon. Working with tears running down our faces, we did what we could and were joined in our grisly task by shocked and silent farmers with their own labourers. White worked beside black and by the time it was all sorted out, black and white skins were stained alike with blood and the detritus of shattered human bodies. How I wished that Ivor Richard, David Owen and many of the other well-known figures who condemned Rhodesia as a racist state could have been there to share in our agony.

That night TV (inevitably I called him Television) Gundani and I sat in my office and got very drunk.

After eight and a half months in charge at Macheke I was feeling the strain. We had brought Brian and Graeme out of boarding school so that we could spend more time together as a family, but I often wondered whether I had done the right thing. Macheke was becoming a dangerous place to be. Since the initial attack on Royal Visit, not a week had gone by without at least one terrorist-inspired incident in my area and most weeks had produced far more than one. Nor did ordinary police work come to a halt for the war. Jannie Jordan, my original patrol officer could no longer take the strain and left the Force to go farming. I relied ever more on Sergeant Gundani to take some of the load off my shoulders and Television rose to the challenge. Ordinary murders, rapes, robberies and road accidents still had to be dealt with and although the powers that be had streamlined docket work, with serious cases we still had to go through the rigmarole of traditional police procedure.

My life at this stage seemed to be an unending treadmill of meetings. I was on the road virtually every day, going to Mtoko for JOC meetings, Marandellas with other members in charge, Mrewa and Wedza for liaison visits and both Headlands and Rusape to find out what was going on in Manicaland. I also arranged regular briefings for my farmers and police reservists. It was all very tiring and at one stage, Missy gave me a serious lecture on the dangers involved in using my little Renault. With all that travel, she felt that my luck was bound to run out, but the R4 had become a trademark and I pointed out that it still gave my farmers a lift to see me running around in that funny little vehicle.

That won't help me or the kids when you hit a landmine', she retorted acidly but I could only shrug my shoulders. I could see her point and God knows it was a strain using the Renault but I didn't see that I had much choice. Obviously there was a fair amount of stubborn pride involved but I really did feel that I was helping to boost morale in the district.

So I carried on using my 'staff car' but it wasn't the only area of concern for my worried wife. I was desperately tired, my nerves were taut with strain and my bad temper was never far from the surface. Missy and the kids probably bore the brunt of it, but my station staff also took to tiptoeing around me in order not to be noticed. On one occasion, I hurled a typewriter at an unfortunate constable and the telephone engineers were called out regularly to replace handsets that had been slammed down and broken in furious frustration.

I don't know whether it was my bad temper, my lack of patience or a basic flaw in my leadership qualities that caused the problem, but for a while I seemed to go through patrol officers like a knife through butter. They came, stayed for a few weeks or months and left — some on transfer and others resigning to take up civilian careers.

It baffled me because the patrol officer post at Macheke was a dream posting. Second in command at the station, the P/O dealt with crime and was responsible for a small proportion of monthly returns. His other duties were usually those I found boring, or I didn't feel inclined to perform myself, but his workload was never onerous.

For all that, my turnover was far too high and it worried me. Jannie Jordan was a bright lad but before he left to go farming, his wife came to see me in my office.

'We can't take it any more, Mr Lemon', she said accusingly. 'Jan has to do the work while you wander around, drinking with the farmers and generally having a good time.

You never give him a hand and seem to think more of your blacks than you do of him.'

I stared at her for a moment or two, completely lost for words. Barbara Jordan was very young and it was true that I had piled most of the routine work on her husband, but that was his job dammit! I didn't think I was unfair about it. As for 'enjoying myself' I was tempted to exchange roles with her little darling for a while. See how much enjoyment he could get out of salvaging shattered bodies or comforting weeping widows while their wide-eyed offspring looked on.

Taking a deep breath, I smiled gently at the furious young woman. To a certain extent I could understand Jannie's frustration, although I would have preferred him to make the complaint himself. However, we were all under strain and the tensions of our daily lives showed themselves in many different ways. Mildly wishing Barbara luck in the future, I diplomatically expressed the hope that her husband's next employer would prove more appreciative of his obvious talents.

'See', she said as she flounced out of the office, 'you never take anything seriously'.

Back behind my desk I muttered a fervent prayer that my next patrol officer would prove a little more suited to life as a copper in what was fast becoming a particularly 'hot' area.

But there were lighter moments to life in Macheke and at times I was able to enjoy being a policeman again. One Sunday we were taking a break from the war by having friends around to lunch. Sitting in the shade of a huge avocado tree, we ate, drank and relaxed as a normal family. The boys played cricket on the lawn and for a few all too brief hours, war and police work was forgotten. Then, inevitably the telephone rang.

Toc Arnold — himself a former copper — reported that a woman had hanged herself from a tree on his farm. Could I arrange for the body to be collected?

I could do better than that. As part of streamlining the system, new procedures had been laid down for obvious suicides and all I had to do was ring the Marandellas magistrate at home. He readily gave permission for the body to be buried so I rang Toc with the news and went back to my guests. Two days later, Sergeant Gundani brought the dead woman's husband into my office.

'I am sorry, sir', Television looked grave. 'He insists that she didn't hang herself. He strangled her.'

The last thing I wanted was another murder docket on my hands. Case files were piled high in my pending tray, Jannie Jordan had gone and I had no patrol officer to deal with routine matters. I struggled to remain calm.

'Does he realise what he is saying, Sergeant? Does he know that if this is so, he will be hanged himself?'

The little husband nodded nervously. Yes he knew what would happen to him but it was surely his just deserts. With his own hands (he held them up for my inspection) he had murdered a good woman and his children were now without a mother. Truly he deserved to be punished.

It all looked cut and dried and I don't suppose too many coppers would have turned down such a straightforward case, but I was busy. For most of that day Sergeant Gundani and I tried to shake the little man's story but he refused to budge. He had strangled his wife after an argument and in all conscience, couldn't allow the matter to be closed without the truth being known.

Eventually there was nothing for it but to have the good lady disinterred and a postmortem performed. Dispol wasn't happy with the idea but after satisfying himself that I had done what I could to avoid the eventuality, he arranged for a visit by the Government Pathologist.

Dr Kevin Lee was hardly the popular conception of a 'corpse cutter.' Rolling up to my station in an open sports car and a cloud of dust, he was dressed in jeans and a colourful shirt while sporting a beard that wouldn't have looked out of place on the fiercest of Selous Scouts. Grinning broadly at my obvious surprise, he introduced himself and off we went to Toc Arnold's farm and the allegedly murdered woman.

I have attended many postmortem examinations in the course of my police career. They are never pleasant but can be interesting and are an inescapable part of police work. The one that followed was surely the most bizarre PM ever witnessed by curious copper. The dead woman had been hauled out of her grave and lay on the ground, wrapped in a sheet. Grim-faced relatives greeted us with stony hostility and the afternoon silence was disturbed by unenthusiastic bird song and the hum of flies. It was fiendishly hot and the sickly smell of putrefaction hovered about the scene.

'Damn; I forgot the fly spray', Kevin Lee muttered as we climbed out of the car. 'Someone will need to keep the brutes away with a branch or something.'

That someone was me. For the next 15 minutes I stood in the sun, waving a leafy branch over the woman's body while the leading pathologist in Rhodesia performed his grisly task. He did a full postmortem and at the end of it, looked up at me with a wry smile.

'She topped herself', was his cheerful verdict. 'See, the hyoid cartilage is intact. Had she been strangled, that would have been crushed. There is no doubt about it I'm afraid — her hubby is telling you fibs.'

I wasn't pleased! Quite apart from the time wasted, I had been forced to stand in the sun looking patently ridiculous while this young popinjay did unspeakable things to the dead woman. It had not been pleasant and my feelings toward the lying husband were hardly charitable. He shifted his feet somewhat sheepishly when I had him brought into my office.

'It was my fault, sir', he mumbled. 'She died after we quarrelled, so I killed her even if I didn't do it with my hands.' He held them up again and I almost screamed at him to put the bloody things away. 'I deserve to be punished.'

There wasn't much I could do other than send him home with all sorts of warnings ringing in his head. As he shuffled out of the station, I exchanged glances with Television Gundani and we both broke into somewhat hysterical laughter. The little man had at least made me forget the war for a while and I wouldn't have missed Dr Lee's open-air PM for the world.

It was shortly after that incident that the harsh reality of a terrorist war was really brought home to me. Following an ineffective farm attack in Virginia, I was questioning the farm labourers with Neil Dart, a detective section officer from Marandellas. My colleague was known for his unorthodox working methods and when it became obvious that one young man wasn't telling us everything he knew. Neil became impatient.

Excusing himself, he took the unhelpful one into a nearby house, accompanied by a hard-faced detective sergeant. I looked somewhat helplessly at Sergeant Gundani and he shrugged. We were but uniformed coppers and Special Branch had their own way of doing things.

Ten minutes later Neil emerged from the house, slipping something small but bulky into his pocket. Behind him came the detective sergeant and the farm labourer, the latter now grey-faced and sweating, his hands noticeably trembling as he struggled to keep them out of sight.

'They went thataway', the SB man told me smugly. 'My little *tokoloshe* always works.'

As a result of what the labourer told him, two terrorists were killed in the Mtoko area and when I asked Neil how he had done it, he showed me his fiendish little machine — his *tokoloshe* as he called it. It was a wind up generator with two electrodes attached and capable of inflicting a powerful electric shock. It was a basic instrument of torture and my policeman's instincts were momentarily outraged, but Neil must have sensed what I was feeling. Perhaps he saw the revulsion in my eyes.

'Don't you take the high moral tone with me, boy', he warned in level tones. 'Innocent people are dying all around us and more will die and horribly. You are on the edge of this bloody war so you can do things the honourable way if you want to. I deal with bloody horrors every day and do not have time to work to the letter of the sodding law.'

Frowning in obvious anger, he went on.

'The trouble is that the gooks don't play by the rules. They use whatever methods are needed and that is why they will eventually win this war and drive us from our homes. We fight by the book because at heart we are Christian bloody gentlemen and worry about peoples' sensitivities. When we finally wake up to what is happening around us it will be far too bloody late.'

For a long time I fretted about that little incident. Neil Dart was a friend of mine but I should really have reported his actions to my superiors. On the other hand, he was a vastly experienced SB officer who had seen far more action than I had and there was an awful logic to what he said. Neil had an enviable reputation as an excellent cop, but could torture be justified in the circumstances? I didn't know and it worried me. In time I was to see other incidents of violence toward prisoners by men who I regarded as decent fellows. I saw captives and witnesses almost drowned with their heads in buckets of water. I saw others beaten, kicked and brought to the point of madness or death before being allowed to speak.

There were many occasions when I longed for the level, interrogatory techniques of Peter Stanton, but his war was a specialist one, while the war in Macheke was brutal, bloody and without rules. With hindsight I can understand and appreciate the Special Branch attitude and by their own lights, they were perfectly justified. They fought a far more brutal war than the rest of us and their methods were bent to adapt to the circumstances. Looked at from a distance, there was no justification for this brutality, but those SB men were not allowed to look at things from a distance. They were in the forefront of the war effort and who was I to criticise them for what I regarded as mere savagery.

That young man in Virginia had known far more than he was telling us and by extracting the information by whatever means, Neil Dart had almost certainly saved innocent lives. I wasn't sure that I could stoop to inflicting pain in order to glean information but in time, my holier than thou attitude was to be severely tested.

13

A man of war

England at the end of a good summer is an enchantingly beautiful place. The sun shines soft and warm while the countryside is incredibly green, particularly to anyone who has just come from the harsh African winter. My cricket tour with the Kongonis made a wonderful break from the war in Macheke. The games I played were in Sussex and I enjoyed the lush green tranquillity of the countryside as well as the warm hospitality of the English people. I also spent time in Gloucestershire with Missy's parents, taking the opportunity to revisit my old haunts around Stroud and Cheltenham. It was great fun and I could feel my body relax, but found it almost impossible to get my mind away from the horrors at home. I couldn't help checking road verges for possible ambush positions and found myself missing the comforting weight of an Uzi or my trusty FN.

Nor did the attitude of the British people help. Many of them seemed to half-heartedly support the Rhodesian cause, but they were so wrapped up with football scores and the state of play in Coronation Street that they didn't really give a damn about the slaughter that was taking place. Even though it was Britons who were dying, it was all too far away and we might have been living on different planets.

The media were another source of irritation. They referred to the Smith government as a rebel regime and to the terrorists who were ravaging our country as freedom fighters or guerrillas. The IRA on the other hand were apparently genuine terrorists, even though their atrocities paled into insignificance beside those of ZANLA or ZPRA.

But it was the attitude of young people in Britain that really disturbed me. Family discipline seemed to have disappeared and teachers literally went in fear of their lives in some schools. Respect for one's elders was no longer the norm and chivalry towards women was regarded as patronising by the women themselves. It was all in marked contrast to the generally well-mannered attitude of Rhodesians, black or white and it left me worrying for the future of my own country. How could we rely on these people, even if there was a settlement?

Another worry was the poor state of morale in the British police force. The bobby was far better paid than he had been in my day, but pride in the uniform or police traditions had completely disappeared. Most of my former colleagues were scathingly dismissive of the service they were part of and I felt a sense of relief that I had left when I had. I couldn't have worked in that sort of environment.

To make matters worse, the police were no longer respected by the general public, they served and almost everyone seemed to delight in running down their own country.

I spent one interesting evening in the police pub at Stroud and wasn't overly surprised to note that words like 'coon', 'darkie' and 'spade' were still in vogue among my former colleagues. Racist incidents were reported on a daily basis in the newspapers and I couldn't understand how these people were calling us racists. It was all so different to the general sense of national pride I had left behind at home. Rhodesians were proud of their country, their flag, their fighting men of whatever colour and their prime minister. I couldn't help wondering why our proud, battling country should be forced to grovel for favours to the general decline that was Britain in 1977.

Yet the break undoubtedly did me good and whether I was relaxing in Gloucestershire or chasing a ball on the tranquil sward of Sussex, it was a far cry indeed from the grim, blood-soaked land I had left behind. In the evenings I would spare the occasional thought for my farmers and their families, sitting in darkened lounges, firearms close to hand and their ears cocked for early warning of impending attack or news of someone else's terror from the Agric-alert. In the peaceful surroundings of the Cotswolds, such scenarios seemed somehow unreal. Here it was television drama, warm beer and litter in the streets. There were few problems to disturb the even tenor of my days, yet there was still a war going on and there were times when I couldn't help wondering how it was going.

Tucked up in my bed at night, I would hear again the distant thunder of landmines and my sleep was often disturbed by horrific dreams of shattered bodies and shocked eyes. But any break from trauma is its own panacea and I was beginning to relax completely when the horror was brought back to me by a report on the BBC news.

A bomb had gone off in the Manica Road branch of Woolworths in Salisbury. Manica road was the artery that cut through the crowded black shopping area of the city and I could picture the carnage. Twelve Saturday morning shoppers — all of them black — had been killed in the blast. Seventy-six others — all of them black — had been injured and the suave white BBC newsreader described the perpetrators of this outrage as 'Zimbabwean guerrillas.'

I wanted to weep. These were not guerrillas. They were terrorists pure and simple. I knew what would be happening back home. I could picture the torn bodies and hear the moans of survivors. My heart bled for them all and to listen to such savagery being described so blandly by this uncaring Englishman left me weak with furious disgust. I mentally composed an angry letter of complaint to the BBC, but abandoned the idea. It wouldn't have achieved anything. I was a white Rhodesian — a member of Smith's allegedly fascist police force. Anything I said would be dismissed as colonialist ranting.

On the other hand, exiled black Rhodesians belonging to ZANU and ZAPU were frequently interviewed on British television and the sycophantic attitudes of the interviewers towards these manipulators of murder disgusted me. I suppose it is all too easy to hold sneaking admiration for shadowy fighters against authority when one is a long way from the terror of ambush, house attack or mindless landmines. The Americans have always done it with the Irish Republican Army and the British do it with anyone when it suits their purpose.

For me, my long awaited overseas trip was ruined by the Woolworth's blast (another victory for terrorism?) and a few days later I boarded a flight from Gatwick and headed back to the sunshine, the war and a whole new packet of problems.

A great deal had changed in Macheke during the four weeks I had been away. My African police were pleased to see me and Television Gundani pumped my hand as though I'd been absent for years. It was all very pleasing but on my first day back, Missy quietly mentioned that Tim Peech wanted to see me.

'He knows where I am', I told her blithely. 'If it is important, he can see me in my office.'

After all, I was the member in charge!

Missy frowned and looked worried.

'I think you might find that things are different now', she warned. 'Tim has achieved a great deal over the past few weeks and I don't think you are going to like the new arrangements.'

In the event, I went out to Salama and saw Tim who was enthusiastic about his plans for Macheke. Missy had been right though — I didn't like them.

'I've fixed things with the army', Tim told me happily. 'All our lads are transferring to the police reserve and will automatically become members of PATU.'

I raised my eyebrows but he ploughed on remorselessly.

'Don't worry. I sorted it all out with Dispol. We have divided the blokes into individual sticks, each covering their own immediate area. I am building a control base here on the farm and the sticks will only work in Macheke, Virginia or the surrounding areas except in times of obvious emergency. I've appointed James Leask as my second-in-command and we have named our unit, the Macheke Local Defence Force.

So it was that the LDF came into being. They were run from Salama, where an existing police reserve base was expanded to include an operations room, ablutions and a dormitory for men on stand by duties. Tim Peech was appointed to the newly created rank of Police Reserve Group Leader and my nose was badly out of joint. The LDF was recognised as Tim's own outfit and although as a reservist, he nominally fell under my command, I knew in my heart that my days as an amateur general were over.

Tim was now running the operational scene in Macheke and although I should have been delighted at the opportunity to become a policeman again, I was definitely piqued. I had really enjoyed security work in spite of my initial antipathy toward the idea. Now the responsibility was to be taken away from me and I didn't like it one little bit. I made my feelings known to Chief Superintendent Peter Bellingham, the new OC at Marandellas and I think he sympathised, but he was more pragmatic than I was and had a better idea of the political influence wielded by farmers like Tim Peech.

I had to admit that Tim had the white population of Macheke eating out of his hand.

With his good looks, powerful personality and military knowhow, he led the LDF to a number of successes and I could feel my own influence in the community dwindling by the day.

Yet this was inconsistent thinking on my part. I had not wanted any part of the war effort. I had wanted to be a copper and do my job as such without interference. Now my wished had been handed to me on a plate and I was upset about it. Power gleaned from responsibility had slipped away and although I knew it was illogical, I felt as though I was a complete failure. Suddenly I understood how politicians must feel when their public support collapses.

For all the innate antipathy I felt towards him as the usurper of my leadership role, I couldn't help liking Tim Peech and we got on extremely well. We had our disagreements — usually over deployment of the LDF — but these were invariably settled over a beer and we even played cricket together on occasion. We should have been friends but I was feeling too much like a child whose sweeties had been taken away.

As the base at Salama grew, so did the reputation of the LDF among the black population. Farm workers and tribesmen began to bring in information on the movement of terrorists or stock thieves and the need for a regular policeman to be stationed at the base became ever more urgent. I approached Peter Bellingham on the matter and he promised to see what he could do. The end result was that Salama became an official police post — complete with guard dog — and was granted a staff allocation of one patrol officer and two ground coverage details. Tim readily agreed to construct accommodation for these men on the existing building and as it was in a vulnerable position beside the main Virginia road, sandbag fortifications were erected. The inevitable flagpole went up and a security fence was put up around the entire base.

It took some weeks of haggling with PGHQ on Dispol's part, but eventually he rang me with the news that my new patrol officer was awaiting collection in Marandellas.

'He is a bit of a rough diamond', Bellingham warned, 'but I think you will be pleased — eventually.'

I was a little concerned by his hesitant qualification of that last sentence but he was right. I was — eventually — well pleased with his choice.

David Scott Bradshaw had done his nine months of national service with the Support Unit and then transferred to the regular force. If nothing else, service with those wild Black Boots had taught him to play hard and live for the moment. There were a number of disciplinary problems outlined on his record of service and these had culminated in an escape from police custody wherein he had stolen the Mtoko member in charge's staff car and cheerfully deposited it in the Nyamapanda swimming pool.

Reading quickly through the awful details, I wondered whether it was wise to send such an undisciplined young hooligan to the wilds of Salama and Bellingham obviously entertained similar doubts.

'Read Bradshaw the riot act before you start', was his advice. 'He's a hard worker but will need firm handling.'

The dreaded P/O Bradshaw turned out to be a rangy young man with an acne-ravaged face and the smile of an angel. On the way back to Macheke I gave him the prescribed lecture and he beamed with sublime innocence at me. He had heard it all before.

Bradshaw quickly settled in at Salama and the locals readily took to him. For all his wild manner when in his cups, Braddles was a personable young man and the local ladies took his little boy looks to their hearts. Food packages and fruitcakes would arrive en masse at the police post so David and his two cut throats lived like kings.

One of his assistants was my old friend Dzorwa, now a sergeant and very conscious of his responsibilities. He was a hard, efficient copper but I worried about Dzorwa. All the bright friendliness that I remembered from my time at Marandellas had disappeared, to be replaced with a grim-faced ruthlessness that was disturbing indeed.

Yet Braddles had no difficulty in handling Dzorwa and they made an excellent team Scouring the bush and farmlands, they acted on information, rounded up suspects and spent many hours in lonely interrogation. Although Neil Dart's cruel machine was always in the back of my mind, I made no effort to check on their methods and their results were spectacular. A number of major operations were mounted with the LDF and forces from other areas, many of them proving extremely fruitful in the matter of kills.

Fireforce, the terrifyingly successful, military reaction team were called in on one enormous punch-up that took place near Mount Bogota and most of my staff listened intently to the battle on the station radios. The scene was co-ordinated by the fireforce commander, riding high above everything in his Alouette K-car and I could only marvel at his demeanour in such a tense situation. He spoke in almost conversational manner to the men on the ground and even when we could hear the murderous slap of rounds narrowly missing the helicopter, he never once raised his voice. I wondered whether I could ever hope to achieve that level of professionalism.

Thirteen ZANLA terrorists died in that battle and everyone involved was complimentary about my young patrol officer's courage and efficiency during the action. It was far and away the most successful contact we had enjoyed as a district and in spite of my injured feelings at being left out of the planning stages, I joined in the celebrations afterwards.

The bodies and captured equipment were brought into the police station immediately after that battle and as I looked down on the terrible aftermath of war, I felt a surge of despair. There were thousands of these men out there — men who would kill or be killed without worrying about the consequences. Men who would murder and torture innocent civilians. Men who in my own experience had acted with extreme barbarism and an almost inhuman disregard for the sanctity of human life. These were men who would kill me and mine without compunction and rejoice in the opportunity. To these men and their kind, I represented more than just an enemy. The colour of my skin and the uniform I wore made me a target of particular relish and I felt a crawling sense of horror at the thought of my family ending up in their hands.

Picking up an AKM, I absently moved the working parts backward and peered into the breech. It was obviously well cared for and I wondered how many more weapons of war were hidden in the wild countryside that surrounded my home. Our own weapons were old, battered and well past their sell-by date. Although they packed more of a wallop than the Kalashnikovs, the FNs were far more cumbersome and ammunition was becoming ever more difficult to get hold of.

I think it was on that sad inspection of the football field at Macheke with dead men all around me that I finally realised just what odds my beleaguered little country was facing. We were fighting an unending wave of these young men. They were hardened by their life in the bush and driven on to supposed glory by their leaders — themselves safe and living the good life in Lusaka, Maputo, Washington and London. Even as we cut them down, others would pour in to their places, some with reluctance but many with the conviction that their cause was a just one and the ends used to achieve that cause were permissible in the circumstances.

Nor was it only the terrorists we were fighting. They had support from most of the world and although we believed that we had the moral high ground and even though we prosecuted the war as honourably as was possible in the circumstances, the outside world wasn't going to allow victory for Rhodesians.

In his own way, Neil Dart had been right. If we were to survive, we had to descend to the level of our enemy. It was a dog-eat-dog situation and if we continued the way we were going, we would all die eventually and our families would die with us. A feeling of deep despair flooded through my system even as my men were celebrating around me.

One dead terrorist had literally lost his head to a Chinese stick grenade and I remembered tales I had heard about the SAS and Selous scouts 'doctoring' terrorist weaponry on their forays into Zambia and Mozambique. The stick grenade usually has a four second fuse, but this one had exploded as the ZANLA man pulled the string. Cruel, barbaric methods on the part of Rhodesians perhaps, but methods that in this case had prevented the dead man from killing members of the security forces. The more I thought about it, the more I was coming around to Neil Dart's way of thinking.

The contact on Mount Bogota had been an overwhelming success for Tim and his men of the LDF. I couldn't begrudge them their joy in victory, so we celebrated together and drank to more successes and more kills. A little ruefully I remembered the idealistic young copper I had been a few years previously. In those days I had been naive enough to believe that I wouldn't need to be involved in the war, yet here I was, celebrating multiple killings with a band of blackened, bloodstained cut-throats.

My values were certainly changing.

Successes continued and the Macheke kill rate mounted. Braddles worked like a man possessed and the reputation of the LDF spread to all corners of the country. Similar schemes were proposed elsewhere but none of them really got off the ground. To set up such a fighting force required a man with boundless energy, a powerful personality and the strength of will to overcome the most difficult of problems.

There were few men like Tim Peech around, even in Rhodesia.

Nor were there many like David Scott Bradshaw. Braddles worked very long hours without supervision and the results he achieved heartened the entire community. Heedless of risk, he travelled deep into the tribal lands at any time of day or night and he seldom took time off.

When he did, the results could be spectacular. He wandered into my office one morning, haggard and pale from lack of sleep.

'I could do with a couple of day off, Boss', He told me somewhat unnecessarily. 'D'you mind if I head into town for a while?'

I had no objections and a short while later Braddles was in again, freshened up and dressed in his best city outfit. Grinning from ear to ear, he informed me that James Leask was taking him into Salisbury and I stifled a twinge or two of misgiving. Leask and Bradshaw were a potentially explosive combination, but both of them needed the break.

I made no stipulation as to how long my young hooligan could have off. I knew he wouldn't take undue advantage and he had certainly earned the break. Nevertheless, after four days I was beginning to fret. Surely he couldn't have deserted? But James was notorious for his occasional three or four day binges and was sure they would soon be back.

At least I thought I was sure. A little wearily I answered the telephone on my desk.

'Is that Superintendent Lemon?' It was a grimly officious voice on the other end of the line.

The bars on my shoulder put me three ranks below the one he had bestowed upon me, but sensing trouble I hesitantly agreed that I was the said superintendent.

'Do you have an Inspector Bradshaw under your command, sir?'

My sigh was probably audible in Mrewa. Now I knew why I had been 'promoted.'

'I do indeed.'

The voice softened a little.

'I'm afraid he is in a spot of bother, sir.'

The caller was a captain in the Military Police and I couldn't help hoping that he would never discover my real rank.

'Mr Bradshaw and a mate of his demolished a Guard Force pub last night and are languishing in our cells at the moment. I understand they have been at the sharp end for a while and are under strain but we really can't allow this sort of thing.'

'God preserve me from the self righteous', I thought but kept my voice as pleasant as possible.

'Of course we can't, Captain.'

How I longed to get my hands around Bradshaw's skinny neck.

'We must uphold standards mustn't we?'

The soldier seemed mollified by my crass hypocrisy.

'In this case, sir, I am prepared to let them go with a warning, provided you will take responsibility for the pair of them.'

I sighed again, possibly with even more feeling than before.

'Yes, of course. Let me have a word with Mr Bradshaw and I will ensure that there is no more trouble.'

'Thank you, sir', he said and after a brief and somewhat acerbic few words with my chastened patrol officer, I replaced the receiver and got on with my work.

David Scott Bradshaw was probably the most diligent police officer I have ever had the pleasure of working with, but he could sure be a headache at times.

A common complaint among Rhodesian whites in the 1970s was that blacks showed no gratitude for the wealth and prosperity, brought to the country since the arrival of the Pioneer Column. They argued that in 80 odd years, Rhodesia had been transformed from a vast area of untended bush into a vibrant modern country that not only supported itself against all the odds, but also supported many black nations to the north.

So why the whites asked, were their efforts so unappreciated? I had heard the argument many times and one evening Missy and I sat down to discuss it. Had we — the white race — done so much for the country and were we right to feel affronted by the lack of appreciation for our efforts? Or had we plundered our way into what had already been a peaceful and prosperous country.

I had been brought up on Rhodesian history, but Missy's education had been in England where the curriculum didn't include details of colonial conquests. Her views were therefore more balanced than mine, yet she contended that Rhodesia's troubled history was merely an excuse that the more rabid seekers after black rule used for their own ends. The answer to our national problem lay more in the humiliation felt by black Rhodesians for the positions they had been given in everyday life. They were automatically slotted into subservient roles in society and this engendered bitterness, particularly among those who were capable of greater things.

She cited Sergeant Gundani as an example and I had to admit that Television was a considerably better policeman than many whites I had served with. Even so, unless radical change was made to the system, he couldn't advance any higher than sergeant major, which would keep him subservient to even the lowliest of patrol officers. I was in full agreement with Missy's views on police promotional procedure, but I believed that all three sectors of Rhodesian society had made mistakes that were now ripping the country apart. The whites had been oppressive and inconsiderate about African culture. The Matabele were naturally aggressive and continually spoiling for a fight against black or white alike. The Shona on the other hand had always been apathetic about their role in society and were only showing their teeth now that matters had gone too far.

All three racial groupings came from vastly different cultural backgrounds and none of them understood the others. Just as the British seemed unable to comprehend the problems of Rhodesia, so Rhodesians — black, white, Matabele, Shona, born or naturalised — were just as unreasonably thoughtless about each other's creeds and beliefs. Would cultural differences ever be swallowed up and forgotten or would tribal loyalties ensure that the difference between races in our little country would always remain in place.

It was an unanswerable question that made us both a little despondent. But life had to go on and in the meantime, I had a troubled little farming area to look after.

14

And of peace

Tim Peech's dreams and plans for the future of Macheke extended far beyond the formation of a Local Defence Force. Tim wanted peace — peace for his children and other children in the area; peace for his neighbours and peace for every Rhodesian of whatever colour living in Macheke.

Long a champion of black rights in the country, he formed a partnership with his labour force on Salama and they were quite the most contented workers in the area. He and Michelea (pronounced Michelle) hobnobbed openly with black friends and neither gave a tuppenny damn for public opinion. Tribesmen from the Mangwende often brought snippets of information to Salama and many of them bypassed the police post, preferring to deal directly with Tim.

He in turn often drove directly into the TTL, never bothering about the danger to himself and never using a mine-protected vehicle — many weird examples of which were appearing on rural roads. Tim used his farm truck and roamed among the kraals, speaking to the people and trying to convince them of the need for peace.

'We are not going to win this war by fighting', he confirmed my own lonely thoughts one day. 'There are too many gooks and we play by the rules. They don't so they will keep us on the run, no matter how many we kill.'

Where had I heard that before?

'The only way we will achieve any sort of solution to the problem', Tim went on, his eyes alight with almost messianic fervour, 'is by sitting down and talking with these blokes. No matter how abhorrent we find their methods, they have their own beliefs and will keep fighting for them as long as we do.'

One of our leading politicians, Alan Savory had recently expressed similar thoughts and caused a furore in political circles, but Tim didn't care about that. Savory had become unpopular throughout the country for his radical views, but Tim was the uncrowned King of Macheke and would say what he liked. He was determined to broker a peaceful solution, firstly in his beloved Macheke and then if possible, throughout Rhodesia. To this end he approached senior men in both the military and political hierarchies and convinced them that he should be given a free hand to do his own thing, starting off in the Mangwende TTL. Having already seen his influence in forming the LDF, I wasn't surprised by his success but I was distinctly apprehensive about his safety.

Quite apart from his rounds of the kraals, Tim left a number of notes in strategic spots around the tribal land. These missives, couched in his own fluent Chishona, invited the ZANLA cadres to meet him for talks. Personally I didn't share his faith in his own destiny and continually urged him to be careful, my warnings backed up by Mike Rayne, the detective inspector in charge of SB operations in the area. Tim laughed us off but arranged for two of his most trusted farm workers to be sworn in as police reservists and issued with G3 rifles. They accompanied him on his rounds and seemed as blissfully unaware of danger as their boss was.

I was never quite sure what those hard men of the LDF thought of their commander's antics. As a soldier and leader of men, they would have followed him anywhere, but so many of them were out and out racists with an implacable contempt for anyone who wasn't white. I still do not understand how they reconciled their beliefs with Tim's desire to love and be loved by our black, fellow citizens.

On 3rd March 1978 the Transitional Government came into being and Tim promptly invited Bishop Abel Muzorewa, a member of the Executive Council and Premier-elect of the country to address a crowd of Mangwende people and convince them of the need for peace. It was a momentous occasion. Curious tribesmen began arriving at the site chosen for the meeting well before first light and the entire Peech clan (Tim, his father and brothers Chris and David) supplied meat and cool drinks for the crowd. Heavy African music blared continuously from loudspeakers and there was a festival atmosphere about the proceedings.

The LDF were out in force and for once I won a small victory over their deployment. Tim had wanted them to wear police reserve 'blues' and leave their rifles at home, but I insisted on them being armed and the blokes themselves backed me up. Nevertheless, an unofficial amnesty was declared for the occasion and more than one hard-eyed, woolly-haired and coldly aloof young man could be seen among those assembled to hear the Bishop speak.

Studying some of these hard-bitten characters, I couldn't help wondering where their Kalashnikovs had been stashed and was sorely tempted to haul a couple of them away for interrogation. It was galling to think of the time already spent in hunting these men and the lives that had been lost in the process, only to have them mixing freely with locals and even partaking of the traditional beer laid on for the occasion.

After keeping everyone waiting into the afternoon, the Bishop finally made his appearance and spoke at length, with Tim translating for the few whites (mainly LDF personnel) who were present. It was the usual flowery ambivalence of a typical politician but when it was over, the diminutive man of God received an enthusiastic round of applause. The people of Mangwende had suffered sorely over the previous months and many of them had lost loved ones to the guns of one side or the other. They wanted peace at any price and were prepared to show their support for anyone who would promise it. When the speeches were over and the crowd was dispersing, Tim turned to me and there was the light of a visionary in his eye.

'Wasn't that marvellous?' He enthused. 'What did you think of the Bishop's speech?'

'Well...', I was loath to voice my reservations in the face of his obvious enthusiasm. 'He was okay, but he sounded like a typical...'

I had been about to say 'politician' but one of the senior men forestalled me.

'Kaffir', he grated to complete the sentence.

Although Tim laughed with the rest of us, he looked distinctly uneasy. If he had not realised it before, the comment must have made him realise that the main obstacle to peace wasn't the ordinary tribesman, but the white farmer. That same white farmer who had been harried to the point of obstinacy by continual attacks from terrorist, politicians and those caring citizens whose ill-considered opinions were for ever being broadcast by the world media as 'informed comment.' The farmers had endured a great deal and were more worried about the future that most of us.

It was shortly after that meeting that Tim finally had direct contact with the opposition and he was obviously delighted. A short, printed note invited him to a meeting but he refused to tell either Mike Rayne or myself where it was to be held.

'They asked me not to.'

We had to be content with that.

To this day, I am not sure whether that meeting took place, but I was aware that Tim's enthusiasm took a sudden knock. He became almost subdued, but whether this was due to the meeting being aborted or the intransigence of those he met with, I didn't know. Whatever the reason, Tim seemed morose and ill at ease for a while. This was unlike him and we all worried but his state of mind didn't stop his campaigning in the Mangwende. He was gaining ground with the rank and file tribesmen and I don't think I was at all surprised when Mike Rayne told me that the ZANLA hierarchy was becoming perturbed about Tim's activities. A 'hit squad' had apparently been sent into the country with orders to eliminate this threat to their operations and I was horrified at the news.

'Have you warned him?' I asked Mike and he shrugged.

'Of course I have but you know Tim. He thinks he can walk on water, so I don't know what else we can do.'

'Get him ordered out from the top', I suggested but Mike was unconvinced.

'I don't think Tim would listen to Ian Smith himself', he mused. 'He feels that he is some sort of bloody Messiah and I don't think anyone can stop him now.'

But one man on his own had no chance against the hard men from ZANLA. Tim might have — almost certainly had — convinced local cadres that peace was possible, but the commanders in Mozambique had only death on their minds. On his way back from a meeting in Mrewa, Tim took a detour into the Mangwende to visit a headman who had asked to see him. It was an obvious set up and on the way, his truck was stopped by a group of armed men. Tim Peech was dragged from the vehicle and his escorts fled, pursued by whip-lashing bullets. Tim had a radio pack set with him but the first we knew of his capture was a garbled telephone report from the two terrified reservists.

The entire LDF was immediately mobilised but we had no idea where to start looking for their leader. Worried looking men milled aimlessly around the base and frustrated tension grew until it was almost unbearable. That evening we heard from Tim himself. As the sun set, he came through on the radio to Salama where most of us still sat around, morosely silent and wondering how best to proceed.

'I am with the comrades', Tim's voice was shaky with strain. 'I am perfectly okay and would ask that no efforts are made to find me for 24 hours.'

He wouldn't say more than that and long before the specified time was up, Tim Peech was dead — struck down and humiliated by the very people he was trying so desperately to help.

Mind you, I don't suppose the tribesmen could be blamed for their actions. They were as terrified as the captive white man. After being harangued at length by the terrorist commander, they were given strict and terrible instructions. One vicious slash of a panga hamstrung the police reserve leader and in his pain, the locals were lined up in front of him. Each and every person, rounded up for the occasion was instructed to beat him with a pickaxe handle and those that didn't show the necessary enthusiasm for the task were beaten themselves.

How long it took Tim Peech to die is a matter of conjecture, but it was hardly a fitting end for a very brave man. A man who wanted nothing but peace for his homeland and a good life for everyone living in his beloved Macheke.

He was a great man in his own way, Tim Peech. A man of vision and unshakeable ideals. A man who put the welfare of others before his own and a man who was a natural leader of other men. He was also a good soldier and a marvellous character. He and I had our fights and there were times when I hated the sight of his little blue truck drawing up in front of my station, yet I had nothing but the highest admiration for the man himself. For all our mutual antipathy, we shared many views on the future of our country and now that he has gone, I only wish I had been more magnanimous and less pig headed when he formed his little fighting force. We could have achieved so much more had we really been working together.

Fit, strong and a fine fighting man, Timothy Michael Steele Peech was above all, a man of peace.

15

Missionaries and murder

There was something chillingly different about the sound made by an exploding landmine. During my first few days in Macheke, I once spent two hours searching the railway line for the source of an explosion that turned out to be a heavy-duty tire bursting on the main road, but I quickly learned to recognise the real thing. When a landmine blew, the sound was a deep, thunderous roar that rattled the windows and made my bones ache with reaction. It was a sound that seemed to linger on the air for minutes and it was a sound that was the inevitable prelude to more horror.

War and the killing of man by man is a terrible business in any circumstances, but of all the fiendish killing machines that have come out of armed conflict, mines are surely the most devilish. Completely impersonal, they kill friend or foe alike and it is a terribly needless way to die.

Early one morning, I felt rather than heard the sound of a mine going off and half an hour later, Sergeant Gundani and I stood surveying a deep crater in a remote farm road. We were well south of the police station and in an area that had seen little terrorist activity. Initially there was no sign of whoever or whatever had triggered the blast and I assumed — and hoped — that whoever laid the mine had accidentally set it off and blown himself to smithereens. That was before I saw the foot.

It was an ordinary black foot, neatly severed at the ankle and not wearing a shoe. There was no blood and no sign of the rest of the body — just one desperately sad-looking foot. The only other relic of the victim we found was a piece of twisted handlebar with a cycle bell still attached and working well. The GMO later decided that the foot had belonged to an elderly man but nobody ever came forward to claim the grisly remains, nor was he ever identified.

The TM46, Soviet-made landmine, normally used by ZANLA needed 400 pounds of pressure to set it off, so whoever he was, the unknown victim had been desperately unlucky. From the size of his foot, he couldn't have been a big fellow. Possibly an itinerant tinker or someone looking for work, he had been on his way through the farms when his life had ended in the one searing second, he had been involved in the war.

That incident was horrific but I shrugged it off as a normal part of my everyday work. I had become hardened to violent death and it no longer upset me. It was early in 1978 and I had been in Macheke for 18 months so I felt that I had seen it all. Only the previous day, Missy and I had been discussing the possibilities of a move. Every year we were asked to give our thoughts on possible transfers and the stations we would or would not like to move to. On this occasion, we agreed that whether I wanted a move or not, (I wasn't sure) I needed one. Never a big man, I was desperately thin and hardly a night went by when my sleep wasn't disturbed. If it wasn't an alarm, a stock theft report or a panicked query on the Agric-alert, it was a nightmare. My dreams were explosively horrible and I had come to dread the onset of darkness.

The situation was definitely getting me down, but unless I applied for a town station, I was going to face the same problems anywhere else. Besides, Brian and Graeme were doing well at Macheke School (Brian won the Best Bowling cup that year) and I didn't want to move too far away.

Marandellas seemed the best bet. I had recently passed my promotion examination to Inspector and although the security situation in the larger centre was only marginally easier than it was in Macheke, at least I wouldn't have to take it all on my own shoulders. I might even be allowed to take over the enquiry section and be a copper again.

My patrol officer at the time was Simon Thorpe, while Braddles had moved on and been replaced at Salama by Chris Carroll. Simon was a pleasant young man whose father was a former assistant commissioner, although Simon didn't share Thorpe Senior's devotion to the police force. Much to his horror, he was transferred to the Support Unit and that rather set me thinking.

The Unit had come a long way since those early days at Nyakasoro. Numbers had been increased to battalion strength and they had recently moved into a brand new barrack complex at Chikurubi outside Salisbury. Their war record was impressive and from being a ragtail cowboy outfit in the early seventies, they now walked tall among Security Force units. Almost entirely black, they had amassed more kills inside the country than any other outfit and in addition to that, they were very well paid. As well as a daily danger allowance, they were entitled to untaxed travelling and subsistence while in the field and that was no mean bonus.

As member in charge at Macheke, my time was almost entirely taken up with security work so I decided that I might as well be paid for it. Missy was doubtful when I put the idea to her, but I pointed out that we could buy a house in Marandellas and pay for it with the extra money earned from my bush work.

Simon Thorpe's dad pulled strings to have his transfer changed and he eventually became a traffic cop in Salisbury, but I submitted a long report applying to a permanent move to the Black Boots.

For a man who had not wanted anything to do with soldiering, that was a major step indeed.

In June 1978, the entire population of Rhodesia was shocked to the marrow by another massacre of white missionaries, this time in the Eastern Highlands.

According to the morning sitrep, a 20-strong gang, announcing themselves as ZANLA soldiers arrived at Elim Mission in the Vumba Mountains. Moving into the mission at eight in the evening, they rounded up nine white missionaries and four children, one of them a three-week-old baby. One middle-aged woman, her hair still in pink curlers, was publicly raped before having an axe buried in her skull. A man had his face hacked open and was then kicked to death. Children were beaten, kicked and bayoneted. It was the worst single killing of whites since the war began and the details made sickening reading.

After the missionaries and their families were dead, their bodies were left where they lay on the mission football field. One survivor, forewarned by his house servant had barricaded himself in a room and thereby survived the massacre, but when the killing was over, the ZANLA men rounded up 250 mission pupils and harangued them on the evils of the internal settlement.

Again the rest of the world blamed the Selous scouts, but — perhaps I was biassed — I couldn't see what they had to gain. That sort of outrage couldn't benefit the Rhodesian cause in any possible way. Besides, no mere servant would have been aware of Selous Scout plans before they were put into effect. They were far too professional for that.

No, the Elim Mission massacre had to be the work of Mugabe's thuggish henchmen and like the rest of my parishioners, I was appalled and sickened by the bestiality of it all. What made it worse was that the Elim Pentecostal Church who ran the mission, had all along refused to be identified with the Rhodesian government in any way. In spite of their isolated position, they had refused military protection for the mission in order to show that they were not involved with the war. In the end, that proved a fatal mistake. Their headquarters in Cheltenham issued a statement forgiving the perpetrators, but for those of us closer to hand, it wasn't so easy.

My farmers were understandably up in arms and I held meetings in Macheke and Virginia in an effort to calm everyone down, although my heart wasn't really in it. As far as I was concerned, whatever faction had been responsible for the killings at Elim Mission, they were true terrorists and not worthy to call themselves soldiers.

As the situation throughout the country worsened, flippancy became my only form of self-defence. No matter how brutal the scene or how much blood and gore I waded through in order to do my job, I always had a grin or a ready quip to steady my own fluttering emotions. This led to some strange looks from those who watched me at work and on one occasion, Missy snapped at me to take life seriously for a change. She was a wise woman that wife of mine, but my cavalier attitude merely disguised deeper feelings and I was close to cracking up. The continual horror and carnage among innocents was wearing me down. I was never far from tears and hatred was building in my soul.

Strangely perhaps, the hatred wasn't directed purely at those whose path through the countryside was marked by so much rape and pillage — those shadowy figures who moved by darkness and whose deeds plagued my life with their sheer depravity. No, I hated even more those faceless men in Lusaka and Maputo who sent them on their missions of murder. Nkomo, Mugabe, Sithole and their henchmen — they shouted their messages of hate into media microphones and were backed up by politicians from all over the Western world. Their words fuelled the anger that was boiling in my country and while they continued, many more innocents would die.

I reserved my especially bitter feelings for the politicians — particularly those in Britain — who with their overt support for the terrorist cause, seemed so determined to encourage the killing.

As well as understandably causing outrage throughout Rhodesia, the Elim Mission massacre widened the rift with Britain. There were no words of condemnation from Westminster and the Americans seemed equally struck dumb at this latest example of cold-blooded bestiality from our enemy. Nevertheless, both countries continued their tacit support for the terrorist cause.

For us, faced as we were with an ever-increasing diet of horror, it was impossible to be as tolerant as those overseas and the growing bitterness led to more and more brutality in Security Force actions. The number of civilians 'killed in crossfire' kept increasing and at times I couldn't help wondering just what dastardly deeds that phrase might be concealing.

In Macheke, the situation since Tim Peech's death had grown ever more volatile. His men were intent on bloody revenge and they saw every man, woman and child in the Mangwende as being responsible for the murder of their leader. Peter Bellingham came out from Marandellas to address the farmers with me, but it fell to a couple of the older hands like Ewen Farrar and Athol Brown to calm them down and prevent wholesale slaughter in the TTL.

Terrorist activity in the area had been concentrated almost exclusively till them on Virginia and the northern farms, but — fortunately perhaps for the general good of the community — it suddenly switched to Macheke itself. South of the main road and close to Chiduku Tribal Trust Land, ambushes became more frequent and isolated farmhouses came under night attack.

At this stage, communications throughout the operational area were in danger of breaking down. One of the main drawbacks to operating on a border between two provinces was the fact that I was controlled by two JOCs and this proved very difficult. Officially, Macheke was part of *Operation Hurricane* and fell under Mtoko, but many of our incidents emanated from Weya or Chiduku, both of which were part of *Thrasher* and controlled from Rusape. There was supposed to be regular liaison between the operational centres, but it sometimes happened that one JOC hadn't had time or sometimes hadn't bothered to inform the other of an operation. And all too often, my blokes were caught in the middle.

LDF operations in the Weya were becoming ever more frequent and I had frequent rows on their behalf with senior officers at both Mtoko and Rusape who demanded that we seek permission for everything we did. I could see the logic of this, but all too often, operations were mounted from Salama and I wouldn't be told about them till it was too late.

None the less, I was nominally the boss so I carried the can, but it could be very wearying. Peter Bellingham tried to protect me from wrath from above, but I was becoming ever more bloody-minded and his efforts on my behalf were not always appreciated. I argued with him too!

It was perhaps inevitable that heavy drinking became very much part of life in a district that was continually under tension. Parties became ever more frenetic and marriages began to fold under the strain. My own was going through a bad patch but Missy and I had a war to fight so we soldiered on, supporting each other through the worst moments and hating each other when things were quiet. Quite what our children thought about it, I don't know. It was perhaps inevitable that they had grown far closer to their mother over the previous two years, although the boys seemed proud to have a father at 'the sharp end.'

The country clubs did a roaring trade throughout the week, even though they were only licensed to open on weekends or for special functions. The Macheke Hotel also did well and was rapidly establishing a reputation for itself throughout Mashonaland. Genially presided over by Matt Carson, the hotel wouldn't have appeared out of place on the film set of Shane or High Noon. It had an air of faded gentility about its rooms and the bar was pure Wild West, even down to batwing doors.

The customers were every bit as outlandish as their surroundings. Guns were casually stacked in one corner and on more than one occasion during my tenure as member in charge, shots were fired — either through the windows at targets unknown, or at bottles behind the bar.

But by its very nature and the times we lived in, Macheke Hotel was often the stepping stone to tragedy. Drink driving wasn't regarded as a heinous offence in war-torn Rhodesia and the road to the east was long, straight and very fast. Many a customer set off after a convivial evening and didn't arrive at his intended destination. On one awful occasion, I was personally involved.

Chris Carroll was my P/O at Salama. I always felt a little sorry for Chris as he had a desperately hard act to follow in Dave Bradshaw. Braddles had ended up a hero to the entire community and nobody — least of all myself — had been pleased by his transfer. But that's the way with any police force. As soon as an officer gets on top of his job and builds up a good rapport with his public, he is transferred. So Braddles had moved on and Chris Carroll had taken his place.

Although he was a pleasant young man, Chris didn't have the personality or the incredible capacity for hard work of his predecessor, but he seemed capable of handling the job. One Saturday afternoon, I found him knocking back beer in the Macheke Hotel and I could see that a 'session' was brewing. Having no intrinsic objection to that, I joined in with a will, but I had only a few hundred metres to go to get home. Chris was 15 kilometres from Salama and he had an almost new Land-Rover with him. Rhodesians might have been cocking a snook at the world where sanctions were concerned, but our vehicle situation was desperate and I struggled to maintain my station fleet.

As the afternoon wore on and the alcoholic haze above the bar thickened, I began to fret about that Land-Rover. I wasn't particularly concerned about my patrol officer. He could look after himself. It was the prospect of explaining the loss of a vehicle that really bothered me. Eventually I called Chris across and much to his dismay, relieved him of the ignition key.

'How will I get home?' he howled. 'There is a party on tonight and I wanted . . .'

I gestured unsympathetically around the bar. A number of patrons were from Virginia and would be passing Salama.

'Someone will give you a lift.'

Content that the problem was solved and my Land-Rover was safe, I returned to my beer.

Chris did get a lift but he never reached his party. On the way home, the truck in which he was a passenger overturned and poor Chris Carroll bled to death in less than a minute. It was a tragically needless death and for a while, I felt extremely guilty about my part in it. Chris' family were upset with me when the story came out, but both Missy and Matt Carson were on my side and their support sustained me through a couple of difficult weeks.

On my second Christmas in Macheke, I decided to do my bit towards race relations in the area, even if it meant offending a few of my farmers. I took my senior staff to lunch at the Macheke hotel. Simon Thorpe and Missy came along, but it was the first time that the hotel dining room had seen black faces at the tables. After some initial embarrassment, my sergeants tucked in with a will however and beer flowed in copious quantities.

Good old Matt didn't turn a hair. He paid the routine visit to our table, asking whether service had been to everybody's satisfaction and one inebriated three-striper joked that he would rather have *sadza* — the maize porridge of Africa — than the baked trout on his plate.

'Not a problem, sir', Matt told him courteously and a few minutes later, a bowl full of fluffy white *sadza* was placed in the centre of the table, much to the delight of my men.

He is dead now, but he was never at a loss, Matt Carson, and I suppose that is the mark of a good hotelier.

Brian Pym was the detective chief inspector in charge of CID in Marandellas. Unpopular with colleagues and public alike, he wasn't known for his sense of humour, but we had worked together on a number of cases and he was smiling ambiguously as he came into my office. Placing a sheet of paper carefully down in the centre of my desk, he made himself comfortable in the chair opposite and gestured for me to read the paper. I took but a moment to realise that it was a full-scale plan of Macheke police camp, including each and every building, the football field, landing ground and petrol pump. An obscure store cupboard was drawn in and my house was carefully annotated. The artist must have taken hours to draw the plan.

'Where did this come from?' I asked and Pym stretched his mouth into what passed for a smile.

'It was recovered by the SAS on one of their externals in Mozambique. They brought back similar plans of Grand Reef and Inyazura. Grand Reef was stonked a couple of nights ago as you know, so we reckon you or Inyazura will be next.'

The news as such didn't worry me too much. A number of small police stations had been attacked over the previous few months and there had been little damage sustained.

The attacks seemed designed to keep up the pressure of terror and were probably directed more at affecting morale among junior staff than doing any real damage to the police force.

What did worry me was how the unknown draughtsman had been able to draw up so detailed a plan without being detected. There was always a flow of witnesses, accused persons, friends and relatives moving through the camp and I mentally chided those early Macheke coppers for planting the great fir trees, I so enjoyed. They would have provided ideal cover for the unknown mole, but I don't suppose the Pioneers foresaw this sort of eventuality. I put my thoughts to Pym and he nodded.

'What do you want me to do about it?' I queried over a cup of tea.

'Not much you can do', he replied. 'Make sure your night guards are alert, I suppose. If they think they might have their throats cut, it should keep them awake for a change.'

'Who do you think drew this plan?'

I looked at the CID man with some surprise. The drift of his question was obvious but I had not for one moment suspected one of my own men. I treated them well dammit and they all seemed happy in their work. Surely there couldn't be a traitor among them? Yet now that Pym had brought the idea to mind, it seemed obvious. Any one of my men would have had ample opportunity to draw the plan, either in bits and pieces or during the long boring hours of a night or weekend shift.

But which one? Sergeant Gundani and I kept strict discipline on the station and in my somewhat nervy state, more than one luckless detail had felt the lash of my tongue, but would that make anyone risk life and career by passing information on to the terrorists? It didn't seem likely, particularly as he would be putting his own family at risk in the event of a station attack.

Pym nodded grimly when I mentioned my doubts.

'What about Constable Mike?'

A few weeks previously, two Special Branch sources had named a 'Constable Mike at Macheke' as being politically suspect and a thorough investigation had taken place. Constable Hozheri was the only detail appropriately christened and he had been interviewed at length. A cheerful, efficient young man, Hozheri had always been full of life and humour so I was loath to suspect him of treachery. Comparisons were made with his handwriting, but these proved inconclusive and nothing could be pinned on him. However, my doubts thereafter increased and poor old Hozheri was kept on a very tight rein indeed.

The attack when it came was short and cataclysmically violent. Like most farm attacks, it occurred just before midnight and the attackers fired from the kopje behind the house. I was jolted from sleep by the most appalling bang and tumbled out of bed, grabbing for my rifle. Missy took a P1 pistol from the bedside cabinet and I prowled around the house in my underpants, desperately looking for something to shoot at.

Another thunderous explosion seemed to batter at the foundations of the house and my stomach contracted to the whooshing shriek of a rocket overhead. I fired six or seven panic-stricken shots into the kopje but it was merely a gesture. I wasn't sure where the rockets were coming from and to shoot in any other direction would mean the possibility of hitting houses.

And that was it. No more rockets came out of the night and my fire wasn't returned. Throwing on a tracksuit, I ran for the charge office where the duty constable — not Mike Hozheri who had been relieved from night duties — was wide-eyed with fright and the camp guards were under a table. I was pleased to see that their weapons were cocked and ready to repel boarders. No traitors among this lot at any rate.

Nobody had been hurt so I hurried to check the rest of the camp. The AP were all okay although many seemed shocked at the violent sounds of conflict and a number of them suggested an immediate retaliatory raid on the nearby township. Considerably cheered by their fighting spirit, I hurried to the patrol officer's house. Simon Thorpe was away on a course, so I bundled his diminutive and badly shaken wife into a blanket and took her back to our house for the rest of the night.

A check of the camp the following morning revealed no obvious damage and it seemed that two rockets had been fired and rushed harmlessly over the buildings to expend themselves harmlessly between ourselves and the town. Not for the first time, I blessed the fact that in general, our enemy were even worse in the practice of warfare that I was. They held all the aces and if they had only been able to shoot straight, those of us loyal to Ian Smith's Rhodesia wouldn't have stood a chance.

Apart from the lack of injury or damage, there was a lighter side to that incident. It took place during school holidays and the boys were not only home, but they had a friend staying with them. Young Anton Kruger lived on a farm in the very north of Virginia and his mother had been only too pleased to have him with us for a few days. She felt he would surely be safer in civilised Macheke and it was ironic that it was here that he first heard the sounds of enemy attack.

Or would have, had he been awake. In spite of two enormous thunderclaps of sound — in spite of the stomach churning whoosh of the rockets — in spite of the thunder that was my FN answering back, three young would-be heroes as well as Deborah slept through it all.

Not quite true I suppose. Brian actually sat up as I ran through his room in search of a vantage point.

'Are we under attack Dad?' he mumbled.

When I affirmed that we were, he went back to sleep. There wasn't a further peep out of any of them until the next morning when they were annoyed with me for not waking them up. Brian didn't even remember our brief conversation.

Truly children can be difficult to understand!

Obert Mufuunde was a stockily decrepit figure of a man. He had one wall eye, smelled very bad and possessed a sense of humour that brightened the darkest of days. He had been a wandering informer on my behalf for well over a year when he slouched into my office to tell me about Monte Cassino mission.

'The *vakomana* are in there, sir', he held out one grubby paw for money. 'I have seen them myself.'

I was sceptical, not only because Monte Cassino was a mere three kilometres from the police station but also because Obert often manufactured information when he was particularly broke — which was most of the time. I didn't really mind as the money came from a special float, kept specifically for informers, but Obert's inconsistencies had led me to take much of his news with a pinch of salt.

On this occasion he seemed very positive, so after parting with a couple of dollars that I knew would be squandered on beer and women, I passed the information on to Brian Pym at Marandellas. He sounded equally unconvinced but promised to check it out with the JOC at Rusape. A few hours later, I had two hard-eyed SB men in my office.

'Where did you get this int from?' one of them demanded.

When I told him, he asked for Obert but that worthy had disappeared into the fleshpots and couldn't be found.

It was my turn for demands and I wanted to know what was going on. After a momentary hesitation, the senior detective showed me a scribbled report from the German priest at Monte Cassino. In the missive, which had apparently been smuggled to Special Branch by a roundabout route, the priest reported that a six-strong ZANLA group was using the mission as a base. The group apparently held frequent indoctrination sessions for the students and the priest himself was regularly sent out to buy brandy. He didn't know the terrorist plans, but they were led by a man known as Gamela the Silent and seemed content to remain at the mission.

The priest had shown considerable courage in reporting the matter to Special Branch, but in view of the difficulties he had to be experiencing, it seemed unlikely that we would get any more information.

'That's why we need your fellow', I was told. 'He can go back into the mission and find out what is going on.'

But Obert was long gone and although I sent search parties out for him, I knew we wouldn't see him again until his need for money overcame his natural caution and aversion to civilisation.

The news from Monte Cassino was worrying. A terrorist presence there would certainly account for the spate of ambushes we had been experiencing on the main road and probably for the attack on my station as well. But it was all very well knowing where the terrorists were holed up, but what were we to do about it? Monte Cassino had its own thriving school and killing any terrorists present without killing kids as well was likely to prove impossible. The SB men were gung ho enough to want a fight but my thoughts were for the staff at Monte Cassino.

The mission had long been a favourite spot for me and I called in for tea whenever I was passing. Sister Placidis was the nun in charge and she always welcomed me with a ready smile and excellent chocolate cake. I had enjoyed long chats with this lovely lady and the 700 or so students at the mission had always been equally friendly. Neatly dressed, polite and full of ready laughter, they epitomised African youth at its very best and my visits to the mission always renewed my flagging confidence in the future of my country. Now the place was under terrorist threat and it seemed there was little I could do about it.

Pym came out from Marandellas to assist in formulating a plan and I called in James Leask — promoted to command of the LDF since the death of Tim Peech. A Support Unit section was working in the Chiduku and their commander, S/O Mike Bullen sat in on our discussions.

The eventual plan was simple in outline, but entailed considerable risk on my part. Staff and pupils at Monte Cassino were accustomed to my visits, so it was agreed that I would drop in casually and try to find out what was going on. We had to be sure the terrorists were really there before we could even think about launching an attack.

The plan meant going in virtually unarmed and this seemed a little risky, but I couldn't think of an alternative. My Chishona wasn't good enough for me to pick up undercurrents that might indicate a terrorist presence, so I would need someone with me. The obvious choice was Television Gundani. When I explained the situation to him, he cheerfully volunteered.

'D'you mean that 'skelm' Obert was right for once, sir?' he grinned. 'Maybe I won't kick him quite so hard when I next see him begging around the camp.'

Two LDF sticks were deployed into observation points in the hills surrounding Monte Cassino and Mike Bullen held a couple of sections in readiness at Macheke. They would react as immediate back-up in the case of trouble, but I couldn't help reflecting that three kilometres was a terrifyingly long way in certain circumstances. Television and I were going to be very much on our own.

Choosing three o'clock on a very hot afternoon as the ideal time for our venture, I took my battered R4 and Sergeant Gundani into Monte Cassino Mission. Dressed in district patrol uniform of grey shirt and khaki shorts, I left my Uzi at home but carried a pistol, tucked into the dashboard recess. Television kept his own P1 hidden about his person, as patrolling AP were normally unarmed. This was to appear as routine a visit as possible even if we were both sweating with nervousness.

I felt like the original Daniel as we drove in and my eyes were wide open for lions. Studying the gaunt hills around us, I prayed that the blokes up there could pull us out of the mire if things went wrong, although I couldn't see how it might be done. They were a long way off and we were on our own.

'Sunray two-one-three, this is PATU Alpha.'

The vehicle radio crackled into life and I answered with some relief. It was nice to hear a friendly voice.

'Go ahead', I cleared my throat to rid it of a nervous 'frog.'

'We have you visual Sunray. Go well and we will be watching out for you.'

It wasn't much but at least we weren't entirely alone. Murmuring an acknowledgement, I glanced at my companion and we grinned somewhat nervously at each other. We had developed into an excellent team over the previous months, but this was our sternest test yet. Mentally bracing my shoulders and whispering a prayer to whoever might be listening, I drove up to the front door of the mission.

Our arrival caused immediate consternation. The first nun I spoke to went deathly pale when she saw us and stammered a confused answer to my request to see Sister Placidis. School children milled in the vestibule and if the hair on my neck bristled, it wasn't so much from fear as from the unexpected hostility that surrounded us. The usual cheeky smiles and high-pitched chatter had been replaced by tense, grim faces and those blank eyes that are the defence of a subdued people against the forces that threaten them. It was horrible to witness.

Even Sister Placidis was a long way from her usual, cheerfully welcoming self. Ushering us hurriedly into an office that wasn't hers, she didn't offer tea and was in an obvious hurry to get rid of us. Trying to make conversation, I could imagine the panic, taking place outside the closed door and wondered what was happening. Would the opposition escape through the rear of the building or would they decide to do something about the member in charge and his assistant. My stomach crawled with anxiety and my hand kept straying to the pistol I had hidden in a pocket. I half hoped that something would happen, if only to ease the mounting tension.

'Is there anything you want to tell me, Sister?'

I put the question gently but Sister Placidis shook her head. Her eyes were suddenly full of tears and my heart went out to her in her obvious dilemma. Missionaries were caught in the middle of the fight for Rhodesia. Their charges fought for both sides of the ideological divide and their calling required them to give succour to whoever needed it, without worrying about political views or way of life.

Still speaking gently, I reminded the frightened nun that my sons had been confirmed in the mission only the previous month and that it was her duty to tell me if anything untoward or against the law was going on. I told her of my understanding for her position but emphasised that my own responsibility was to the community as a whole. I had to worry about the greater good rather than the threats or needs of individuals.

None of it did any good. Sister Placidis was frightened and looked at me in stony-faced silence. This was a complete departure from her normal voluble hospitality and I felt desperately sad when I left that bleak little office. The war was destroying us all and making common criminals out of folk like this good nun. Sister Placidis had devoted her life to the welfare of Rhodesians in general, but was now being asked to make an impossible choice between opposing factions and ideologies.

Only a few months previously, the Roman Catholic Archbishop of Umtali, Donal Lamont had been sentenced to ten years hard labour and then been deported for failing to report the presence of terrorists. I had little sympathy with the Archbishop who had always used his position as a leader of the church to harry the Rhodesian government, but now my favourite nun was putting herself into the same situation. I had no doubt that if the presence of Gamela and his merry men was confirmed, Sister Placidis would also be prosecuted.

It seemed desperately tragic and my heart was heavy as we left the mission. When we arrived, there had been staff and pupils milling about all over the place, but they had disappeared and we departed to a funereal silence that was as depressing as the interview I had just conducted.

The LDF men in the hills had spotted considerable activity in the mission grounds, but they had seen no weapons and we were virtually back at square one. However, neither Sergeant Gundani nor I were in any doubt that Obert and the priest had been telling the truth. Monte Cassino had definitely been infiltrated.

The problem remained however. How did we get them out without creating a bloodbath? Our visit would have told Gamela that we had our suspicions and he probably realised that the mission was under observation from the hills. This would make him extra cautious and increase the danger of the situation.

I found it almost impossible to get Sister Placidis' anxiety out of my mind. Although I hated the fact that she was actively assisting the enemy, I could sympathise with her predicament. I knew her reasonably well, but we had never discussed the war so I had no way of knowing where her sympathies lay. At the same time, there surely couldn't be anyone in the country who wasn't aware that we were fighting a cruel and ruthless enemy. Whatever her political views, Sister Placidis would be torn between her duty as a Rhodesian citizen and her responsibility toward the children in her care.

In the past, like most of my countrymen, I had railed against missionaries like Bishop Lamont or the deliberately controversial Sister Janice McGauchlin, but now I was personally witnessing the cruel dilemma faced by a nun who had only her faith in God to guide her. The position for all of us was untenable and although I agreed with James and the others that we keep the mission under observation for the foreseeable future, there was nothing we could actually do to alleviate the situation.

So we watched and waited for something to happen.

Sitting with my feet up on my desk, I pondered the situation. Two LDF sticks — strange how I no longer thought of them as PATU — were in the hills above Monte Cassino, but I couldn't keep them there indefinitely. The Unit was still camped on my football field waiting for something to happen, but the scene had gone cold and I wondered when to stand everyone down.

The telephone rang and I took my time over answering it while I wrestled with my dilemma. If the terrorists were still in the mission, they were keeping very quiet and we could do nothing about the situation until they showed themselves. In the meantime, I was wasting a great deal of manpower and...

'Lemon.'

I have never been noted for my telephone manner and my mind was far away. Mrs Crombie's brisk, no nonsense tones brought me abruptly back into the real world.

The Crombies were an elderly farming couple who had moved down from the Mayo area a few months previously. Mayo had been subjected to an all-out assault by ZANLA terrorists with the result that almost all the farmers had pulled out, leaving the land to whoever was willing to risk working it. Mr Crombie had taken a job as groundsman for Macheke School and rented a small spread south of Monte Cassino where he and his wife ran a few head of cattle and raised exotic monkeys. He was a small, garrulous fellow who liked to drink tea in my office while poring over the wall maps and plying me with unanswerable questions on the security situation. His wife was a large lady with fierce blue eyes and an intimidating manner.

'Good morning Mr Lemon', she began in conversational tones. It was quarter past seven in the morning and I waited for her to report stock theft during the night. It was the most common reason for my telephone to ring so early in the day.

'We are under attack and my husband has been shot on his way to work.'

This little bombshell was delivered in such calm, matter of fact tones that had it come from anyone other than Mrs Crombie, I might have thought it a joke. After all, it was broad daylight and long past the normal hour for farm attacks I pictured the gate to the Crombie farm. It opened on to a main road and was surrounded by open countryside. No, she had to be having me on.

Yet with this good lady, it couldn't be a joke and even as doubts flashed through my mind, I heard the dull thunder of gunfire through the receiver in my hand. I struggled to remain as calm as she was.

'Hold on Mrs Crombie. I will have a reaction stick there within minutes.'

Less than five minutes later, Mike Bullen and his Black Boots were hurtling down the road past Monte Cassino and I followed with Sergeant Gundani in my Renault. The scene that greeted us at the farm gates has haunted my sleep for years.

Old — he was in his sixties — Mr Crombie had been alighting from his truck to open the gate when the terrorists opened up on him. Bullets smashed him back across the vehicle seat and one or more of his killers had moved in to finish him off at close range. A terrifying hail of 7.62mm intermediate calibre rounds had almost cut the little man in half. I felt my stomach heave as I looked down on his body. With the retching came a blinding surge of anger. The death of this innocent old man could so easily have been avoided. I had no doubt at all that his killers were the Monte Cassino lot and my feelings of sympathy for Sister Placidis evaporated with Crombie's death.

The Support Unit headed off on spoor while I went inside the house to comfort Mrs Crombie. Indomitable lady that she was, she looked after me, pouring tea down my throat and lacing it with something from a most appetising bottle. We talked quietly and I couldn't help comparing her dignified courage with the craven attitude displayed by my friends in the mission. Anger grew in my chest. Our conversation was interrupted by the radio and it was the LDF section leader calling from his observation point, high above Monte Cassino.

'They are moving out, Boss', he reported laconically. 'Lock, stock and barrel, the whole bloody lot of them are on their way.'

I was confused.

'Who? The gooks?'

'No', came the astonishing reply, 'the mission inhabitants. Staff, pupils, nuns and the priest — their cases are packed and they are assembling outside the building, obviously waiting for transport.'

For me, it was one of the most incredible incidents of the entire war. As soon as news of Crombie's killing filtered back to Monte Cassino, someone in charge ordered an immediate evacuation. I don't know whether they thought we would return, intent on vengeance or whether they were frightened of the terrorist reaction, but buses were ordered and by midday, the entire mission complex was abandoned.

Cattle were left in the barns and crops forsaken to rot in the fields. Classrooms, dormitories, laboratories — even the chapel — were left open, to be eventually looted and pillaged by thieves.

I never saw Sister Placidis again.

The Support Unit lost the spoor of Crombie's killers and Mrs Crombie left Macheke to live with her daughter. The exotic monkeys were removed and the little farm was abandoned and forgotten. It was a small tragedy in the horror that was Rhodesia, but for me it was a turning point in my feelings. Crombie's murder had been so senseless and avoidable that I couldn't get it out of my mind. The actual killing had been particularly vicious and while terrorist sympathisers might claim that the old man was a white man living on land that belonged to blacks, that held no water where I was concerned. He did a good job for black and white children alike and never wished harm on anyone. At the time of his death, he wasn't even armed. Hardly a threat to freedom was old man Crombie.

A corollary to Crombie's death occurred that very same evening in the form of a telephone call from the Roman Catholic Archbishop of Salisbury. The Right Reverend Patrick Chakaipa introduced himself and asked me to mount a guard over the empty mission buildings at Monte Cassino.

It took a supreme effort on my part but I remained very polite. Explaining to the Archbishop exactly what had happened and how it could have been avoided, I told him in graphic detail how I felt as a Catholic myself. Furthermore, I flatly refused to supply much needed manpower to guard his abandoned chattels.

In time, a guard was mounted on Monte Cassino, but it didn't come from me. I heard no more about the Archbishop's call and watched in minor bemusement as local farm workers and tribesmen homed in on the mission. Beds, curtains, crockery and sundry items of equipment disappeared at an alarming rate. I didn't care. For the first time since I had become a copper 14 years previously, I ignored blatant theft and felt no guilt about doing so.

Shortly after that I cracked up. It had been on the cards for some time and I woke one morning with terrible pains in my chest. My immediate thought was that I was having a heart attack and Jenny Schlachter was called in to whisk me off to Marandellas Hospital.

After giving me a thorough check up, the GMO pronounced me fit as a horse, but suffering from stress. It wasn't a fashionable disease in those days and his recommended cure was an immediate transfer to the bright lights of Marandellas.

So it was that after 23 eventful months, I left Macheke and moved into an easier life running the enquiry section at the district headquarters. I was no longer the boss, but I was waiting on promotion and quite enjoyed the easing of responsibility. I could go home at night and know that my sleep wouldn't be disturbed by the howling alarm of the Agric-alert as friends faced rockets and bullets from the darkness. I could play cricket every weekend and watch my kids in their own sporting endeavours. I was a family man again with time to spend on my children, while at work I dealt with the normal varieties of villainy and no longer had to witness or write up the horrors attendant on terrorist attacks.

It was a great relief but for all my enjoyment of being a copper again, I found myself missing the gut-wrenching excitement of war and the responsibility of knowing that people relied on me to take charge at a scene. I even missed the personalities — many of whom had made my life difficult over the preceding months. I would picture them in my mind and wonder how they were doing.

There was Tim Peech of course, long my *bete noir*, but a man undeserving of the fate that had overtaken him. I knew where Tim was, but my heart grieved for the loss of a man who could have been so much. There was David Scott Bradshaw, wild and undisciplined but a joy to work with. There were the farmers — James Leask and Mick Rose, the local hard men, Ewen Farrar with the accent of an Old Etonian, family estates in Scotland and the clarity of thought that made him an automatic leader among the older folk. Toc Arnold, Keith Baisley, Peter Robart-Morgan and Andrew Clark — all men I had worked with, fought with and admired. Their women had also done a sterling job — Daph du Preez who ran the WFR, Jenny Clark who kept everyone cheerful with her gurgling laughter and of course the incomparable Jenny Schlachter — a woman who provided inspiration for an entire community at a time when nobody else could do it.

Suddenly I missed them all and wished I was back as their member in charge. Back to be sniped at in public meetings, back to be complained about to politicians and my own senior officers. Back to take charge of the most awful situation that any copper can face — to lead a community, subject to constant harassment and killing, stock theft and store burning; a community whose morale had been terribly affected by the murder of their natural leader and a community that continually threatened to explode into an orgy of violent revenge.

In Marandellas I was just another police officer and had no control over events in Macheke and Virginia. Marandellas was experiencing its fair share of security trouble, but I was no longer affected by everything that happened and no longer the man with direct influence over the destiny of a community.

How I missed that but I certainly wasn't finished with Macheke. My knowledge of the place and its people was about to lead me into more excitement and almost end my career in considerable disgrace.

16

Violence and fear in the Mangwende

As 1978 continued so did the butchery. On 3 September, the Air Rhodesia Viscount 'Hunyani' was shot down by a heat-seeking missile while taking off from Kariba. The aircraft came down in the Vuti African Purchase Area and as if that wasn't bad enough, many of the survivors were butchered by a ZIPRA gang.

Few people survive an air crash and to go through that and find yourself alive, only to face death all over again at the hands of AK-wielding thugs was surely taking horror to the ultimate degree. Of the 66 people who took off in that doomed aeroplane, 48 were killed in the crash and ten were gunned down by the terrorists. Among the eight ultimate survivors was Doc who had been our family dentist in Kariba and had some terrible tales to tell. One particularly poignant twist to his story was the account of a middle-aged woman, gunned down in the act of tearing her petticoat up to bandage survivors.

This time the Selous Scouts couldn't be blamed as Joshua Nkomo appeared on British television to claim responsibility for the shooting. To make matters worse, he laughed about the killing and claimed that the Viscount was a military aircraft. This was arrant nonsense and even the British must have realised it. If it was possible that this atrocity could have anything beneficial about it, then perhaps it may in the way the incident — and Nkomo's attitude — brought the whole country together in defiant hate. John da Costa, the Anglican Dean of Salisbury, preached a damning service in the Cathedral in which he lambasted the international community for their 'deafening silence.'

It seemed that Western politicians were only vociferous when it came to the alleged exploits of the Selous Scouts. They seemed curiously reluctant to condemn the shooting down and subsequent butchery of so many innocents. We couldn't help feeling that this was because they were frightened of offending Nkomo.

Throughout Rhodesia, attitudes hardened noticeably and even those who had been half-hearted about the war became bellicose and bitter. Personally, I just felt sad at the blatant hypocrisy of British and American politicians. The shooting down of the Viscount was bound to lead to more bloodshed, more atrocities and infinitely more hatred, yet these craven men and women didn't appear able to see what was happening. And these were the people who ultimately controlled our destiny.

That would not be the last such air atrocity either. On 12 February 1979 ZIPRA terrorists shot down another Air Rhodesia passenger aircraft, Viscount 'Umniati' and on that occasion all 59 passengers and crew members died.

As 1978 drew to an end, my own life seemed to be moving along in a weary haze. After the tensions and trauma of Macheke, Marandellas was very tame, even though it had a security problem and people were dying. A sub-JOC had been set up behind the station and camouflage uniforms outnumbered grey shirts and tunics among station personnel, but I couldn't work up any enthusiasm.

Shortly after my transfer I was promoted, but this made little difference to my life. I exchanged my shoulder bars for 'pips', had a poached-egg badge sewn on to my cap and was issued with a Sam Browne belt and leather-covered cane. I was now entitled to salutes from the masses and was sent on a course at the University of Rhodesia, presumably to equip me for the responsibility inherent with my newly acquired status.

The course provided an interesting couple of weeks, but I couldn't help wondering what relevance it had to the situation prevailing in the country. There were people dying horribly out there, yet we were delving into the motives and morality of policing and the effects of education — both old-fashioned with its overtones of brutality and modern with liberal sharing of responsibility between teacher and students — on African teenagers. A man who would one day become chief justice of the fledgling country lectured us on the future of law in the 'new' Zimbabwe and we were subjected to a continual tirade of vituperation from the university students.

Some of those on the course with me seemed surprised at this unexpected hostility, but after my experience at Monte Cassino, I somehow expected it. Although most older members of the black community accepted that progress to majority rule was going to take time, the students demanded it right then and there. They were young, they were intelligent and they were hungry for a cause. They looked on us as tools of an unjust administration. It was an administration denying them their birthright and as such, we were natural targets for their hatred. Students have always been thus, no matter which nation they belong to and these students were black Africans — urged on by the world to take what was said to be theirs and take it by whatever means were available.

Whoever was responsible for organising the course could have alleviated the situation by including some of the newly promoted black officers, but that had not been done and our white exclusivity only increased the antagonism towards us.

In fact, black advancement in the police force was at last taking place. Eight sergeants and sergeant majors had come through a rigorous selection procedure and were in the process of being made into 'instant' senior officers. Three of the eight — Govati Mhora, Nebbie Madziwa and John Chademana — were former colleagues of mine and I wished them well as they shot up the promotional ladder.

Many of my white colleagues were not so pleased. Instant advancement to higher command was regarded as reprehensible and the injustice of keeping good men in the lower ranks for so long was conveniently forgotten. Most policemen understood the need for change, however, and the progress of the eight 'pioneers' went largely unremarked. They were sent all over the world on a series of courses and seminars. Their heads were crammed with facts, figures, cultural statistics and regulations while they advanced with meteoric regularity through the rank structure. Although all eight eventually reached the highest echelons of the force, it was perhaps inevitable that there would be casualties. Nebbie and Govati Mhora fell by the wayside in a corruption scandal that included the first black commissioner and Chadders later left under a cloud amid allegations of buffalo poaching.

A couple of weeks at the university with the rest of us might well have proved more beneficial to all concerned.

One part of that university course that I really enjoyed was a visit to Air Force Headquarters at New Sarum. There we saw the disassembled fuselages of eight Bell 205 helicopters. These were larger than our Alouettes and could be used as troop carriers as well as general work horses. They had enjoyed considerable success in Vietnam and these particular aircraft were painted a virginal white so that their country of origin remained a secret.

Apparently they were part of a larger consignment and we were all cheered by the thought that somebody out there loved us, even if it was only for our money.

For Rhodesians the year was coming to a worrying end. After some of the most traumatic months in the nation's history, the Transitional Government decided in November to form a 'Coalition Government of National Unity'. This was supposed to create political stability after the advent of black rule, but it merely disturbed the already anxious white population and emigration figures rose to unprecedented levels. The main worries for whites were the possible effects on health and education, so most of those taking what had come to be known as 'the yellow route' or 'chicken run' were young family folk — the very ones we needed to fight the ever escalating war.

Alan Savory, still having his say against government policies, described the emigrators as taking the 'wise old owl' run and I couldn't help feeling that he was probably right.

In December, the fuel storage depot in Salisbury was rocketed by a small group of ZANLA cadres and the resultant fires blazed for nearly a week. South African fire fighters were eventually called in to assist with dousing the blaze, but even more significant than the economic cost of the attack was the effect on white morale. For many it was the final straw. The war was no longer confined to rural areas and city businessmen began to wind down in preparation for a quick exit when the country finally capitulated to the opposition.

In this unhappy situation, I was having my own problems. I wasn't happy in Marandellas. My marriage was struggling, I was drinking too much and I didn't get on with my boss. How I longed to be back in Macheke. When I pestered Dispol to chase up my request for transfer to the Support Unit, he was told from PGHQ that 'if Lemon doesn't wind his neck in, he will end up in the Unit.' My protests that such a move was exactly what I wanted were greeted with horrified incredulity. Nobody volunteered for the Support Unit.

Those few months in charge of the enquiry section at Marandellas were bad months for me and my self esteem sank to an all time low. I spent my evenings propping up the bar and moved through my daily chores like an automaton. Once again I was heading for disaster.

Nor did the fact that I was now an ordinary policeman spare me from the horrors of war. On one occasion, I was called to a particularly bestial scene in the Soswe TTL when two district assistants from the Department of Internal Affairs were abducted by terrorists. A number of local girls were rounded up and the DAs were forced into sexual depravities with some of these women in front of everyone else. Eventually the DAs and the violated ladies were shot, while those who had orchestrated the horror made good their escape.

The district was under martial law at the time and it was decided to make an example of locals who had been feeding the terrorists. I was sent out with a small party of men to conduct a reprisal operation. The Military Court (what do soldiers know of justice?) had decreed that one particular village should lose 25 head of cattle and our task was to round up the beasts, shoot them and set fire to the carcasses. To most Africans, cattle are wealth and this seemed a harsh way of inflicting punishment for an offence which in all probability, they had been forced to commit. I was a copper however and my duty was clear.

As the man in charge, I read the court findings to the kraal head and when that was done, everyone waited for me to get the proceedings under way. After a momentary hesitation, I walked up to a big, piebald ox and shot him in the forehead. The FN packs a two-ton wallop but the brute just shook his head like a boxer taking a big punch. For a moment I thought I would have to shoot him again, then his knees buckled and he fell slowly on to his side, gazing reproachfully at me as he died. I felt sick. This was hardly war and certainly not justice.

After my shot all hell broke loose. The others opened fire on individual beasts and even above the thunderous sound made by a dozen heavy rifles, I could hear the bellowing of wounded cattle and the shrill yells of excited men. Huge bodies crashed to the ground around me and choking dust billowed over the landscape. It was like a scene from the bowels of Hades and after my initial shot, I leaned on my rifle and watched, trying to keep my mind aloof from the carnage. None of it did anything for my sense of patriotism and for the first time in 14 years, I felt ashamed to be a policeman.

Eventually I could stand it no longer. I wanted to vomit. My men were still yelling with the joy of killing and I moved a short distance away to get dust and the smell of slaughter out of my nostrils. The tribesmen looked at me with blank faces and hating, sullen eyes while their women wailed in the background. Dead cattle were stacked up in the dust and panic-stricken beasts struggled to escape, many of them displaying horrific injuries from the gunfire.

Even when the firing stopped, the horror wasn't over. Feeling completely apathetic, I ordered the villagers to pull the carcasses into one large pile, which was then doused with petrol and diesel before being set alight. The stench was terrible and by the time I got my party back into the truck, the killing lust had worn off even the most bloodthirsty of them. We drove back to Marandellas in uncomfortable silence.

For me it had been a terrible experience. By doing what we did, we sank to the level of the terrorists we were fighting. It was brutal, depraved, barbaric and totally unnecessary. As I said to Missy that night, if the same thing was happening all over the country, we no longer deserved to win the war.

'You are a copper and there will always be jobs you dislike doing', she consoled.

It didn't help. I felt unclean and thoroughly ashamed to be a member of the 'Force in the Great Tradition.'

Old man Jeffries was a retired bank manager who lived alone, ten kilometres out of town. Nominally a farmer, he survived on his pension, allowing the land to be worked by his staff. They planted a few acres of straggly maize as well as a bit of sorghum and rapoko around their houses, but in general the farm was left untended.

Although years of living alone had left him cantankerous and reclusive, Jeffries had spent many years in Kenya, a country I knew well, so I was one of the few policemen he would talk to. During my first stint at Marandellas, I had paid the occasional visit to his property and we had reminisced over lunch about the good old days when 'men were men and elephants were plentiful'. Now that I was back at the station with rank to my name, I looked forward to another visit but things had changed on the Jeffries property.

Jeffries had a young black man working for him and it was immediately obvious that Ephraim was more than a mere servant. Apparently the old fellow had taken him in as a child and paid for his upbringing, which was fair enough, but he had a confidently obsequious air about him and I disliked him on sight.

Ephraim's mother had worked in the house and I couldn't help wondering if there had been more to her relationship with Jeffries than was normal for a maid and her employer. It seemed to me that the old man looked after the boy out of a minor sense of guilt, although he certainly showed no paternal pride in Ephraim and seemed almost frightened of offending him. However, it was none of my business and after a strained initial visit, I left the shabby little farm alone.

It was a report of stock theft that drew me back and that was more out of curiosity than anything else. My first surprise was that Ephraim was virtually running the place. He had 30 odd head of cattle on the farm, as well as a few scrawny goats — not the sort of animals likely to make him popular in the white farming community. Although he lived in the farm compound, he seemed ever more proprietorial toward the big house and treated Jeffries with thinly veiled contempt. He had reported two cows taken by the thieves, but I hadn't been on the scene more than ten minutes when the sergeant in charge of the stock theft team reinforced my own suspicions.

'The *mombies* were killed here on the farm, sir'

Sergeant Pepukayi drew me aside to show me clumsily disguised bloodstains.

'There is no sign of the meat and there have been gooks in the area. Perhaps they have been living here and Ephraim has been feeding them.'

It was a serious accusation but seemed justified by the indications and I put it to Jeffries himself. He waxed indignant and ordered me off the property, but he was nervous and I wondered how much he knew of the matter. When I left, I took Ephraim with me and that provoked another uproar from the old man. He threatened to report me to everyone from the prime minister downward, but his protestations were too theatrical and my suspicions were hardening.

Back in the station, Ephraim was blandly indifferent to my questioning. He knew nothing about terrorists, he told me. He was an innocent mission boy — that was the wrong thing to say to me after Monte Cassino — and his cattle had been stolen. It was my job as a policeman to find the stolen beasts, return them to their rightful owner and prosecute the thieves. His gentle smile made my hackles rise, but there was nothing I could do. For all his chubby features and relaxed manner, Ephraim was a hard nut and I wondered how much help he had been giving to the enemy. The area in which he lived had been subject to farm attacks, arson and vehicle ambushes of late, so it seemed highly probably that those involved had been operating out of the Jeffries property.

I voiced my suspicions to Special Branch and they also had a go at Ephraim but were no more successful than I had been. He was released without charge and I don't suppose I was terribly surprised to be called out a few nights later with the news that Jeffries' homestead was on fire.

By the time I arrived on the scene, the building was blazing well and there was no sign of the old man. A tearful Ephraim was wringing his hands and exhorting us to do something, but his eyes were hard and I wondered how much he had had to do with the matter.

The next day we found Jeffries' body curled up in a corner of the gutted building. It was merely a charred husk and there was nothing to indicate anything other than an accidental fire. That should have been the end of the matter but Sergeant Pepukayi was suspiciously nosing around in the compound when he found a clip of 7.62mm intermediate ammunition. This he brought to me with a triumphant grin on his face and my suspicions were confirmed. Both sides in the Rhodesian conflict used 7.62mm bullets but the Security Force FNs had the long rounds while the Kalashnikovs, favoured by our opposition, used intermediate or short ammunition.

Despite Ephraim's protestations of innocence, 'the Boys' had definitely been present on the farm and were almost certainly responsible for burning the house and killing Jeffries. I requested a postmortem and wasn't at all surprised to learn that the old man had been bayoneted and left for dead before the fire started.

He left the farm and all he possessed to Ephraim and although I interrogated that young man for many hours, I got nothing further from him. He met all my questions with the same bland, hard-eyed smile and eventually had to be released yet again.

As he left the station, I burned with futile anger. Ephraim had outwitted us all and I had no doubt that if he had not been involved in the actual killing of his mentor, he had certainly known what was happening and made no effort to prevent it. Jeffries had been good to the boy and had probably been actively sympathetic toward the terrorist cause. He had certainly condoned their presence on his farm, but he eventually paid for this generosity with his life. He died horribly and I couldn't help wondering yet again, whether the Afrikaans attitude toward farm labour wasn't the correct one. The Boers treated their people with rough paternal severity and were generally respected by their staff. Jeffries had gone to the opposite extreme and been murdered for his pains.

Ephraim continued to live on the farm and as far as I know he is there still. The full story of Jeffries' death never did come out and I don't suppose anyone other than those directly involved will ever know what happened. The farm itself was less than 20 kilometres from Monte Cassino and I couldn't help but wonder if its destruction had anything to do with Gamela the Silent, but that was probably paranoia on my part. I saw that worthy's hand in every violent act. There were other terrorist groups operating in the Marandellas district and Gamela was probably back in Mozambique by then.

The inquest verdict on Jeffries' death was that he died 'at the hands of armed terrorists' and that was that. A cantankerous old man had died and was unmourned among his neighbours. They categorised him as a 'terr sympathiser' and the general attitude was that he had received his just deserts. The natural generosity of spirit that had always been a hallmark of Rhodesians was rapidly being eroded by the war and we were all quick to condemn.

When Dispol walked into my office with a docket in his hand, I could see from the tension in his face that this was not going to be a pleasant visit.

'Your blokes at Macheke have gone on the rampage', he handed me the docket. 'Read that, then I want you to investigate.'

'That' was a collection of complaints from residents of the Mangwende. From the statements, it appeared that the mounted section of the LDF had run amok in one area of the TTL and indulged in an orgy of beating, burning and torture that would have shamed Gamela the Silent himself. There were allegations of assault, arson, attempted murder and indecency. I read the complaints with mounting horror.

Later that morning I discussed the file with Pete Bellingham. I had always looked on him as a first class 'book' policeman, but far too soft in practice. During the 18 months he had been my Dispol in Macheke, he had all too often bowed to pressure from farmers and politicians, thereby leaving me out on a limb and trying to face such people down on my own. Bellingham was an ambitious man and I could sympathise with his desire not to rock the boat, but his lack of decisiveness occasionally left me isolated and bitter. On this occasion however, he seemed grimly determined.

'I have no doubt that some of these complaints are gross exaggerations', he told me. 'But if there is any truth at all in them, I want the culprits punished. In the circumstances, you are definitely the man for the job.'

I suppose I should have felt flattered, but my heart was deep in my boots. I knew all the blokes involved. Some of them — all of them dammit — were my friends. We had been through a great deal together. We had drunk together, played together and fought together. Now I was being asked to investigate them on charges that might well send some of them to prison.

'Why me, sir?' I queried hesitantly. 'I mean . . . I am involved with these blokes. I know their families.'

'That is precisely the reason why I want you for the job', Bellingham was obviously determined. 'They will clam up with anyone else but you might just get through to them. Besides, locals in the Mangwende know you as a police officer rather than as a soldier. If they see that we are taking their complaints seriously, they will speak to you.

'I want you to carry out the investigation in police uniform rather than camouflage. Let the people know that we are on their side and they won't feel it is all being covered up in the war effort.'

I couldn't resist the question.

'And will it be, sir? Covered up, I mean. If I find the evidence, will this government of ours prosecute white men for assaulting blacks? Particularly white farmers from Macheke.'

'If there is a case to answer, they will answer it', Bellingham said firmly and in that moment he went up in my estimation. I knew only too well the political firepower that Macheke farmers could range in their support and the actual investigation would only be half the problem. Would Dispol keep his nerve when the storm broke, or would I be left to face it out on my own yet again?

Whatever the case, it seemed that I was lumbered, so after asking that Sergeant Gundani be detached from all other duties to assist, I set off in an unprotected police van for Macheke and the Mangwende.

It wasn't an enjoyable investigation. In different circumstances, I would have been only too pleased to be back in harness and doing what I was trained to do. This was common or garden coppering — investigating, interviewing and putting a case together. This was what I enjoyed most, but everything was far too personal and my investigations were being carried out in a war zone. The Mangwende had long been lost to the Rhodesian cause and I had no doubt that we were working under the watchful eyes of an enemy who had shown no compunction in murdering Tim Peech — the last white man who had tried to help the local people.

For six long, nervous days, Sergeant Gundani and I wandered through the dusty heat of the tribal trust land. We took statement after statement, interviewed witnesses in smoky huts or beneath the branches of conveniently shady trees. We used tape measure and drawing materials to make detailed sketch plans and I filled one entire pocket book with scribbled notes. As the evidence mounted, so my spirits sank even further. It all looked very damning and I knew that the most difficult part of the investigation was yet to come.

If ZANLA allowed us to get that far!

I carried a briefcase containing a cocked and loaded P1 pistol, but Television was unarmed and we both felt very conspicuous in our grey shirts. It was many years since regular members of the BSAP had been on ordinary police enquiries in the Mangwende and locals frequently greeted us in wide-eyed amazement.

What were we doing? Where was our escort — our weapons, our back up sticks, our 'military' Land-Rover? They shook their heads in bemused incredulity when we explained why we were in the TTL.

As the investigation progressed, I came to the conclusion that although many of the complaints had indeed been exaggerated, there was a hard kernel of truth involved that couldn't be ignored. The woman who claimed to have been indecently assaulted was particularly convincing. I interviewed her in the presence of her husband and they impressed me. Far from being simple tribesfolk, they were both teachers and highly articulate. She showed me fading wheals on her legs and arms which she claimed had been made by riding crops and was in the act of showing me more intimately located marks to confirm the rest of her story when I hastily intervened. That was the doctor's province and I wasn't going to risk further complications.

Inevitably perhaps, the most difficult task of all was interviewing the LDF men involved. Having worried from the start about my approach, I went to each house in turn, accepted tea and put my case as straightforwardly as I could. In almost every instance, I was met with courteous disappointment in my attitude by the men themselves and outraged hostility from their wives. I was a 'sell out', a 'kaffir lover' and a 'waste of white skin.'

I could sympathise with the distraught ladies and loved them none the less for their outbursts, but my mission was with their husbands. I needed statements after caution if my docket was to be watertight, but nobody was prepared to oblige. Eventually I appealed to James Leask. I had approached him at the start of the case and kept him informed of my movements, but he wasn't particularly sympathetic and I couldn't blame him. He wasn't directly involved in the case, but he was still in command of the LDF and the accused men were his responsibility. I hoped that he was also still my friend and if anyone could persuade these blokes to talk with me, it was James.

Lovely Sally Leask made my visits to Medlar farm somewhat uncomfortable, but James was pragmatic. After lengthy discussion between us, he arranged a compromise. I would carry out a simultaneous interview with all the men involved and at the end of it, they would each give me a statement, presenting their own side of the case.

The price for this co-operation was that when my docket was completed, I would outline the available evidence to James. The Macheke and Virginia communities were up in arms at what they considered a gross betrayal by the police. If James could convince them that I had been absolutely fair, it might help to alleviate the simmering tension. It was obvious to both of us that such collaboration could lead to serious repercussions for me if anything got out, but it seemed worthwhile in the circumstances. I knew only too well the strains and tensions in the area and if I could help to ease the pain of this latest trauma, it might bring a bit of common sense back to the hotter heads among the farmers.

So it was that I recorded the necessary statements after caution and in time, a carefully prepared docket was submitted to the Attorney General. As agreed, I copied my summary of evidence to James and thereby kept my side of the bargain, but in doing so, I started a train of events that came close to landing me in jail.

But that was all well into the future when I finally shook hands with the five men involved, made my farewells and headed back to Macheke with Sergeant Gundani. In spite of the tension involved, it had been a satisfying investigation and I knew I had done an excellent job. I would recommend prosecution for various offences against each of those involved and they were all aware of my intentions. Now it was time to celebrate, so at his request, I dropped my worthy assistant off at his home and made for the Macheke country club with a briefcase full of accumulated evidence and a now unloaded P1 pistol.

I was singing when I left the club. The sudden release of tension had been an excellent reason to party and I had partied to the full. In beery disharmony, I pointed the van towards Marandellas and home, content that I would be in bed by midnight. Ten kilometres out of town, the night exploded into a winking kaleidoscope of coloured lights. I heard a muffled bang, but in my somewhat befuddled state, it took me long moments to realise that the sparkling lights were tracer bullets arcing from both sides of the road and heading in my direction. I was under attack! My pistol was still tucked away in the briefcase so there was nothing I could do but put my foot down hard and hurtle through the ambush.

Pulling up half a kilometre down the road, I took the pistol out and switched on the vehicle radio. While I was wondering whether to report the incident or leave it till the next morning, I heard a police reserve stick reporting that they had come under fire in the same area. I butted in with my own version of events and arranged to meet up with the reservists. As we spoke, it became obvious that the shots fired at me had whistled over their nearby road block position but they were not having that.

'Those shots were aimed at us', I was firmly told. 'The gooks were firing from that big koppie on the other side of the road.'

It didn't seem important who had been the intended recipient of the shots fired, but to emphasise his point, the stick leader fired a burst from his FN at the koppie in question and somewhat to my surprise, fire was immediately returned. We scattered for cover and I wondered whether I had been subject to a drunken dream and ought to get on home to bed. My sense of self-righteousness was restored when another stick came on the air to say that they had just been shot at and fired back in the direction of the main road.

Leaving them all to their little war, I headed back to Marandellas. The officer in charge, Chief Inspector Mike Farrell was waiting up for me and he wasn't in the best of humour. Mike and I didn't get on well at the best of times and on this occasion he had been roused from his beauty sleep. I was still fairly inebriated and he was spoiling for a fight.

'Were the tracer rounds red or green?'

I presumed he was referring to my ambush and gazed at him in open-mouthed astonishment. I didn't know what colour the damned things were. When one is under fire, the colour of the rounds that are threatening to take one's head off does not seem particularly relevant. Hardly bothering to conceal my disbelief at his naivety, I went on home for a well-earned sleep.

By the time I arrived, it was well after midnight so I removed my shoes and tip-toed up a long corridor toward the bedroom. Carefully pushing the door opened, I crept inside to find myself blinking down the wrong end of my own FN. My ever-nervous wife had woken to the sound of creeping footsteps and quickly grabbed my rifle to defend herself.

I couldn't help reflecting that having been shot at by the enemy and then by the police reserve, to be finally potted in error by my own wife would surely be an ironic end to my already eventful day.

That my vehicle had indeed been ambushed was confirmed by two holes in the roof of the cab and a huge scorch mark in the tarmac where a rifle grenade had exploded directly behind me.

'You were bloody lucky', Mike Farrell affirmed but as I pointed out somewhat sarcastically, nobody had believed me at the time.

The docket outlining the evidence against the five LDF men went through to the Attorney General, but once again the Macheke community wielded too many guns for mere coppers. In spite of my careful presentation, most of the charges were dropped and only one man eventually came to court on a very minor charge of common assault against the lady teacher.

In court, the man's advocate produced the summary of evidence, I had given to James Leask and prosecuting advocate Adrian de Bourbon was understandably incensed. He wanted me charged with conspiring to defeat the ends of justice and from his point of view, this was probably justified. Had he been allowed his way, I would have been jailed and/or dishonourably discharged but fortunately for me, less jaundiced views prevailed. I was brought before a board of officers to answer the charge that I had 'acted in a manner unbecoming to a member of the Force.'

That was bad enough.

How well I remember my feelings on the day of the hearing. Police disciplinary proceedings have all the pompous ritual of military courts martial and are every bit as intimidating for the offender. My case was heard in Salisbury on 26th August 1978 and was due to start at 2.30 pm. I drove in to town alone, although Missy had volunteered to accompany me, and having arrived far too early, spent a miserably unhappy lunch hour wandering sightlessly around the crowded streets of the capital, wondering what was going to happen to me.

I could understand and even sympathise with de Bourbon's desire to see me punished and knew that I had been lucky to escape an appearance before the High Court. A judge might well have sent me to prison, and I wasn't sure that I could have coped with that. My motives might have been good, but in my heart I knew I was guilty as charged and intended to plead that way.

The possible consequences went round and round in my brain. I might be reduced in rank. I had only just become accustomed to being saluted and rather enjoyed the razzmatazz attendant on being an officer. Going back to S/O or even — heaven forbid — P/O, would be a major blow to my pride, but I could probably cope with that. A more serious worry was the possibility of ending up behind bars. Even a few days in police cells would probably be more than I could bear. I have always had a horror of being penned in and any inspector doing a spell 'in the box' could be assured of a hard time indeed.

Even a heavy fine didn't bear thinking about. I had been spending money like water of late and we couldn't afford to throw any more away. Overwhelmed with despair I wandered the streets feeling distinctly sorry for myself. My situation was entirely of my own making, but in my efforts to be fair with the people of Macheke, I had let my family down and probably doomed us all to disgrace and penury.

A few citizens noticed my uniform and approached me with queries, but I fear I was hardly a good advertisement for the BSAP. My answers were abrupt and ill-considered, but my mind was a long way from those to whom I was speaking. At that moment, I was a very lonely man indeed and for the first time ever, I truly regretted coming home to Rhodesia.

Standing like a felon in front of a senior assistant commissioner, a chief superintendent and a superintendent, I pleaded guilty to the charge against me. Rigidly at attention, I listened while the facts were read out by the prosecutor, Chief Inspector Roger Lebish, a man who had also served at Macheke in the past. A female secretary took notes and everyone wore grave expressions.

When it was my turn to speak, I tried to explain the motivation behind my actions, but I couldn't tell from their expressions whether I was getting through to the three senior officers. It was a nerve-wracking procedure and I stumbled frequently in my presentation, while SAC Eric Saul, known throughout the force as a harsh disciplinarian, watched every movement of my face. When I had finished, he questioned me at length and I answered as best I could, my mind numbed by the enormity of what I had got myself into. At last it was over and the Board adjourned, leaving Roger and I to discuss everything but the matter on hand until they returned.

In the event I was treated very leniently. Eric Saul read me the riot act but added his own understanding of my motives and predicament. Trembling a little in my shiny boots, I waited dumbly for sentence.

'I shall have to be hard', the SAC went on and my heart sank, 'We cannot allow this sort of thing to go on and this board must be seen make an example', he continued.

'You are therefore fined 50 dollars.'

I could hardly believe it. I had been expecting ten times that much. I marched out of that room in a daze and outside, Roger shook my hand.

'You were lucky', he commented and I couldn't help but agree. I had been lucky — desperately lucky.

Back at Marandellas, Dispol was relieved and my family were over the moon. Missy had agonised with me in the days leading up to the trial and we were all thankful that it was over. Jenny Schlachter phoned to find out what had happened and a few days later, I received a cheque for $50 from Macheke Farmers' Association in appreciation for all I had done for the community. It was a lovely gesture on their part and ensured that whatever my feelings about their political influence, the people of Macheke and Virginia will always mean a great deal to me.

Many years later, I was told by former Detective Chief Superintendent Ray Ritson that I had been made a scapegoat for the incident that so nearly cost me everything.

'They needed someone to deflect attention from what your LDF blokes had done', Ritson was the investigating officer in my case. 'You were convenient and were lucky that Saul knew what was going on and wouldn't play ball. You would have been crucified had anybody else been president of the board.'

And for the record — in spite of all our hard work, in spite of the heartache, fear and physical danger that investigation had produced for Sergeant Gundani and myself — the one LDF man who came to trial was acquitted of the charge against him. It was a blatant miscarriage of justice and when I had time to think about all that had happened, it made me very bitter.

Fortunately, perhaps, I didn't have too long for reflection. Two days after my trial, I was posted to the Support Unit on an immediate transfer.

I was about to become a Black Boot.

17

Charlie Nine

It could only have happened in Rhodesia. I duly reported to Support Unit Headquarters, to be told that there was no instructor available to train me. It sounded all too familiar. The barracks at Chikurubi were fascinating but there was only so much I could do there. After inspecting all the facilities on offer and having my camouflage uniform tailored to fit me properly, I wandered into town. There I invested in a black leather briefcase as befitted a company commander in the BSAP Support Unit.

The police hostel in Fife Avenue offered excellent accommodation, but the residents had little in common with the policemen I usually worked with. These were 'uniform carriers' with little interest in national problems and were interested only in enjoying life to the best of their ability. There was no talk of sitreps or the security situation at the bar and for all these young men seemed to care, the country might have been entirely peaceful.

Looking around me of an evening, I burned with unjustifiable anger. Didn't these uniformed popinjays know that innocents were dying out there? It was desperately unfair of me, but my emotions were stretched at the time and I was extremely worried about my ability to succeed as a Black Boot.

Another worrying feature about life in Fife Hostel was the absence of black faces. All the residents were white and the main topic of conversation at the bar was the inadequacies of everyone black. Whereas there had been an easy sense of fraternisation between races in my previous stations, here in the city there was a distinct sense of segregation, the ethnic groupings only getting together when it was time to work. I couldn't help wondering how much confidence the general public could possibly have in such an obviously divided force.

The civilian population of Salisbury also seemed very different to my farmers. They wore suits and ate out in fancy restaurants. They seemed quite relaxed in their daily lives and survived without firearms. I saw no guns in the city and vehicles on the streets were all fancy saloon cars, with nary a sign of the mine-protected monstrosities that were springing up everywhere in the farming areas.

The only sign that there was trouble in the country was the fact that anyone entering a shop was liable to be searched. Perhaps the war hadn't really hit these people yet.

In fact, apart from the rocket attack on Salisbury fuel depot, there was little for city folk to worry about. There had been the odd skirmish in Harare Township, but these were fleeting affairs and the terrorists involved had generally been quickly mopped up by highly trained police SWAT (special weapons and tactics) teams. According to the daily sitreps from Comops, the entire country was facing imminent disaster, but for a visitor to the capital city, life seemed to be going along in its normal pleasant fashion. I found it very difficult to understand.

As an inspector, I was to be put in command of a full company of fighting men and this was a daunting prospect. For a while it seemed that India was to be mine, then Tony Merris of Charlie Company decided to return to normal duties and I was given his merry men to do with as I pleased.

'They are a bit of a shower at the moment.' The Unit Chief Inspector told me cheerfully. 'Tony's heart has never really been with the Unit and they have been allowed to drift along, but they have the makings of a damned fine company.'

Hardly reassuring words from my point of view and when I looked up the position of 'C' Company on the Unit 'kill' board, my heart sank even further. During the year they had registered very few kills, their tally putting them well down the list with only two other companies below them. However, I was to become 'Charlie Nine' and for all my doubts in my own ability, I was determined to do well.

But I still wasn't trained. I wasn't even fit and Black Boots had the reputation of being able to run other units off their feet. How could I hope to inspire a company of men with my thickening waist and lack of fighting experience. Eventually I collared Chief Superintendent Fred Mason — as second in command, he was Badger One — and pleaded to be given some idea of what I was supposed to do.

Seeming surprised by my enthusiasm, Fred sent me out with Badger Four — Superintendent Sakkie Mackay. We drove to Enkeldoorn where Echo Company was working, then on to India at Fort Victoria. It gave me some idea of operational logistics but it wasn't really what I needed. My first real lessons came when I spent a week with A Company at Sipolilo.

'They train hard in Alpha', Mason warned me. 'The CSM is Sam Chikovore and he is a hard man indeed. You should see some action with them.'

It wasn't like that. Sipolilo was going through a quiet period and I saw no action, although I did admire Alpha's training programme. They did everything at the double and used live ammunition in their tactical exercises. Running for kilometres with a rifle in my hands and a bunch of sweating, singing cut-throats around me or crawling on my stomach with bullets crackling about my ears, I reflected that I had to be learning something.

Later on I asked Chikovore — a scowling bear of a man — whether they ever had accidents in their live firing exercises.

'Only one in my time', he growled. 'The bloody fool stuck his head up to see what was going on.'

I could feel myself blanche at the big man's casual attitude, but didn't question him further. My rapidly waning confidence might not have been able to take it.

Battle camp at Shamva was the next stage in my training. Companies went through it two at a time on a regular rota and I was to spend a week in residence as an observer. I lived in an abandoned farmhouse with the instructors and a couple of South African police officers.

In spite of government denials, the SAP were still sending men up to Rhodesia on a regular basis. Officially acting as extra instructors, they were obviously learning what they could about genuine COIN operations before they faced the real thing in their own country. There were a number of genuine mercenaries serving with various units in the Rhodesian Security Forces but the SAP were the only official ones I came across and I presumed that their military counterparts were performing a similar role with our army.

They made interesting companions, but battle camp itself was a disappointment. I did everything with the instructional staff and enjoyed a comfortable bed and excellent meals in their mess. It was hardly battle conditions as far as I was concerned, but during the week I learned a little more about the war that was raging throughout the country.

I tried out various terrorist weapons including the little known gurunov heavy machine gun and spent time with men moving through the jungle lane, desperately trying to spot the 'enemy' before they did. With only Chief Instructor Rusty Hustler to witness my shame, I went through the jungle lane myself, but I was a disaster and succeeded only in reducing Rusty to fits of semi hysterical laughter. It made me wonder why a man who loved being a policeman would volunteer to become a proper soldier.

I also tried ambush and counter-ambush drills where the object was to jump from the side of a slowly moving lorry and land on my feet, alert and ready for instant action. I had seen it done in war films but in practice it wasn't as easy as that. Every time I launched myself into space, I landed badly, either twisting an ankle or knocking the breath out of my body and blushing in confusion as the cumbersome rifle clattered out of my reach.

On the rifle range, I witnessed the horrific striking power of claymore mines and the 20 millimetre cannon, while learning the technicalities of mortars, MAGs and every other weapon used by the Security Forces. At the end of the week, I was pronounced fit to take over an operational company.

At least as fit as you are ever likely to be', added Rusty Hustler with a gloomy shake of his head.

Driving back to Chikurubi, I glanced down at my gleaming black boots and it was my time for a shake of the head. From being a peace-loving copper who wanted nothing of warfare, I was now part of an elite and somewhat notorious fighting unit. My camouflage was snugly tailored, my leatherwork gleamed a deep, midnight black, medal ribbons shone brightly on my shirt and the Unit's martial eagle emblem — the *gondo* — was prominent on my left sleeve.

In short, I was a fully-fledged Black Boot and expected to take command of approximately 120 uniformed bandits, all of whom would have experienced far more in the form of warfare than I had.

I couldn't help wondering what I had let myself in for.

It was Rusty Hustler who showed me the magazine. Flipping the glossy publication across the table, he gestured at me to read it.

'You will be interested', he promised. 'It is all about your home town.'

The magazine had been brought back from Mozambique and was published and printed in Britain. Issued by ZANU as a promotional paper, it reported the 'Battle of Marandellas' where 19 Rhodesian helicopters had allegedly been shot down and Security Force casualties were listen in the hundreds. Even if this imaginary battle had not purported to have taken place in the town I knew so well, I wouldn't have believed the story. The Rhodesian government was often economical with the truth when it came to playing down military setbacks, but there was no way they could have hidden that sort of disaster. Besides, I had only recently come from Marandellas and I knew that we didn't have that available manpower in the whole district.

Nevertheless, the magazine was professionally produced and printed on good quality paper. It contained carefully posed photographs of stricken men and machinery so that anyone not knowing the true situation would probably believe exactly what they read. It seemed that the terrorist propaganda machine was considerably more advanced than our own and that was a depressing thought.

In June 1978, the new government of Rhodesia — the first one dominated by blacks — was installed but US President Jimmy Carter refused to lift sanctions. The country was renamed Zimbabwe-Rhodesia and its first prime minister was Bishop Abel Muzorewa. I was never quite sure how the bishop reconciled his religious beliefs with such a high political profile, but he duly flew to America for a meeting with Carter, which did no good whatsoever.

Margaret Thatcher had become British Prime Minister at much the same time and Rhodesians felt that a Conservative government would prove far more sympathetic to our cause than had their predecessors. Thatcher immediately dashed such hopes by announcing new initiatives, with the Patriotic Front coalition of Mugabe and Nkomo more closely involved. Thatcher's announcement was supported by other Commonwealth leaders, meeting in Lusaka. Informed comment had it that Thatcher had been willing to accept the Internal Settlement as a *fait accompli*, particularly as British observers had declared the recent general election as being as free and fair as it was possible to be. Like so many British politicians, Thatcher had her mind changed for her. After talking with the leaders of Australia, Jamaica, Nigeria, Tanzania and Zambia, she insisted that the two terrorist leaders had to be part of any new government.

In view of Australia's blatantly racist immigration policies at the time and the political chaos holding sway in the other countries involved, Rhodesians found this particularly difficult to swallow.

Thatcher went on to decree that Britain would produce a new constitution providing for genuine majority rule and prepare another plan for free and fair elections, monitored by Commonwealth observers. The beleaguered Rhodesian government countered with feeble spite by deciding that black apprentices should be liable for call up like their white counterparts. This was counterproductive in that many young blacks left the country for military training with Mugabe or Nkomo, rather than fight for Smith and his white government.

Through all the political wrangling, the war for Rhodesia went on.

The maps were pinned to a large sheet of ceiling board, propped up in one corner of the room. I studied them warily, suddenly very alone and conscious of my lack of tactical experience.

I had arrived. I was the boss. It was my first day in command of Charlie Company. Tony Merris had stayed on for an extra week to help me along, but now he was gone and all my men had been deployed the previous evening.

Assistant Commissioner Don Rowland — commander of the Unit and known to us all as Badger — had been a mute witness to the company handover and at breakfast that morning had imparted a few gems of specific advice. One of them came vividly to mind as I studied the map board.

'Always make sure that there is someone in camp to make your decisions', Badger rumbled around his bacon. 'Either you or your deputy must always be at hand in case something unexpected crops up.'

It was sound advice but even as I pencilled large red arrows on to the map, I debated ignoring it. The previous evening I had sent two sections into the Mondoro TTL on the spoor of a small terrorist band that was heading directly north. I had positioned the rest of my company in a line of 'stop groups' stretching right across the TTL. The Mondoro was the last tribal area, south of Salisbury and it was vital that we kept the capital free of an enemy presence. Terrorist attacks in Salisbury had a crippling effect on morale in the entire country, so responsibility lay heavily on my shoulders.

Yet even as I studied the coloured pins that indicated the position of my troops, a glaring hole became apparent at one end of the stop line. Calling my Special Branch liaison officer across, I pointed out the problem and he grimly agreed with my assessment.

'If they slip through there we will lose them', Jack Simons muttered and we subsided into pensive silence.

The obvious answer was to use a vehicle as a mobile stop group, but that posed further difficulties. The only one available was my own and my deputy was with the pursuing troops so I was stuck in camp. I had been so determined to start my Support Unit career with a success that I had been profligate with my resources. The end result was that all I had left to plug the gaps with was Jack and myself, a police reserve radio operator and two sick constables. But this was no time for hesitancy and I decided to gamble. The radio operator might have only been a reservist, but he assured me that he was quite capable of holding the fort. So taking the less unwell constable with us, Jack and I sallied forth to war.

As company commander, I had my own armour plated, open Land-Rover and Jack drove while Constable Chibvongodze stood up in the rear, his MAG resting on the roof and ready to fire. I sat in the passenger seat with a map on my knees and a nervous fluttering in my breast. It wasn't the first time in my career that I didn't know what I was doing.

Map reading has never been my strong point and what had seemed straightforward back in camp now looked merely confusing. The entire TTL was flat and featureless. Driving very slowly, we prowled through this grim, brown landscape and although I tried to look confident, I wasn't even sure that we were in the correct area.

Feeling sure that we were completely lost, I was concentrating on the map when Jack yelled a warning, wrestling the heavy truck to a halt as he did so. Above my head I heard the aggressive thunder of Chibvongodze's MAG and directly in front of us, a line of men scattered for cover. Even through my bemusement, I noted the rifles slung across their shoulders. Banana-shaped magazines took a few moments to register on my mind and in those few moments, the battle was on.

My first problem was to get out of the Land-Rover. In my haste, I couldn't get the door open and when I did, I had a fleeting glimpse of Jack lying behind a bush and four of the enemy running hard in different directions. Instinctively I took off after one of them and it was only when I heard the flat crack of rounds passing over my head that I realised how badly I had boobed — again!

I was in a ploughed field, totally exposed and the man I had been chasing had gone down in heavy cover to shoot at me. Once again I had disobeyed all the rules and had a fleeting thought that my reign as Charlie Nine was likely to be the shortest in history.

Crossing open ground in such circumstances has all the qualities of a nightmare and I seemed to be wading through treacle as I forced myself forward. Hostile bullets crackled angrily around me, but at last I felt scrubby bushes tugging at my trousers and hurled myself earthwards with a gasping sigh of relief.

Once again the Hollywood producers had it wrong and I envied men like Clint Eastwood and John Wayne who could go down with a minimum of effort, roll over and regain their feet while firing from the hip. This was real life. My collision with hard earth drove the breath from my body with a painful whoosh and it took me nearly half a minute to regain my scattered senses. In that half minute, the man I had been chasing made good his escape.

Gasping, wheezing and angry with myself, I fired a few shots into the undergrowth, just to show that I knew what I was doing, but the terrorist was long gone and I heard my ricocheting rounds whining into the distance. Tiring of this futile exercise, I made my way somewhat more circumspectly back to the Land-Rover to find that Jack had killed one terrorist while Chibvongodze's MAG had jammed. After a brief conference, we loaded the dead man into the Land-Rover and resumed our patrol, keyed up now and anxious for another chance at the enemy.

It was Jack who saw them first. We were cruising slowly past a bush school when he pointed out three armed men moving cautiously through the scrub. They were heading for the school buildings and were miraculously unaware of us. Again I saw the curiously shaped magazines and my stomach tightened in nervous anticipation. We were less than a 100 metres from them when Jack cut the engine and glided to a halt. Debussing as quietly as we could, we prepared to engage the enemy while Chibvongodze continued to struggle with his recalcitrant machine gun.

When adrenalin is running fiercely through the nervous system, it is incredibly difficult to shoot straight and I don't think our opening salvo hit anyone, but it caused immediate panic. The three terrorists again took off in different directions. One ran for a small line of teachers' houses, another went for the school itself while the third man ran in our direction.

In open country, loud noises are often difficult to pinpoint and this fellow had his bearings way out of line. Galloping madly towards us, he held his Kalashnikov tightly across his body and his face was taut with panic. My own nervousness evaporated and my brain was suddenly clear. I glanced at Jack and he returned the look with a slight smile. Without a word passing between us, he rested his rifle in the crook of a small tree while I fired across the bonnet of the Land-Rover, my elbows wide apart and supporting the heavy weapon in approved text book manner. I aimed for a point directly above the rifle, held across the running man's chest.

Taking a deep breath, I steadied myself and fired. Jack fired at the same moment and the terrorist went down as though he had been hit on the head by a giant hammer. There was nothing theatrical about his death. He just fell in a heap and we sprinted in search of the others.

Running ahead, I made for the house I had seen the terrorist enter, but at the front door my path was blocked by an elderly teacher and his trembling wife.

'You cannot go in there', the man stuttered. 'My mother in law is very ill.'

I didn't hesitate. I had been shot and returned the fire. I had killed a man and I was on a high. The blood lust was running hard through my system and at that moment I could have taken on the world. Pushing roughly past the frightened couple, I cautiously entered the front room with Jack Simons on my heels.

The room was empty but beyond it was a bedroom containing a double bed, chest of drawers and wardrobe. There were no apparent hiding places and no sign of the sick mother in law. Feeling vaguely disappointed, I moved toward the bed, a single shot rang out and I felt my trousers flutter violently just below the crotch.

'Jesus, Jack', I turned on my companion. 'That nearly took my balls off.'

'It wasn't me.' He yelled back. 'The bastard is under the bed.'

We made a concerted dive for safety and I slammed the door shut behind me. The terrorist was trapped. There was one small window to the bedroom and I shouted at the approaching Constable Chibvongodze to watch it while we took cover below the level of the veranda.

'Tell him to come out, Chibvongodze', I called and the constable relayed the request in Chishona.

The only answer was a burst of automatic fire through the door. Splinters flew and I flattened my face in the dust. Suddenly aware that the teacher and his wife were standing helplessly out in the open, I screamed at them both to get down.

Over the next five minutes a strange sort of stalemate ensued. The terrorist couldn't get out but nor could we get him out. We needed to take him alive so that Special Branch could get some idea of the terrorist threat in the area. Chibvongodze relayed my promise that he wouldn't be harmed if he surrendered, but this was met by another hail of defiant gunfire. My colleagues looked to me for guidance. I had to do something.

At least my initial nervousness had gone and tiring of the impasse, I moved around the building and tossed an M962 grenade through the window. As mere fighting coppers, we were not issued with stun grenades and the explosion was cataclysmic in that confined space. Steel shards whined off flimsy walling and even as the noise died away, I heard the teacher moaning behind me at the destruction of his home.

In that tiny room, I felt sure that the grenade must have killed the enemy so I moved forward and carefully eased the door open, only to fling myself to the floor as another hail of bullets threatened to cut me in half.

'The bastard's still alive', I shouted unnecessarily to Jack and he actually laughed.

Adrenalin was rushing through us both and I think he was enjoying himself. So to be honest was I. My abhorrence of war had been forgotten in the excitement of battle.

But there was still a job to be done and I was determined to get the business over as quickly as possible.

The fourth member of the terrorist group was getting ever further away and like a gambler riding his luck, I wanted more kills.

Another grenade went in through the window and while it might have shredded everything in that cramped bedroom, it did nothing to dampen the aggressive instincts of the trapped terrorist. More bullets cracked, whistled and whined around our heads and this time, I angrily returned fire through the window. I don't think I hit anything and my rifle promptly jammed.

The FN rifle is a marvellous piece of equipment. As it causes a round to explode, cordite gases build up in the firing chamber, throwing the spent cartridge case out and forcing the working parts back into the firing position. Something had gone wrong and the mechanism only came half way back so that I was reduced to manhandling the cocking handle before I could fire each shot. Only afterwards did I discover that the gas regulator had been dislodged in my exertions and too much gas was escaping, lessening the pressure to the point where it could no longer move the working parts.

Training or a little reasoned thought would have made this patently obvious, but I was basically untrained and in no mood for reasoned thinking. Swearing monotonously, I slammed the working parts backwards and forwards and fired again and again through that open window. The only result was a withering return fire from the apparently unscathed terrorist.

Tiring of the futile activity, I instructed Chibvongodze to pass one final message for the bloke to come out and when that had no effect — except for more bullets — I tossed in a phosphorous grenade. That beastly little weapon took a moment or two to take effect but a few minutes later, the entire bedroom was burning fiercely. We waited anxiously for the terrorist to emerge, our fingers tight and trembling on hot triggers, but he continued to fire back until he could fire no more.

The roaring flames finally burned themselves out and all we found of a very brave enemy was a charred husk and the red-hot framework of an AK47. The fourth terrorist walked straight into one of the stop groups and was duly despatched and my career as a Support Unit Commander had begin with a bang. As we drove back to camp with the bodies and captured weaponry, I felt oddly drained but couldn't help remembering the moment when I first faced my new company only three days previously.

I had been nervous and uncertain after my encounter with Augustine Totohwiyo, while in front of me 116 battle-hardened, grim-faced warriors gazed back impassively, their contempt for this elderly brown boot readily apparent. I was the one wearing the fancy hat but each and every one of those hardened fighting men knew that he was worth at least two of me. Struggling to control my nervousness, I had resorted to bluster.

'I might be older than any of you,' I told the assembled company truthfully enough, 'but I can outrun, outfight, outdrink and outfuck every damned one of you.'

Brave words and their collective sneer told me that Charlie Company found it difficult to take me seriously, but that one eventful morning in the Mondoro was to change all that. Lemon's Luck was running high and I had lived up to at least one of my foolish boasts. One hundred and fourteen fighting men had achieved nothing in the exercise while my three-man party had flattened the entire enemy group. It was a memorable start to my Support Unit career and while I was never called upon to live up to my other boasts, that morning well and truly established my fighting credentials with the hard men of Charlie Company.

I had often wondered how it would feel to kill a man. In theory it is a traumatic moment, but all I felt during that Hollywood-like morning in the Mondoro was a fierce sense of excitement. With my own hand, I had killed two men and felt no guilt about it.

At the same time I could only wonder at the motivation of a man who chose to burn to death rather than surrender. Either he was more afraid of what we would do to him — which said something for the propaganda ranged against us — or he felt so strongly for his own cause that he was prepared to give his life in the most painful manner imaginable.

The forces we fought against in the war for Rhodesia were often portrayed as craven and cowardly, but I wasn't sure that I could have allowed myself to die so horribly — even for my country.

For days I brooded on the manner of that one man's death, but my uneasiness was eventually forgotten in the excitement of my new life as Charlie Nine. I put in a report to Headquarters, asking for the teacher to be compensated for his wrecked possessions, but for all his obvious fear at the time, I wasn't overly concerned about him. He had lost everything but like sister Placidis in Monte Cassino, he could have helped and the fact that he didn't, merely indicated where his sympathies lay.

18

War in the Wiltshire

Although I was officially still a copper, I might as well have been in the army. The Support Unit was made up on the lines of an infantry battalion. The Commanding Officer, Don Rowland was known by his radio call sign, Badger. Badger One was a chief superintendent and Badger Two a senior superintendent. They were assisted by a load of minor Badgers — all superintendents — to watch over we poor cannon fodder who did the hard work.

Apart from Badgers various and other staff officers, plus the sick and wounded at Chikurubi, the Unit was broken down into 12 fighting companies (A — L) and a half company operating on horseback. There was also Headquarters Company which was responsible for discipline and training. The code name for the Unit was 'Mantle' and the radio call sign at Chikurubi was 'one five one.'

Inevitably the pub there was 'The One Five One.'

Chikurubi Barracks was said to be the finest military establishment south of Cairo and to an ordinary copper like myself, it was an impressive set up indeed. There was housing for 5 000 people, sports fields, a cinema and even a hospital with its own well-equipped operating theatre — often in use since the start of the war. There were separate sections for training staff, ordinance and transport, while roads throughout the complex were wide and beautifully maintained.

A ferocious looking assault course brought me out in anticipatory sweat, while the parade square was almost as large as my entire police camp in Macheke. The main administrative block was surrounded by velvety green lawns and in the front entrance, a flag-bedecked Roll of Honour board stood proud before the salutes of Black Boots entering the building.

Saluting in the Unit was the real thing, too — not the casual gesture, normally used by policemen. Longest way up and shortest way down, every salute was made with military precision and obvious pride. The men visibly enjoyed their role as fighting coppers and I felt a tingle in my spine whenever I came through the entrance boom and acknowledged the guards. They might have been notorious as wild hooligans among the rest of the BSAP, but as far as these men were concerned, there wasn't a copper anywhere to compare with even the lowliest of Black Boots. I was one of them now and it didn't take long for me to start sharing their arrogant pride at being members of an elite.

In spite of my spectacular start, I had a great deal to learn about life in the Unit. I had been a copper for 15 years but that was soon forgotten. In spite of my lofty ideals, I became a soldier, pure and simple. The trouble was that I had only a sketchy idea of soldiering and the various drills remained a complete mystery. Fortunately I have always been a quick learner and a little to my surprise I began to enjoy the military rigmarole.

Once I had learned the ropes, I revelled in parading my company for inspection prior to deployments. To lead Charlie Company in full regalia while we marched past the saluting dais gave me a good feeling and to know that I was their commanding officer made me very proud.

My navy blue lanyard had been replaced with a much more flamboyant affair, woven with company colours of blue and gold. With my tailored uniform, medal ribbons and martial eagle insignia, I felt very much the dashing cavalry officer and a long way indeed from a Cotswold Bobby.

Even my everyday equipment was different. I had been issued with a full set of military webbing, five extra magazines for my rifle and a CZ nine-millimetre pistol to wear on my belt. My magazines were kept loaded with a tracer round in every five round, so that I could direct fire at night and all in all, I felt like a hardened fighting man. If it didn'thing else, the extra hardware gave me a psychological boost and suddenly I began to feel undressed if I didn't have my rifle to hand and that damned great pistol strapped to my waist.

Deployments into the operational area were for five weeks at a time and were followed by eight days of R and R when the war could be forgotten. Before going back into the field, the company was put through a rigorous retraining programme at battle camp that was conducted with the virtual certainty of combat in mind, rather than the vague possibility of action I had hitherto enjoyed.

My problem at battle camp was to learn everything from scratch without displaying my inadequacy in matters military to my men, but I muddled along somehow and don't think I made too much of a fool of myself.

On a normal day in the field, we were up before first light for 'Stand-to', everyone moving silently to allotted positions from which to repel an enemy attack. I would do the rounds with the CSM, checking every man's state of readiness and picking on the occasional unfortunate to ensure that his rifle was loaded. I particularly liked to chat with the mortar men huddled in their specially prepared pit, bombs held ready to slip into the ugly tube. Stand-to was very much part of military tradition, but I was assured that it was very necessary. If it didn't do thing else, it made me feel like a proper soldier and gave me confidence for the day ahead.

The next item on the morning programme was a long run. I determined from the start to exercise with the company, but to begin with that was an ordeal I could certainly have done without. The only concession I allowed to age and seniority was that I ran without my rifle. The rest of them didn't and in an effort to balance the scales of fitness slightly more, I insisted that whenever possible they sang lustily throughout the run. Even so, I struggled to keep up with those desperately fit young men.

Breakfast followed the run — in the mess tent for senior details while the rest ate *sadza* around small fires. Then came morning parade. If I was going to be a soldier, I was going to soldier to the full and for the first time in my life, I was on the easier side of ceremony. I savoured the parades, carefully inspecting both turn out and weaponry, often finding fault even where no fault was readily apparent. In busy times, there might be only a section of men on parade, but my sense of power increased dramatically when I had the entire company at my command.

If there was nothing more immediate to attend to, a brisk drill session was the natural corollary to parade. I kept a careful eye on the CSM during these manoeuvres, trying to learn how and when he bawled out his instructions. Foot drill was an important part of a Black Boot's life and the newly born, warrior side of my personality stirred to the measured tramp of boots and the singing of marching songs. Folklore in the Unit included one comment made by the Regimental Sergeant Major of the RLI when preparing for a presidential funeral parade.

'Come on, you men', the RSM roared at his well-drilled troopies. 'You're being made to look supremely scruffy by a bunch of fighting kaffirs and that will never do.'

The 'fighting kaffirs' were Mantle Headquarters Company, putting on their usual display of immaculately prepared and executed drill movements. The story had done the rounds and in spite of the racist overtones, the entire Unit chuckled at having put one over on The Incredibles. I had no wish to ruin that tradition of smartness should it ever be my lot to take a ceremonial parade. I could remember only too well, the hash I had made of foot drill on my promotion interview and I was determined to get things right, so I watched and listened to the experts whenever I could.

The rest of the working day was hardly strenuous. I had a thousand and one little tasks to take up my time, many of them administrative, others merely inspirational. I discussed field deployments with the CSM and my second-in-command, taking advantage of their experience when I could. However, the final decision always rested with me and when my deployments led to success, I felt like a very clever fellow indeed.

When I had time on my hands, I enjoyed dropping sections off in the field and collecting them after a patrol, while my briefings were full of exhortations to courage and steadfastness. I also enjoyed the tactical side of military life and would spend hours in front of the map board, plotting known or suspected enemy positions and calculating how best to improve the kill rate. Coloured pins and chinograph pencils are very much part of a field commander's equipment and I employed them to the full.

The men played volleyball when there was nothing else to do and I occasionally joined in, generally managing to make a fool of myself. As the day waned and darkness crept over the land, it was time for 'Stand-to' again and soon after that, it was supper and bed. This routine varied with the exigencies of the security situation, but I tried to stick to it as closely as I could. Black Boots were chosen for their fighting prowess rather than their intellectual qualities and routine kept them happy.

Discipline in the Unit was strict and I tried to keep it so although I decided very early on that the disciplinary set-up had its priorities wrong. Fit fighting men will always transgress but provided their offence wasn't a heinous one, the men of Charlie Company were offered the choice between formal disciplinary proceedings or being 'tried' by myself and the CSM. Our punishments invariably consisted of crippling PT sessions and/or a fine, the money from which was put into a company fund, which I administered. This extra cash was dished out in the form of emergency loans and special purchases, thus enabling us to buy a brand new football strip within my first few weeks in command. The bright blue and yellow shirts with 'Charlie' emblazoned on the back did wonders for company morale.

As long as they were fed, exercised and knew exactly what was required of them, my men of Charlie Company were a match for any fighting troops in the world.

For me, those first few months as Charlie Nine, were heady days. I might not have wanted to be a soldier, but having adopted the military mode, I adapted to it like a pig in the proverbial. My rifle became an additional part of my anatomy and I wore the heavy pistol on my belt wherever I went. On occasion, I went out on patrol with various sections, 'enjoying' long, aching walks and the sweaty discomfort of lonely observation points. These outings were designed more to enhance my reputation with the men rather than in any anticipation of results, but they certainly increased my fitness.

Around us the war was increasing in both severity and barbarism. In my tented control room, I was kept continuously on the go, planning, briefing, debriefing and making instant decisions that really were a matter of life and death. Days merged into weeks and nights into days. Time ceased to have any meaning and I rarely had any idea of the date. As a company we were kept extremely busy. The operational area was in turmoil and sections on the ground followed spoor, kept observation on suspect kraals and had the occasional punch up with the enemy.

A few of these contacts were successful and our kill rate began to mount, but more often than not, they were fleeting exchanges of fire with figures vaguely seen over long distances. Casualties on either side were few but company medics were kept busy, treating injured or sick villagers and we usually used up our medical supplies long before the deployment was over. Once again it was the civilian population who were bearing the bunt of the war. Hardly a day went by when we were not required to deal with the aftermath of terrorist visits or indoctrination meetings. These invariably followed the same pattern. Terrs would move into a kraal after dark, demanding food and sometimes women for their edification. Posting amateur assistants or *mujibas*' as lookouts, they would make themselves at home before settling down to a few days of politicising the population.

To this end they would round up neighbouring villagers and hold a formal *pungwe* — a meeting where *Chimurenga* songs were sung and the virtues of Robert Mugabe and the Marxist ideal were loudly trumpeted. Ian Smith and his 'oppressive racist regime' were just as soundly vilified by the *vakomana*. The villagers would listen in silence, the words of hate burning like acid into their minds until the message was well and truly delivered. Those who expressed reservations were beaten or held up to ridicule. Recalcitrants were often murdered, sometimes horribly so.

One elderly kraalhead in Mondoro obviously put up strong resistance to the harangue of his visitors and suffered desperately for his loyalty to the ideals he had been brought up with. His eyes were burnt out with embers from the fire, he penis was cut off and he was flayed by degrees. A rugged old fellow, he took a long time to die and his weeping family were forced to witness his agony. Another man had his arms and legs broken before being tied out in the sun, unfed and unwatered until — unable to move — he died of thirst and dehydration.

Punishments were invariably meted out in front of relatives and friends. That way they acted as warning to others who might be tempted to defy the preaching of ZANLA and the men from Mozambique. We would enter a kraal to find residents sitting about in stunned apathy, their faces blank and pinched, their expressions drained of emotion. Children would stare mutely up at us, their eyes wide and vacant with the horror of what they had been forced to witness.

I think we all tried to close our minds to the death and destruction with which we were surrounded. To have allowed oneself to dwell upon the bloodshed would have been to invite madness and we hid our inner feelings behind facades of callous indifference or sick jokes. I was perhaps fortunate in that I saw less of the carnage on the ground than my men and I had a great deal of administrative work to take my mind off what was going on. To keep us all sane, I concentrated on building up company morale and set the men to competing with each other in everything they did.

In my reflective moments — scarce though they were — I realised that my attitudes were changing. In Macheke and Marandellas, my family and friends had been around to alleviate the daily horrors, but in my Mantle camp, I was surrounded by men who had been fighting constantly for years. I had no relief from the tensions of warfare and my state of mind was conditioned by the hard-bitten warriors around me. In short, I was becoming a soldier. I had my headquarter staff of radio operators, transport supervisor and clerk for company and in spite of all the horrors, I revelled in the responsibility that rested on my shoulders.

For a man who had only wanted to be an ordinary copper and had actively avoided involvement in the war, I was somewhat surprised to find that I was enjoying myself.

Like most of Africa, Rhodesia was a chauvinist society, but although men bore the brunt of the fighting, our women were the unsung heroes. Many of them spent as much time in uniform as their menfolk and a huge proportion of police administrative work fell fairly and squarely on the WFR. During the long weeks of lonely bush life, it was always cheering to hear friendly feminine voices on the radio and I know I wasn't the only one who fell regularly in love with disembodied voices. To this day, I think most of those wonderful ladies remain unaware of just how many admirers they had.

A number of women had also taken over jobs, hitherto reserved for men and it was no longer uncommon to find farmers' wives — usually festooned with firearms — supervising the planting, reaping and drying of crops. They dipped cattle, ferried livestock to market and paid watchful attention to prices on the tobacco floors. In the city many offices, shops and larger companies were run by women and as male teachers were called up with a greater frequency, the staff at some schools came to be entirely female.

Weapon training was as much part of a WFR's duty as it was for the men and a letter from Missy announced that her prowess with the rifle had elicited lavish praise from a former British army instructor. I felt very proud of her but I couldn't help hoping that her musketry classification wouldn't end up better than my own.

A humbler but infinitely more important role as far as we were concerned was carried out by the wonderful ladies who operated Forces' throughout the country. In these wayside eateries, servicemen could drop in for coffee, tea and cake or even a full-scale fry up at ridiculously low cost. The canteens were multiracial and having a white skin or wearing 'pips' on the shoulder wouldn't ensure preferential treatment. The women serving were always cheerful and I often called in to these establishments just for the sake of seeing a warm, feminine smile. It made all the difference when the war was getting me down. There was a song going the rounds for a while called 'Cammo clad Angel' and it was really rather apt. Our WFR might not have worn camouflage uniforms, but their drab grey dresses looked pretty glamorous to a man who had been starved of feminine company for weeks on end.

My number two in Charlie Company in those early days was Jonty Court, an earnest young man who if he noticed my military shortcomings, was far too polite to mention them. Jonty was a great help while I was struggling to find my feet and without pushing his own ideas forward, he guided many of my decisions and occasionally kept me from making a complete ass of myself.

After a few weeks in the Mondoro, new orders came through and Charlie Company moved to the Wiltshire — a tribal trust land adjoining an African purchase area. APAs were one step up from TTLs inasmuch that residents bought their own land where they grew crops and ran cattle or goats. We were based in Spurwing Farm on the edge of the TTL, where a once beautiful homestead had been abandoned to the tender mercies of successive Support Unit and army companies.

Spurwing was less than 100 kilometres from Marandellas, but the Wiltshire was an enemy stronghold. The population didn't like us and at any one time, there were upwards of 300 ZANLA cadres roaming the area. Through the years of war, Rhodesian Security Forces were to lose more men than they killed in that terrible little piece of real estate and Charlie Company provided a fair share of both.

My attitude to war wasn't the only part of my make up that was changing. I have always been a little too sensitive for my own good and prone to tears at the most inopportune moments. My mother always put this down to the artistic temperament, she was convinced I had, but my sensitivity was being blunted by the daily diet of horror and atrocity. Tears were giving way to anger and hate. I exulted in finding the enemy and felt a fierce sense of pride when any of my sections reported a kill. Cash bonuses from the troop fund were paid out to successful sections and slowly but surely Charlie Company began to creep up the kill table. To me it was almost like a game and I suppose such an attitude is necessary in times of war, but there were occasions, when I horrified myself

(Right) On parade the Black Boots could give the Brigade of Guards a run for their money.

(Left) Mine-protected transport at the Support Unit's Chikurubi Barracks. (Left to right) Hyena, three crocodiles, an Ojay/Kudu, a mine protected Land-Rover and another Hyena.

(Right) Mine-protected Land-Rover. Note the steel deflection plates fitted behind front wheels. Only the cab was protected.

(Left) Battle Camp at Shamva.

(Right) Crossing a river Black Boot-style.

(Left) Charlie Company being put through their paces.

(Right) Trooper going through assault course at Chikurubi Barracks.

(Left) Punishment drill. Sergeant Machisa looks on while offender sweats.

(Right) Sporting relaxation.

(Above) Operating in the bush. Note mortar-man in pit with Ojay/Kudu and three Hyena mine-protected vehicles in the background.

(Right) Typical bush camp.

(Below) Kit laid out for inspection in bush camp.

(Left and above) Morning parades in the bush.

(Right) multiracial Forces' canteens operated throughout the country. Just seeing a warming feminine smile made a big difference to the troops.

(Above) A Charlie Company Crocodile charges through a swollen river in Matabeleland.

(Right) Charlie Company raises its battle flag for the first time. The author didn't dare ask his men where they had obtained the flagpole.

(Below) Uplifting a call-sign in Matabeleland.

(Above) This Crocodile mine-protected vehicle detonated a landmine with its left front wheel. The occupants escaped unscathed.

(Left) Casevac!

(Right) Burying their dead with full military honours. The Support Unit pays their last respect to Sergeant Major Machanja who was killed in action.

(Left) Bishop Abel Muzorewa playing at being a 'freedom fighter'.

(Below) And his disastrous *Pfumo re Vanhu* — Spear of the People.

(Above) Signing the deal at Lancaster House.

(Left) Rapturous crowds welcome ZAPU leader Joshua Nkomo back home.

(Right) It's all over. Ian Smith and Robert Mugabe walk side-by-side into parliament.

(Left) A foolish school bus driver braved the Insiza River bridge at Filabusi while the river was in spate. The children were almost lost, but Charlie Company got them all to safety.

(Right) Bus is finally washed away.

(Left) Sergeant Mareve and Constable Majiga were each awarded silver batons for their bravery during the rescue.

(Top and left) During the Entumbane troubles in February 1981 when ex-ZIPRA fought ex-ZANLA and both fought the Security Forces. This comprised units of the former Rhodesian Security Forces including the RAR and Charlie Company Support Unit. Four of ZIPRA's BTR-152 Soviet-supplied armoured personnel carriers were knocked out during the fighting.

(Right) This civilian car also became a casualty.

(Left) This house was one of many damaged during the Entumbane fighting.

(Right) A similar mine-protected Hyena served as the author's staff car during the Entumbane fighting.

(Left) Sergeant Mataera admires the author's new issue truck. Leon Oosthuizen is sitting on the caravan's steps.

(Right) Robert Mugabe deploys his dreaded North Korean-trained 5th Brigade into Matabeland. Its mission was the genocide of the Ndebele people. It has been conservatively estimated that they murdered between 15 to 30 thousand Ndebele men, women and children. They called them the *Gukurahundi* and their murderous campaign was called the War of *Gukurahundi*.

(Left) In February 1982 extensive caches of arms of war were discovered on ZAPU properties. In this picture ZANU-PF Minister Emmerson Munangagwa is seen in conversation with police and army officers. The discoveries led to ZAPU MPs being expelled from Parliament and to Joshua Nkomo fleeing the country.

(Right) ZAPU dissidents killed by Zimbabwe's Security Forces. While South African-trained, armed and supported dissidents were indeed operating in Matabeleland, Robert Mugabe insisted that *all* Ndebeles were dissidents who had to be rooted out.

(Left) A 5-Brigade victim buried at the scene of crime in Tsholotsho where he was murdered.

(Right) A Tsholotsho man displays scars where 5-Brigade tortured him with burning plastic.

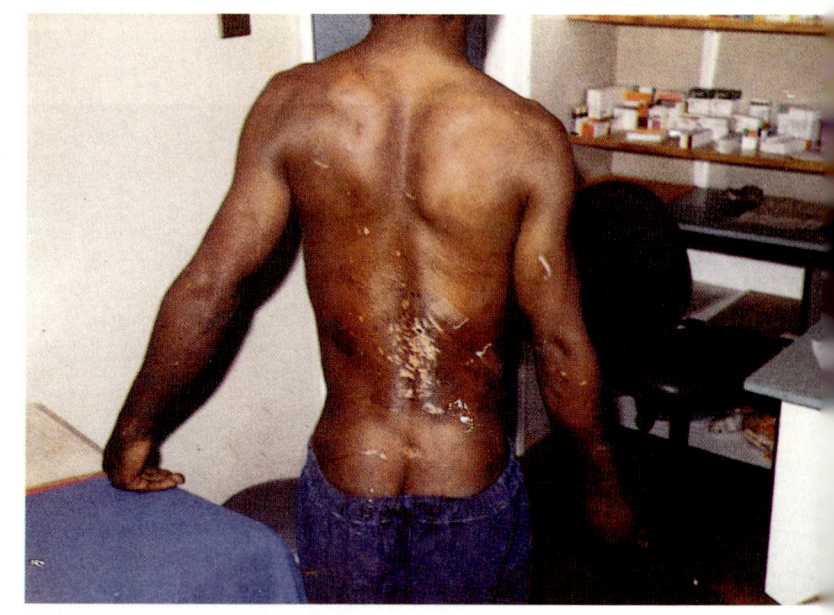

(Left) Women at Nkayi tortured by 5-Brigade for failing to speak Shona and objecting to their daughters being taken for sex. (Right) Her nose was cut off. (Centre) Her arm was broken and mutilated. (Left) Her fingers were hacked. Their husbands and two sons were shot dead. The soldiers ordered they be left to rot where they fell.

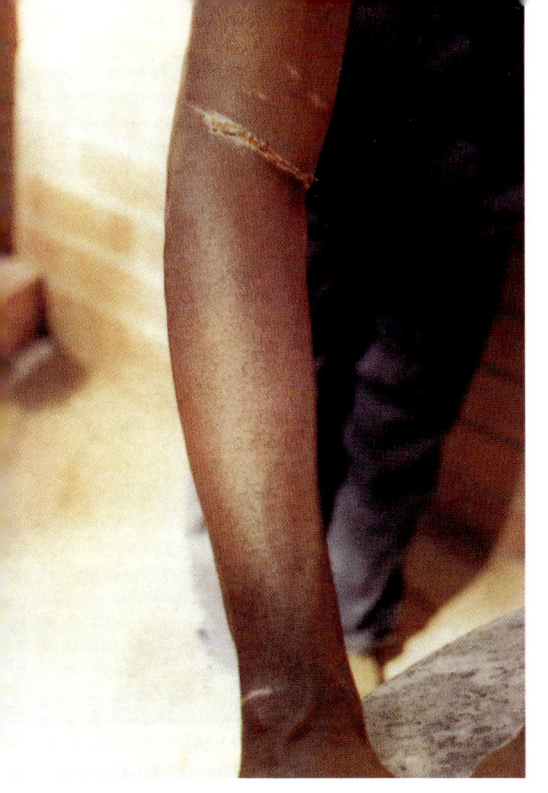

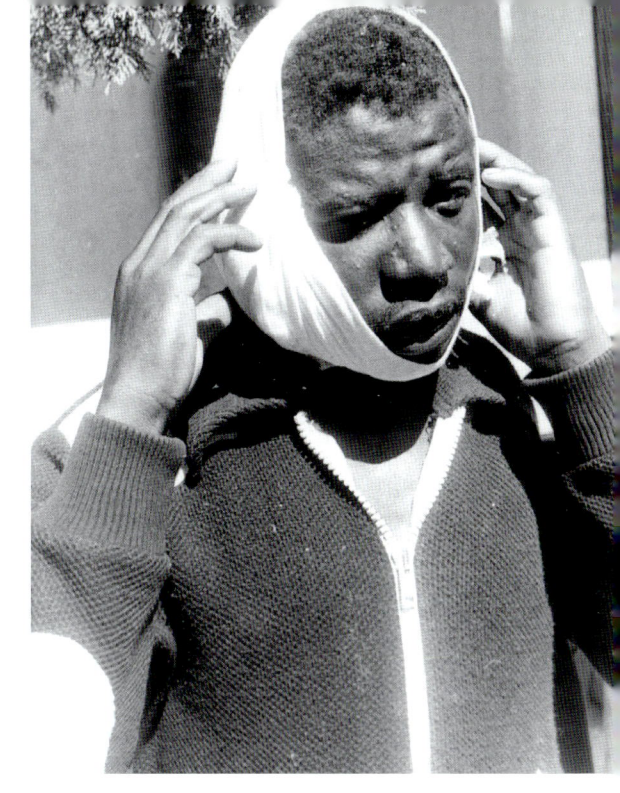

(Above left) This man suffered permanent paralysis in both forearms after 5-Brigade bound him with wire.

(Above right) Men claiming to be ZAPU dissidents (probably 5-Brigade on pseudo operations) hacked of this woman's ears and lips and ordered her husband and adult sons to eat them. The men were then ordered to dig a grave and were buried alive. These horrors were perpetrated in the presence of five children aged nine and under.

(Below) Bones of 5-Brigade victims excavated from the Old Hat Mine, Silobela.

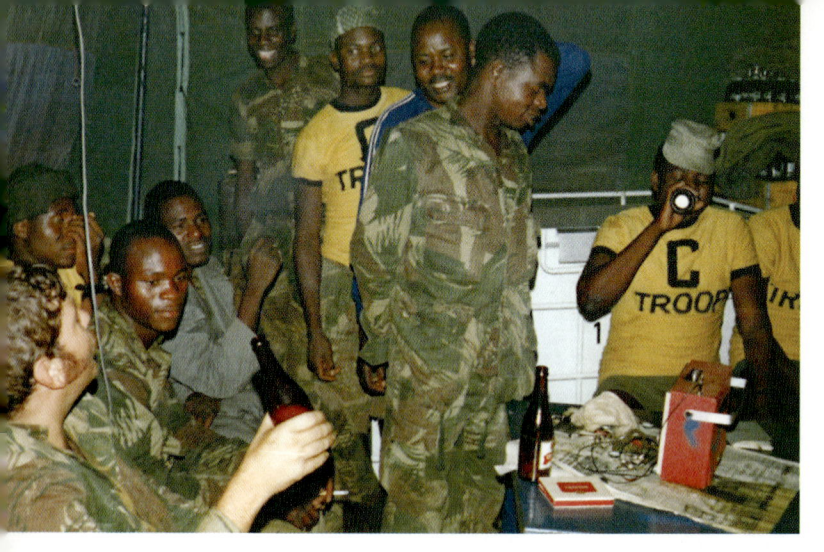

(Left) Black Boots' customary end of patrol celebration when much beer was drunk and T & S was issued.

(Right) Sergeant Mareve leads the celebrations after a football victory over Chisumbanje.

(Left) End of an era. Farewell party at Chikurubi. (L to R) Gus Albertson, Tony Merris, Don Rowland, Dave Callow, the author, Barry Woan.

with my own insensitivity.

I must have been about ten years old when I first fell in love — totally, blindly, sickeningly in love. The lady concerned was five years older than me so my love was unrequited, but we had remained friends over the years. In the late seventies she lived with her family on a farm outside Marandellas.

Matronly but still beautiful, Sandra was a born and bred Rhodesian with a low opinion of black people and a searing hatred for Mugabe and his terrorists.

'They should send us women into the front line', she rasped at me over a Sunday barbecue. 'We wouldn't handle the terrs with kid gloves like you blokes do. We would cut them into pieces and wear the bits as necklaces.'

I smiled at the imagery but Missy looked uneasy. In her quiet English way, she wasn't as bloodthirsty as true Rhodesians and worried about the future for us all. Sandra though was serious in her hate. With her husband and two brothers subject to call up, she was fed an ever-increasing diet of atrocity tales from the operational areas and thirsted for revenge. Even though I saw much of the carnage at first hand, I didn't feel quite as passionate as she did and couldn't help wondering what she would really do if she was ever faced by helpless terrorist or terrorist sympathiser.

'I'll bring you back an ear from our next kill', I offered facetiously. 'Then you can wear it around your neck.'

'You're on', she said and there was nothing facetious about Sandra's sentiments.

A short while later, she presented me with a small jar filled with gin.

'You can pickle the ear in that', she told me. 'I don't want it going bad before you get back.'

I duly took the pickling jar back to the Wiltshire with me and at the beginning of the patrol was laughing about it over dinner in the mess tent.

'So don't forget you fellows', I chuckled to my section leaders. 'I want an ear from your first kill.'

Three days later, one section was involved in a short but bloody contact with half a dozen terrorists. They killed two and when the fighting was over, the P/O in charge asked to speak to me on the radio.

'I've got your souvenir, Boss', he said and such were the moral depths to which I had sunk that I saw nothing reprehensible about the message.

'Good lad, bring it back with you and we'll put it in the jar.'

Sandra would be able to start her necklace.

The ear — nothing more than a strip of shrivelled flesh — was duly pickled in gin and eventually presented to the one-time love of my life. She didn't wear it around her neck as promised, but seemed pleased with the offering and possibly has it still among family heirlooms and souvenirs.

A terrorist war cheapens and demeans everyone it touches — even those not directly involved.

On 10th September, the Lancaster House conference opened in London but most

Rhodesians looked on with cynical amusement. We had seen it all before and few of us expected any cessation in the hostilities that were now part of daily life for all citizens, whatever their political sympathies.

For Charlie Company, Lancaster House made not a single jot of difference to the horrific excitement of our lives. The war went on unabated and we were an integral part of the conflict. As a field commander, I was in control of my own destiny and that of my men. We were given a section of countryside in which to operate and were usually the only troops in that particular area. How I arranged our fighting patrols was left to my discretion and it was an awesome responsibility, although I didn't think about that at the time. I passed positional grid references through to 151 each evening but these were never queried and I was left to do my own thing. Very occasionally, Badger or one of his henchmen would arrive on a routine visit and I would have to explain my actions, but these vastly more experienced fighting men seemed to approve of what I was doing.

With my lack of training or experience, I should have been way out of my depth but my confidence was growing by the day and I felt capable of dealing with anything.

Spurwing Farm had been abandoned by its owners after several terrorist attacks. It had been a beautiful place in its time and whenever I walked through the overgrown garden, I couldn't help wondering what the personal cost had been when the magnificent old house was abandoned to nature and the Security Forces. Not only had there been a swimming pool and tennis court, but the homestead had wonderful views, was beautifully decorated and even had a mirrored bathroom with a bidet.

Families had lived, loved and grown up in that house. Children had played the wild and silly games that farm kids do. Doting parents had dreamed of a peaceful, prosperous future and it must have been a wonderful spot in its heyday. Overgrown and battered, it now appeared terribly forlorn.

I had little time for maudlin thoughts, however. Having learned the lesson from my first day in command, I kept at least one five man section in camp and sometimes there were two or three. My caution was justified when we were attacked on three successive nights halfway through our first stay at Spurwing. On each occasion we were harassed rather than hurt and the attacks were easily beaten off, but the first one nearly brought my personal war to an abrupt end.

As company commander, I had commandeered a bedroom to myself and when the sound of gunfire brought me tumbling from my stretcher, I ran for the door. As I flung it open, some strange instinct of self-preservation made me slam it shut again. At that very moment, a rocket whooshed sickeningly past, the door was smashed open by the blast and I was hurled bodily across the room. A thunderous detonation followed and I was showered with plaster and tiny specks of shattered cement. The missile had missed the opening door by millimetres and detonated against a wall at the far end of the corridor. RPG rockets are primed to detonate on impact and had the nose cone of that hurtling projectile come into contact with my door, the whole thing would have gone up, vaporising me in the process.

Pulling myself shakily from the debris, I breathed a silent prayer of thanks to whichever

Deity was controlling Lemon's Luck. It seemed that He had been working overtime over the past few months.

Out in the Wiltshire, we were not quite so lucky. Constable Raminore took a bullet in the thigh, Sergeant Mandiwa died on a landmine with two colleagues from the Uniform Branch and Constable Ndhliwayo was murdered by terrorists while he was enjoying some well-earned occasional leave.

Like so many off duty members of the Security Forces, Ndhliwayo was denounced by fellow villagers and beaten to a bloody pulp, to die later from his injuries. Black society in Rhodesia was being torn apart by the conflict and neither soldiers nor policemen could afford to trust anyone on their infrequent visits to their home areas.

For me, the death of any of my men seemed terribly personal and I felt a deep sense of loss whenever Charlie Company suffered casualties. When Constable Nzou had his knee shot away in a contact, I was quickly on the scene with a medic and while he was being strapped up, I could feel his agony in my own limb. It wasn't so much the damage to his flesh that hurt me, but the raw shock and pain reflected in his eyes.

Another problem with casualties was that experienced men were replaced by raw recruits, adding to my administrative problems. The newcomers had to be carefully assessed by my senior staff before being assigned to a section and there was seldom time for an adequate appraisal. Nor was there room for passengers in the field and individual personalities had to be considered. On occasions, able-bodied men were kept in camp for weeks because I couldn't make up my mind who they would work best with. These were matters of routine and I could cope with them, but whenever I lost a man for any reason, I felt a deep sense of personal defeat.

To add to my manpower problems, Constable Kamasukiri suddenly declared himself possessed by the spirits and had to take time off for a visit with his family medium in Matabeleland. I was initially sceptical as Kamasukiri was notorious for his aversion to hard work, but older hands put me right. Problems with departed ancestors are by no means unusual among African fighting men and spirit mediums exerted enormous influence on both sides in our war.

Kamasukiri eventually returned fully rejuvenated and ready for anything. I was pleased to see him back.

In the midst of all the excitement, I still found time to play cricket. One memorable weekend, I drove home alone through the Wiltshire (another stupidly irresponsible risk) and turned out for a Marandellas team against the local high school.

Teenagers now, Brian and Graeme were also playing while Missy helped with teas, but my main memory of the game was the feeling of total unreality as we took the field in our white flannels. This was surely part of a different life to my daily diet of gunfire, exploding landmines and shattered bodies. I had the feeling that at any moment, I would wake up and find it had all been a dream.

Playing in that game was Kingsley Harris, an old friend who taught at the high school. A small man with a wry sense of humour, Kingsley was popular with parents and pupils alike. He and his wife Lynn lived in a smallholding outside town, only a few hundred metres from the spot where I had been ambushed on my late night return from Macheke. They had built their house themselves and as they only had a few hectares of land, concentrated on breeding bulls. It didn't bring in much money, but it supplemented Kingsley's salary and with their two small daughters, they were a happy family indeed.

On one of my later stints of R and R, we had Kingsley and Lynn around for lunch and during the afternoon, he and I had a serious discussion.

'I reckon they will come to an agreement this time', he was referring to the Lancaster House conference. 'Hopefully the war will end and . . . do you know what? I have never seen a gook . . . dead or alive.

'I've been on a number of call-ups', he went on thoughtfully. 'I live on a farm and Lynn spends much of her time working in the police station. For all that, neither of us has ever set eyes on what we are up against.'

Smiling somewhat enigmatically, he tapped his pipe out against a tree stump. In spite of the ever-escalating scale of the war, there were many Rhodesians in the same position as my friend Kingsley. We fought a shadowy enemy and for most folk, the battle was a vicarious one, seen only through the media and operational reports.

For Kingsley Harris, this state of affairs wasn't to last much longer. He saw his first terrorist only five days after our conversation. Driving home from school, Kingsley was alone when a ZANLA man stepped into the road and put a rifle grenade through his windscreen. So died a fine man who did his bit for the country he loved and was sincerely mourned by everyone who knew him. The pupils of Marandellas High School (including my sons) lost a fine teacher and Missy and I were both reduced to tears by his death.

But life went on and although I was allowed out of battle camp to attend Kingsley's funeral, it was a very short let up in my personal war. In the Wiltshire, our opposition was made up entirely of Robert Mugabe's ZANLA troops. Most of them had been trained in Tanzania and entered the country through the border with Mozambique. They obviously had the support of local people and were led by a man known only as Sachiweshe. His name cropped up regularly in SB memos but we knew nothing about him as a person. I studied every file I could lay my hands on and held long debriefs with my men after contacts, but for all my efforts, it was difficult to build up a mental picture of my enemy.

It was all very frustrating, but in the meantime I worked hard at being a soldier. By putting even more competition into our daily work, I managed to build up a great sense of personal pride in my men. With so many of the enemy around, the company kill rate continued to improve and Charlie Company came to be considered a crack outfit in the Mantle pecking order.

Missy made us a company battle flag in blue and gold and we flew this wherever we happened to be based. Coming in for R and R at the end of a patrol, we would assemble on the outskirts of Salisbury and I would lead the triumphantly singing convoy through the city, our flag flying and my men grinning all over their faces at the waves of pretty girls. This was the glamour side to a business that was anything but glamorous, but it promoted pride and self-confidence among the men. We were Charlie Company — the best — and my efforts to instil self-belief certainly had a beneficial effect as far as results were concerned.

The first night of R and R was always difficult for me. I would be in a hurry to get home to my family, but Support Unit tradition meant going on an immediate binge to celebrate successes and the boss was expected to be there. Missy and I still lived in Marandellas, nearly 80 kilometres from Chikurubi so I courted sobriety and in any case, my position dictated that I remain slightly aloof from the celebratory excesses of my troopers. My way of getting around this dilemma was to put a handful of banknotes into the kitty, stay for a couple of beers and leave before the party generated into hooliganism.

On one occasion, I mistimed my exit and was forced to look the other way when a laughing constable upended a waiter into a convenient dustbin. The waiter wasn't happy, but my blokes had just come through a long and difficult patrol, so I neglected my obvious duty — again.

There was only one occasion when I was genuinely bored in the Wiltshire and that was when it rained for three weeks. When I say 'rained', I mean it RAINED! For 24 hours a day, seven days a week, the rain bucketed down and when one is living in a tent that is not pleasant. A thick patina of mould covered everything and my little home smelled foul. My clothing was also pretty rank and dress standards slipped drastically throughout the company.

We had moved from Spurwing to a school near Featherstone, but the proximity of stone buildings didn't help. Our makeshift parade ground was under water, the wood boiler couldn't be lit and it was pointless to send patrols into the TTL. The terrorists wouldn't be patrolling and neither side would be able too see the other in all that driving rain.

My main problem lay in keeping the men out of mischief. Two sections slipped away to the Featherstone beer hall one evening and I was particularly severe in disciplining them. They ran, exercised, climbed and sweated — in the rain — until they could run, exercise, climb and sweat no more. One man passed out from the strain and another broke his leg, but I hardened my heart and kept them at it under the lashing tongue of the CSM. They also paid over a large portion of their T and S payments to the company fund and I think the lesson was learned.

It was instant justice and illegal under the Police Act, but I didn't care. It worked. Charlie Company made a profit and the offenders didn't end up with an official black mark on their record of service. Once they recovered from their exertions, the men soon forgot the pain and it seemed a very satisfactory result all round — apart from the broken leg of course.

The rain brought considerable discomfort as well as boredom and disciplinary problems to my life. Cold showers, damp shirts and mud baths are poor compensation for the normal regimented life of a fighting soldier and I briefly debated whether I could set my disgruntled troopers to building boats.

When Bishop Muzorewa took over as Prime Minister of Zimbabwe-Rhodesia, a number of his so-called freedom fighters came in from the bush to be assimilated with the Security Forces. They were formed into military units, separate from but allegedly working in conjunction with regular forces on the ground. Ndabaningi Sithole's men were formed into similar units and a group of them moved into Spurwing when we pulled out.

Known as *Pfumo re Vanhu* — spear of the people — these young men were hardly impressive. One or two might have made passably decent soldiers, but the majority were thugs, pleased to have a uniform, a monthly pay cheque and an easy life. The Support Unit was given the responsibility of training them and although I wasn't involved in that particular exercise, I had two *Pfumo* camps under my command in the Wiltshire. I was under instructions not to use the men from Spurwing Farm, but I did deploy the other lot on a couple of occasions. They caused so many problems with the local populace that I soon found it expedient to leave them in their base where they seemed content to lie around and do nothing.

After a few weeks of having this rabble on our doorstep, reports began filtering in of rapes, murders and general pillaging among Wiltshire villages. This seemed to be criminal rather than political and was in direct contrast to what had gone before. The entire area had long been subverted to the ZANLA cause and the terrorists no longer needed to rob, rape and pillage. Everything they wanted was given freely to ZANLA, so it seemed clear that the new outbreak of criminal activity could only be put down to *Pfumo* re Vanhu.

I spoke to Badger about the matter but he told me to be patient and leave both camps alone. The area around Spurwing Farm was suddenly frozen and shortly afterwards, the sound of pitched battle could be heard all over the Wiltshire. I don't know how many of Sithole's men died in that engagement, nor am I sure exactly who it was that attacked them, but the survivors — and there weren't many — were bussed out of the district and that lovely farm was abandoned once again.

It surely couldn't have been coincidental, but reports of atrocities in the Wiltshire also died down. The other camp remained however and on one occasion I paid a routine visit with Sergeant Dube, a hard-bitten Matabele who had one brother fighting for ZANLA and another with Nkomo. I was speaking to him about it on the way to the *Pfumo* camp.

'What would you do if you met up with either of them? What would you talk about?'

Dube smiled wolfishly at my naivety.

'We wouldn't talk', he said. 'We would kill. While there is *hondo*, we are enemies and must kill each other.'

Dube walked beside me as we entered the camp and his expression of outrage measured my disgust at the squalor that surrounded us. The camp was indescribably filthy and individual 'spears' lolled about the buildings in various degrees of half-dressed inebriation. They gazed at us with hostile eyes and I felt as though I was walking into a pen full of stray dogs — flea-bitten; watchful and ready to rip us to shreds at the first opportunity.

The slovenly inactivity of the camp would have delighted Sachiweshe had he chanced on it. In spite of the formidable weaponry they had at their disposal, these men hardly threatened the enemy and I had the feeling that they would run for their lives at the first sign of danger.

Personally, I didn't care whether the Bishop's gangsters lived or died, but while they were under my command, they were going to look like soldiers, even if they couldn't behave that way.

Prodding a dozing orderly in the ribs with my rifle, I called for the camp commander, only to be told that he was away for the weekend with his second-in-command. Controlling my impatience, I asked for whoever was in charge and a few minutes later was confronted by a scruffy individual with huge shoulders and a torn shirt. Chewing gum with his mouth open, he eyed me with surly insolence. Feeling ever more irate, I demanded to know why the camp was in such a filthy state.

Looking me up and down with studied contempt, the *Pfumo* leader wanted to know my justification for asking. He put it in baser terms but that was the general gist of his question.

'I am your field commander and responsible for everything that goes on in this camp.'

I doubtless sounded pompous but my temper was rising by the moment. Other grinning *Pfumo* had gathered to watch the fun and I didn't like the situation.

'We don't take orders from you', the big man sneered. 'We are not your capitalist lackeys, to be spat on and made to do the white man's bidding whenever he calls.'

In all my years as a Rhodesian policeman, it was the first time I had encountered blatantly racist hostility from a member of the Security Forces. In police and army units, black and white worked together in harmony and relations were invariably good-humoured. To have this thug — probably with the blood of innocents on his hands — speak to me like this was too much for my over-strained nerves.

I had been holding my rifle below waist level with one hand on the barrel and the other gripping the stock. It wasn't a conscious pose, but it proved ideal in the circumstances. Moving without thinking, I smashed the heavy stock upwards, catching Chummy full on the jaw and hurling him backwards. There was an immediate murmur of hostility from the men around me and I was suddenly aware that Sergeant Dube and I were alone among a few hundred potentially dangerous men. If they felt like it they could tear us apart. It was a nasty moment but in the sudden silence, I heard Dube ease the working parts of his rifle backwards. They clattered harshly into the cocked position and the raw sound immediately defused the situation.

'Pick him up and have him taken to Enkeldoorn Hospital', I said shortly to the men around me. 'When I return this evening, I want to see this whole camp spick and span.'

When I returned, the camp was indeed spick and span, but this time I had a full escort at my back, including the giant Totohwiyo with an MAG. My impromptu inspection went off smoothly and the camp commander later apologised for the trouble caused during his absence.

The lout I had clobbered was treated for a broken jaw, but somewhat surprisingly was good as gold when I met him again and almost became a worthwhile 'spear of the people.' Although I had horrified myself with my own brutality, I was learning that in many situations it was the only answer. The war was debasing us all and ultimate survival lay in being stronger and more vicious than one's enemies.

I had some marvellous characters among those hard men of Charlie Company. The CSM and I didn't get on, which was a pity but my sergeants included Dube and Mareve, totally opposite in appearance, but doughty fighters and inspirational leaders. My transport man was Constable Matambashora, a bespectacled 'professor' who managed to keep our ageing vehicles on the road and ready for action in the most difficult circumstances. Mudakureva and Hobe were both constables of above average intelligence and at the other end of the intellectual scale was Augustine 'Totohwiyo. 'Totohs' was no mental heavyweight, but he more than made up for that with incredible strength and the heart of a lion. He seemed to look on me as a teacher on a pupil who has done surprisingly well and I was always reassured to see the big man close by when danger threatened.

Constable Ncube was another comforting character to have around. Built like a piece of uncovered wire, he could track a spider over bare rock and had a laughing unconcern for danger which inspired his colleagues. Other leading lights among the men were Sergeant Mataera, almost as old — and twice as noisy — as me and Constable Makanda who had the voice of an angel and always led the singing on the morning run. Sergeant Major Chiromo was another great character and I often reflected on my luck at having inherited such a fine bunch of men. We were all proud to be members of Charlie Company and none was prouder than I was. As Charlie Nine I was a happy man in spite of the circumstances.

The one place where my metamorphism into a fighting soldier didn't go down well was at home. With my long absences, Missy was developing her own circle of friends and inevitably, they were not my sort of people. The regular round of Marandellas parties still went on and now that I was no longer part of the 'in crowd', I became hypocritically disapproving of their activities. As far as I was concerned, they were living the good life while people were dying in the operational areas and that wasn't right.

Missy's reminders that I had enjoyed the parties just as much myself only a short time before were undoubtedly justified, but I was restless at home and didn't want to settle down to routine. With Missy working and the kids at school, there was little for me to do on my R and R except drink and this I did to excess. I found it difficult to sleep at night and family life was disintegrating under the pressure of my aggressive moodiness.

It was almost a relief to drive back into Chikurubi after my eight days off, accept the salutes of the guards and know that I was back among my own. I loved my family but Charlie Company had become a more exciting substitute for life at home.

The Lancaster House conference brought more disciplinary problems to my working life. While the talks were in progress, all time off was cancelled for those of us in the field. Week succeeded week without a break and the tension began to tell on us all. This led to dissension among the men and I could feel myself becoming ever more tired and irritable. One young constable blew a hole in his foot with an accidental discharge and although I felt the incident was deliberate, there was nothing I could do about it.

On another occasion a knife fight broke out between two experienced constables and

I settled that by putting them into boxing gloves and having them whale seven bells out of each other with me as the referee. More serious was the disappearance of two new recruits. It was eventually presumed that they had deserted and gone across to the enemy, but we never saw them again and their disappearance upset me.

We followed progress in London as best we could, but it was the usual comedy of acrimonious ranting and farcical argument. Margaret Thatcher and Lord Carrington seemed intent on washing their hands of Zimbabwe-Rhodesia as soon as they could. Like businessmen in trouble, they were cutting their losses and putting the best possible face on their own treachery. A little nation that still looked up to Britain was being left to sink or swim on her own and the Brits were obviously determined that the sinking or swimming would be controlled by Nkomo and Mugabe. My own bitterness mounted as pressure against our elected leaders increased.

To my mind, this abandonment of my country was the real obscenity of colonialism. The occupation of any country is a necessary part of evolution and conquest has always been the way nations are born and developed. In the process, countries grow and adapt until they become worthwhile members of the world community. To throw all this away for the sake of vaguely understood liberal ideals was to demean history and the efforts of everyone involved.

The original annexation of Rhodesia had undoubtedly been unfair and no doubt exploitation had been a major part of the country's development, but colonising any country surely imposes certain duties on the nation taking over. Britain — justly famous through the years for upholding the virtues of fair play — was abandoning her responsibilities, just as she had abandoned them elsewhere in Africa. Callously leaving ordinary Rhodesians to the whim of rulers without experience of governing was cold-blooded cruelty.

Evidence of British heartlessness was easy to see in the poverty of life north of the Zambezi. Margaret Thatcher's determination to reduce my country to the same abject state was obvious. It seemed that the easiest way for her to solve the Rhodesian problem was to get rid of it, just as Pontius Pilate did on another memorable occasion in history. In my mind I cursed her, Carrington and their craven henchmen for abdicating their responsibilities and thereby condemning a few million loyal citizens to an unknown and unpromising future. Events in the Wiltshire merely served to emphasise my bitterness.

Civilians living on the edge of the TTL had hitherto been free from terrorist depredation, presumably in recognition of assistance they gave to the liberation cause. Better off financially than the average tribesman, purchase area farmers led a privileged life and their support was necessary for the *vakomana*.

One family must have faltered in this support or offended one of the terrorist leaders, because we found them hacked to pieces outside their looted house. Father, mother, five children and sundry elderly relatives — every one had been cruelly done to death and even the most hardened of my troopers was sickened by the carnage. Once again I was reminded — as if I needed reminding — that ours wasn't a conventional war. We were fighting an enemy who were overpoweringly evil. I was still a copper at heart and I tried to behave with a certain amount of honour, but there were no rules in this conflict and by sticking to convention, I was merely hastening our inevitable defeat.

It is a sad fact of life that — whatever the Good Book says — evil will always triumph over good when it comes to a stand up fight.

Another vicious murder that hit me personally was the death of our company cook. Old William came from the Mondoro and when he asked for a few days off to attend a family funeral, I warned him of the dangers. Charlie Company had recorded a number of kills in Mondoro and feelings would still be running high against us but William was determined to go. He was denounced and shot in the head at a beer drink.

It wasn't only his culinary expertise that was missed. William had been a cheerful old boy, ruling the batmen with a rod of iron and mothering my patrol officers, even cleaning up after them and chiding them when their table manners seemed to be deteriorating. With his death, we needed another cook. I asked the CSM to make enquiries, but he pointed out that potential recruits from the Wiltshire were just as likely to poison us all. There were a number of captured *mujibas* in camp at the time and one of them offered his services as a cook. I wasn't originally impressed.

Daniel Machipisa was an incredibly ugly young man, with one eye and a face badly disfigured in a childhood accident. It wasn't his looks that put me off however. Daniel was also one of the dirtiest and most unhygienic young men I had ever come across. Nevertheless, we needed a cook, so Daniel Machipisa took over the kitchen until we could find a suitable replacement.

Mujibas were youngsters used as scouts by the enemy. They ranged in age from eight to 18 and worked in the countryside as lookouts and spies, inconspicuous while tending cattle and worth their weight in gold as extra eyes to those who were ravaging the land.

Occasionally we would pick up some of these lads for interrogation but they seldom gave us any worthwhile information. In the terrorist hierarchy, they were the lowest of the low and not party to anything useful as far as we were concerned. After we had finished with them, many stayed on in camp for a while, often claiming that they were scared to go home.

I was a little cynical about this excuse. With us, these lads were well fed and cosseted so for many of them, life in a Black Boot camp was infinitely preferable to living at subsistence level in their own kraals. A few might even have looked upon themselves as continuing their duties inside the camp, but we ensured that they learned nothing that could be of use to the enemy.

Daniel Machipisa was a *mujiba* with a difference. Born in the Mrewa area, his disfigurement resulted from an accident with fire as a baby, but he was an intelligent young man. Surprisingly well read for a boy who had lived his life in a TTL, he originally asked to work for me as an informer. I shooed him away with a laugh, but he pleaded for the chance to prove his worth and eventually, I gave him 25 cents and told him to get lost.

I didn't expect to see Daniel again but a few days later he was back with a conspiratorial grin lighting up his ravaged features. To keep him happy, I sat him down for a debrief and passed the information he gave me to SB at Enkeldoorn. Two days later, three ZANLA men were killed by army patrols in the Wiltshire and it was Daniel's information that led to the contact. I immediately put him up for a government reward. Substantial payments were being handed out at the time and many terrorist leaders had money on their heads. Sachiweshe himself was worth a cool $5 000, dead or alive and in those days that was a small fortune.

My request on Daniel's behalf was turned down by the local JOC on the grounds that people like him were wastrels, seeking favour from both sides. In this they were undoubtedly correct but the information had been good and I felt that my funny little *mujiba* deserved a reward. Informing on anyone in wartime carries a serious degree of risk and if we wanted to encourage others, we had to make it worth their while.

My protests fell on deaf ears, so I rewarded Daniel with beer, food and a few dollars before sending him out again. For weeks he wandered the area, a scruffy, demented-looking figure, easily recognisable and ever cheerful. He brought in snippets of information that never amounted to much and I often wondered whether he was doing the same for the opposition. He seemed to lead a charmed life and the only apparent danger he faced was provided by the uniformed police.

On three occasions Daniel was locked up for drunken brawling and I was called upon to get him out. Charges would be dropped at my request and he would be released into my care, only to offend again and end up in the same cells a short while later. Remembering my Kariba brushes with Ron Reid Daly and his hooligans, I couldn't help marvelling at the way my ideals had turned full circle over the years.

Now Daniel wanted to be our cook. The thought appalled but we needed somebody to prepare food for the senior mess and there was no alternative. So it was that Daniel Machipisa — after being thoroughly washed and disinfected — was let loose in Charlie Company's kitchen. If ever his bona fides were established, that was the time. At first, the dishes he served up were so disgusting that liberal doses of strychnine would probably have improved them, but we coached him patiently and in time, he improved and almost became proficient with a frying pan. What he lacked in culinary expertise, Daniel made up for with sheer good humour and he was invariably cheerful, even under verbal attack from outraged diners.

'You are a bloody "*magookoo*", Machipisa', someone shouted at him after a particularly horrible repast — that being the word Daniel himself used to describe any member of the opposition. 'You're trying to poison us for your ZANLA friends.'

But verbal attack never worried Daniel. With a resigned shrug and a grimace of his ravaged face that was really a smile, he would repair to his smoky kitchen and return with the offending dish allegedly improved. Nothing upset him and for all the uncomplimentary remarks that were passed about his lack of talent, we were all rather fond of Daniel Machipisa.

But young men like Daniel are men of restless spirit and one day he approached me with the news that he wanted to go home. Mrewa was one of the areas having a hard time in the war and he wanted to see his family.

'When will you be back?'

I wrote out a note that might prevent him running into undue difficulties with Security Forces and shrugging skinny shoulders, Daniel gave me that funny, twisted smile I had come to know so well.

'Some time, perhaps.'

I knew we were going to need another cook and felt as though I was bidding farewell to an old friend. Very much a *mujiba* with a difference was Daniel Machipisa. I often wonder whether he survived the war.

I think we were all astonished when the Lancaster House conference ended in unexpected agreement. On 12th December 1979, Lord Soames arrived in Salisbury as the new British governor and Rhodesia's long rebellion against the Crown was over. On 21st December — seven years to the day since the attack on Altena Farm — Zimbabwe-Rhodesia once again became the British colony of Southern Rhodesia. Mugabe, Nkomo and the Bishop signed agreement for a cease-fire and an amnesty was declared for all combatants. Britain and the UN Security Council immediately lifted sanctions and our little country was back among the recognised nations of the world.

Details of the proposed cease-fire were announced and we learned that 'free and fair' elections were to be held early in the New Year. These would be overseen by British and Commonwealth monitors and that part of the announcement was met with hollow laughter by Rhodesians. Any elections would be held at the barrel of a gun, no matter which observers were present.

On the other hand, any cessation of hostilities was welcome, as we couldn't afford to keep going much longer. Our equipment was worn out; our vehicles were almost impossible to repair or replace; our manpower shortage became more critical by the day and morale — particularly among the civilian population — was at an all time low. We were a defeated nation trying to keep ourselves alive in impossible circumstances.

When the agreement was announced in early December, most of us involved in the fighting felt that whatever else, it would give us a breathing space and a chance to regroup. Like many of my compatriots, I still had confidence in our national leaders and didn't think we could possibly be let down again.

Not for the first time was I being naive.

19

Cease-fire

An official cease-fire was set down for the first few days of the New Year and the Support Unit was tasked with overseeing it. The details were simple but seemingly unrealistic. ZANLA and ZIPRA forces would come in from the bush and stay in designated assembly points dotted around the country. They would be allowed to keep their weapons and would be looked after in the camps by British and British Commonwealth troops, brought in for the occasion.

Because we were still officially policemen and presumably more trustworthy than our military colleagues, we were given the unenviable task of keeping the Brits safe from their charges. The major problem with this arrangement was that we were required to remain unseen, presumably to avoid giving offence to the *vakomana*.

Charlie Company was given two assembly points to look after. Papa was in the Magunje TTL outside Sinoia and Romeo was at a long abandoned research station, deep in the Zambezi Valley. I did an air recce with a Police Reserve Air Wing over Rekommetjie and quite apart from the fact that we were shot at from the Valley floor and our army observer was sick all over the plane, I decided that it was one AP that would prove impossible to protect.

The research station was surrounded by thick bush, teeming with wildlife and if I put my blokes in nearby, they would be more afraid of wandering lions than the enemy. I couldn't help wondering at the lack of common sense displayed by the faceless bureaucrats who chose such a spot and then expected us to sort things out. Even a brief look at the map would have showed that the location was completely impractical.

I suppose that by then I should have been used to it.

There was at least one group of terrorists in the Wiltshire who had not heard about the cease-fire, or perhaps they were even more prone to doubt than the rest of us.

We were based at another abandoned Enkeldoorn farm and had been having serious trouble with the borehole. I was hot, sweaty and disgruntled, so when Jack Simons heard of a ZANLA section occupying a remote kraal line, I went along to check it out. The cease-fire wasn't yet in practical effect, but there had been a noticeable decrease in terrorist activity since the plans had been announced.

With my usual naivety, I had not been expecting trouble but had become soldier enough to take a six-man patrol with me. They were led by Constable Totohwiyo who I had recommended for promotion to lance sergeant. Totohs would never pass a written examination, but he was respected by his colleagues and would make a fine NCO. Field promotions had become commonplace and I was looking forward to presenting the big fellow with his stripes.

We moved in on the kraal line well before first light and as the sun rose, advanced through waist-high scrub in extended line. Peace might have been at hand but my stomach was suddenly tight with nervousness and I was grateful for the hulking presence of my would-be sergeant, 15 metres to my right. The MAG looked like a toy in his hands and he was a comforting sight.

The fire when it came was frighteningly loud. I don't know whether the initial burst was aimed at me as the only white face in the section, but I distinctly heard the whiplash crack of bullets flying past my head. The earth came up to meet my dive and as always, breath was smashed from my body by the impact. I heard my colleagues returning fire and beyond them, the awful, high-pitched chatter of a RPD light machine gun. Like the song of a laughing devil, it echoed into the distance and I cautiously raised my eyes from the ground to see where it was coming from.

Away to my right, I could hear the classic double-tap of friendly fire and suddenly realised that my nervousness had gone. It was as though with the advent of action, my mind had accepted that the battle was on and there was nothing to be gained by fear. My heart pounded but it was with excitement and I searched eagerly for a target. I wanted to kill. I longed to add to my personal score of dead men and looked forward with relish to reporting more kills on the evening sitrep.

The opposition were no longer human beings. I thought of them as 'scores' rather than men with feelings, emotions, mothers and perhaps children of their own. It was almost as though I was back on the cricket field, determined to score more runs and take more wickets. There was nothing personal in my feelings. I wasn't killing people; I was adding to my tally and in my adrenalin-charged excitement, could no longer tell the difference. I never considered the possibility that I might be killed myself and if I had, would have probably dismissed it as irrelevant in that totally unreal situation.

Had there been time to reflect, I might have marvelled at the change in me. Where had the dedicated copper gone? I had taken an oath to preserve life and was this urge to kill, part of the same man who cried at road accidents or was reduced to heartbreak by the futility of domestic disputes? None of it made sense but I suppose it was part of the horror that is a civil war.

Across open ground in front of me, little puffs of red soil advanced in a rapid line and my face was back in the earth, gritty dust scratching against my teeth. I hadn't heard the RPD coming back into the action, but the dust puffs had been awfully close and this time there could be no doubt — they were directed at me.

The thunder of gunfire ceased abruptly — almost as though some unseen conductor had made the ritual cut with his baton. I was vaguely aware of high-pitched voices from a distant kraal and marvelled that life still went on in the rest of the world. Around me, heads came up and the men looked at each other with the blank-eyed expression I had come to recognise as the aftermath of battle. I probably looked the same. With a determined effort, I pulled myself together.

'Do the roll call Totohs', I called softly and listened while each man reported himself intact and gave an estimation of the ammunition he had left. Nobody had been hurt and when we swept through the enemy position, we found no trace of blood so the contact had been a complete waste of time and nervous energy for all concerned. In that, it was typical of guerrilla warfare. A brief and noisy meeting between opposing forces, then both sides retire to regroup and swap ever more extravagant reports on the incident with their mates. It is only civilians who suffer in a terrorist war. Exposed to the excesses of both sides, they are helpless and have nowhere to hide.

Turning to Totohwiyo, I was about to issue instructions for withdrawal when he grinned broadly and pointed to my right shoulder.

'Too close that one, *Mambo* — too close by half.'

When I saw what he was talking about, I felt a sudden urge to sit down. I was wearing 'slip on' rank badges over my shirt and a bullet had somehow passed between my shoulder and the relevant epaulette. One entire pip had been neatly removed and I had been very lucky indeed. It was difficult to work out the path taken by that particular round and I eventually put the narrow escape down to Lemon's Luck and a freakish ricochet. But it had been far too close for comfort.

In time, my sons stuck the ruined epaulette on their wall as an example of the Old Man's good fortune, but every time I looked at it I couldn't help wondering how long my incredible luck could possibly last.

I had always impressed upon my band of uniformed thugs that although they might steal from all and sundry, they should refrain from doing the same to fellow Black Boots. After all there has to be some sort of *esprit de corps* in a regular outfit and if everyone is thieving from everyone else, it cannot work. It seemed that other companies didn't share my sense of honour among thieves.

For a while we shared our makeshift base on the farm with Bravo Company and although the higher ranks messed together and stayed in the homestead, the troops from each company were kept resolutely apart. Andy Gray was commanding Bravo and he was vastly more experienced in Black Boot ways than I was. When the order came to move out to our respective assembly point areas, there was frantic packing of kit and equipment with the CSMs keeping a wary eye out for theft, but Andy concentrated on his breakfast. As I was leaving first to find a suitable base in Sinoia, I had my Land-Rover and trailer driven to the front of the house while I cleared up the last bit of paperwork. Andy merely smiled at my zeal and enjoyed an extra slice of toast.

Finally bidding him farewell and good luck, I went out to my truck, only to discover that the tow-hitch pin had disappeared and my trailer was therefore immobile. I knew that my own blokes wouldn't have taken the damned thing so the culprit had to be from Bravo. I threw an instant tantrum. Striding back into the house I demanded retribution from my fellow commander and the thief's head on a plate. Andy merely laughed and waved me away.

'You are a Black Boot now', he murmured laconically. 'Dry your eyes and have some tea.'

There is only one antidote to that sort of thieving and when I returned to my sorely afflicted vehicle, the CSM approached with a big smile and a replacement pin.

'Where did you find it?' I demanded and he grinned.

'Don't ask, *Mambo*', was his advice. 'Just be happy that you have a hitch pin.'

Leaving the farm before anything else could go amiss, I couldn't help reflecting that I still had a lot to learn about life in the Support Unit.

Rekommetjie Research Station seemed like an ideal place to house a few thousand of the enemy but the only access road was a little-used dirt road and the closest place to position a clandestine reaction stick was 12 kilometres away. Reaction time would be at least 40 minutes in ideal conditions and this was the rainy season so conditions would be far from ideal.

However, those who knew best had accepted my positioning and I abandoned my worries. My concern was for the safety of my own men rather than the British. Like everyone else involved, I didn't think the cease-fire exercise would work anyway.

Magunje was far more suitable and once we had chosen an abandoned school as siting for the AP, I was able to place a section close enough to arrive within minutes should trouble erupt.

In the fortnight leading up to Christmas, I set up a company base on another farm outside Sinoia and settled down to enjoy the festive season. We had one brief skirmish with a ZANLA group who obviously hadn't heard or didn't care about cease-fire or settlement proposals, but I was able to allow my blokes their first time off in a very long time, albeit on a staggered basis. In the meantime, I made liaison visits to Kariba and Chirundu, went game watching in the abandoned park at Mana Pools and enjoyed a number of reconnaissance flights over the Valley with the Police Reserve Air Wing (PRAW). It all seemed somehow dreamlike, but I was enjoying myself.

On Christmas Eve, I took British army representatives out to the sites, selected as Assembly Points and although we were not supposed to discuss politics, they seemed as uncertain as I was about the cease-fire exercise. In spite of my misgivings, I couldn't help feeling sorry for these pasty-faced soldiers. They were in an alien environment and on a hiding to nothing if things did go wrong.

One young officer in an Irish regiment summed up the situation.

'The Taffies won seven Victoria Crosses at Rorkes Drift', he commented languidly. 'If the wheels fall off with this one, we should do even better, although most of them will probably be posthumous.'

For all of us it was a time of considerable tension.

But as history will show, the cease-fire exercise didn't fail. Much to my surprise, ZANLA and ZIPRA — heavily reinforced by *mujibas* — flocked into the camps and there was little trouble. The only British casualties occurred in road accidents and the only problems encountered by my reaction sections were nocturnal visits by a pride of lions.

I managed to offend a British colonel by refusing to take his men into Rekommetjie until the day after that laid down for occupation, but that was his own fault for delaying our departure time from Salisbury. He seemed out of touch with African travel conditions and we didn't leave the city until well after midday. I wasn't prepared to tackle that wild Valley road in darkness, so we night-stopped at Makuti where the police pub did a roaring trade among Black Boots, British soldiers, journalists and former terrorists.

In spite of the circumstances, we had one hell of a party. I normally insisted on my men remaining teetotal in the field but it was Christmas, we were on the verge of defeat and I wasn't happy with my lot. I relaxed the restriction and everyone enjoyed himself to excess. When we set off for Rekommetjie at first light, I had a monumental hangover and was even more irritable than usual. We carried a ZIPRA liaison officer with us and I made sure that he travelled in the front of my Land-Rover with one of the Brits. If I was going up on a landmine — as seemed highly probable — I was going to have international company.

We didn't hit any landmines and although subsequent press reports stated that our convoy was repeatedly stopped by elephants on the road, this was reporters (themselves seriously hung over) indulging in journalistic licence. We did stop repeatedly on the way in, but breakdowns rather than jumbos caused the halts. Our ancient vehicles struggled on that bush road and I shuddered at the thought of reacting to an emergency in such conditions.

For me, the only bright spot to the cease-fire exercise was that I was able to enjoy both Christmas Day and New Years Eve with my family for the first time in 15 years.

20

Soldiers of the Bishop

One part of the cease-fire exercise that I did enjoy was the reaction of local people in the Sinoia area. Black and white alike greeted us with smiling faces and unfailing curiosity, which was in marked contrast to the sullen, unhelpful attitude of folk in the Wiltshire. What I found curious was that local nationalist sympathies were with Nkomo rather than Mugabe, even though the latter was almost a local boy, having been born and brought up in the Zwimba area.

But everything was changing, so I wasn't particularly surprised when Badger One flew out with Barry Woan to address the company. I called Fred Mason 'the Brylcream Colonel.' If ever I saw a fighting man, totally in love with his own — admittedly dashing — appearance, it was Fred. His camouflage always had the correct degree of fade and his hair was impeccably groomed. He rarely spent nights in the field, preferring to fly rather than use a Land-Rover, presumably because it gave him time to get back to the comfort of the bright lights before nightfall.

Perhaps I am being unfair to the man, but his languidly foppish manner tended to grate, particularly when we were in the middle of a difficult deployment.

Be that as it may, Fred gave us a rousing speech, fervently extolling the virtues of Bishop Muzorewa and denouncing Mugabe as little more than a rabid dog. It seemed that our only chance of ultimate survival as Rhodesians lay with the Bishop, so we were being detached from normal duties in the weeks leading up to the election, purely and simply so that we could electioneer on Muzorewa's behalf. This was against everything I had been taught as a policeman and I sourly informed Fred that I was a copper not a 'bloody political agent', which didn't go down well at all.

The debonair chief superintendent ended his speech by reassuring the whites present that there was no need for panic and that he personally would be sticking it out right to the end.

'I'll be the fellow who switches out the lights', he said theatrically and I couldn't help the cynical thought that he would probably be the first to leave. Again I was probably being unfair but I wasn't too far from the mark. Badger One wasn't the first of our senior officers to take the gap, but less than a year after that speech to Charlie Company, he was living in Britain. Those of us he had so earnestly exhorted to stand firm were yet again up to our necks in muck and bullets.

But once again I am jumping ahead of my narrative.

Inevitably we were sent to the Wiltshire to do our electioneering and my protests that the area was long since lost to the Rhodesian cause were ignored. Before going back however, I was instructed to detach one of my troops and join the Rhodesian Defence Regiment and local police reservists to hunt down a terrorist group in Wedza.

Although the operation was spectacularly unsuccessful (the only casualty on either side was a coloured soldier shot in the backside) I enjoyed myself. Not only was I in command, but I controlled the scene from the top of Wedza Mountain and for once I could ride roughshod over the farming community.

I had turned out as a guest for Wedza Cricket Club on numerous occasions and knew most of the local personalities. They wielded considerable political influence and I was expecting trouble. This was another community like Macheke, but I was no longer an ordinary copper and was prepared for a fight.

Needing all three of the Wedza PATU sticks to assist in the operation, I was immediately confronted by the Chairman of the Farmers' Association. Well dressed and suave, he was obviously accustomed to getting his way with mere policemen.

'Have you any idea what time of year it is?' he demanded sarcastically. 'All of us are reaping and curing so you will have to make do with field reserve sections. You can make up the numbers with your own men and the damned coloureds.'

The RDR was a coloured regiment and notorious for their inefficiency, but they were under my command and this sort of racist remark made me mad. Besides, I was a Black Boot now and answerable only to my own hierarchy. We didn't look on ourselves as mere coppers and I had no fear of being brow-beaten by this self important bigot.

'Okay', I told him mildly; 'you find your own terrorists. My men have more important work to do.' (I didn't mention electioneering!) 'If you are not prepared to help with the defence of your own area then I am not going to do it for you.'

The look on his face was one I shall always remember. Policemen didn't speak to important Rhodesian farmers like that. Turning on my heel, I would have walked away but he called me back.

'All right', he offered in conciliatory tones. 'You can have one PATU stick, but better than that I cannot do. After all, the tobacco crop is vital to the economy.'

I had heard that argument too many times for it to have any effect.

'It won't be vital to anyone if we are all dead', I snapped. 'I want *all* your PATU sticks and if I don't get them, the operation is off and I will ensure that Comops knows why.'

I got my three PATU sticks. It was a petty little incident and hardly worth mentioning in the context of historical events going on around us, but it was a moral victory that gave me considerable satisfaction. More than all the fighting and killing, it marked my metamorphosis from Bobby to Black Boot. In the former category, I was forced to abide by convention, remain polite, keep everyone happy and watch my Ps and Qs. As a Black Boot, I didn't care who I offended. I answered only to my commanders and ultimate victory over the terrorists who were ravaging the land was my only aim in life.

Throughout my years of war and peace in Rhodesia, I felt that our politicians — that meant the farming community — wielded too much influence over the war effort and this was a major factor in our eventual defeat. All too often, urgently needed men were held back to work the land and while I accept that agriculture was a vital part of the economy, there were times when the war effort should have taken precedence over everything else no matter what it cost. All out victory in the war just might have saved Rhodesia, but in the event, there was no chance of that.

Mine is perhaps a naively idealistic view but a number of fortunes were made out of the Rhodesian conflict and little of that money remained in the country. Many leading citizens — including farmers — fled to South Africa, Australia or other parts of the world and without exception, they took their money with them.

In Wedza I won a small personal victory and even if I had made another important enemy, it didn't disturb my sleep. My demands had been justified and as it turned out, that particular farmer soon forgot his pique at being bested by a mere *mujonnie* (white Rhodesian policeman). I heard no more about the incident and our subsequent meetings were cordial and free from tension. He had merely tried to be awkward and this too was typical of his kind. I don't think Rhodesian farmers actually went out of their way to be difficult, but they could make life very unpleasant for we mere mortals.

Back in the Wiltshire, I soon lost all faith in the Prime Minister of Zimbabwe-Rhodesia, Bishop Abel Muzorewa who was his own worst enemy. On one occasion, a mass meeting was laid on at Sadza Township and — God forgive me — I used police transport to bring people in from all over the area. It was a stinking hot day and the meeting was due to start at eleven o'clock. By then 5 000 people were assembled in the sunshine to hear the Bishop speak. Local stores did a roaring trade and so did the pickpockets, prostitutes and loan sharks. I kept a watchful eye out for the opposition but either the weather was too hot for them or they felt that Muzorewa was so far behind in public opinion that they had no need to worry about attending.

Midday came and went, so did one o'clock and by two thirty the Bishop still hadn't arrived. My men were as fed up as were the locals and I certainly wasn't enjoying myself. Beer and meat were normally laid on at political gatherings, but on this occasion there wasn't even a regular supply of drinking water. Tension was growing by the moment and we had the unenviable task of preventing people from going home in disgust.

At 3.15pm the little man finally appeared in his red and white helicopter. He greeted the crowd and they clapped but the only real warmth came from the sun overhead. The speeches that followed took up less than half an hour and our revered leader didn't even manage five minutes before sinking sweatily down beneath the canopy, erected to give him shade. None of the crowd had canopies and they were visibly upset.

Well before 4pm Bishop Muzorewa flew away with his entourage, leaving me with 5 000 disgruntled people on my hands and ensuring that when it came to voting time, he had no chance at all in the Wiltshire.

I really wasn't sure why we were bothering. Our electioneering efforts in the Wiltshire were doomed to failure long before we started. This was countryside subverted to the cause of ZANU-PF. Robert Mugabe was the unseen God whose name was only whispered but whose party symbol of a cockerel would be marked when the time came to vote.

But orders are orders and splitting the company up into small groups, I sent them on the campaign trail. I kept a few sections in camp in case of trouble while Sergeant Mareve and Constable Hove operated on their own, unarmed and in plain clothes. Posing as itinerants, they wandered from kraal to kraal, gauging the mood of the people. They did no active campaigning and their reports were disturbing. Muzorewa out — Mugabe in: that was the universal feeling in the Wiltshire.

I wasn't the only one who became ever more depressed. Sergeant Mataera approached me one afternoon to find out what I intended to do when Mugabe took over the country.

'It is all right for you, sir', he pointed out reasonably enough. 'You can always go to England or South Africa and get another job. For us it is different. We have nowhere to go and for sure, this hyena Mugabe will make life difficult for all those who have been part of the Security Forces.'

Even as we spoke, plans were afoot to cope with that awful eventuality. The higher echelons of Comops formulated *Operation Quartz*, wherein it was planned that in the event of an unfavourable election result, the military would take over the country. With other field commanders, I was called to briefings in Salisbury where Charlie Company was given a role to play. Units such as the Selous Scouts and SAS were tasked to take out the more threatening centres of black power while we were to combine with local army units and our neighbouring Mantle company in an attack on Assembly Point Foxtrot.

Detailed plans were also made for the evacuation of Unit personnel and their families. Vehicles were set aside for the purpose and lists of dependants carefully assessed. Black and white families would head for the South African border in convoy, fighting their way through if necessary.

On a quick visit home, I put the plan to Missy but she was openly scornful.

'We are better off where we are', she said. 'At least we know everybody here, whereas I don't know a soul in your beloved Chikurubi.'

She had a point I suppose. We lived in Marandellas and she hadn't even met the other Support Unit wives. Tough little lass that she was, she had no intention of heading into all sorts of unknown dangers with a group of strangers and was determined to see things out in her own environment. My efforts to dissuade her were halfhearted as I too believed that our future lay in Zimbabwe-Rhodesia or whatever the country would be called next. This was our home and no matter who was in power, it had to be better than Britain or South Africa.

Yet as the three days set aside for the election drew closer, I became ever more depressed and worried. As a nation we were sliding down a slippery slope and signs of panic and confusion were everywhere. Almost without exception, Rhodesians believed that we were heading for disaster.

21

Bitterness and boredom

Two days before the election, I was called to Enkeldoorn for a meeting with General Walls. He was doing a whistle-stop tour to judge the mood of Rhodesians and we were his last port of call before he returned to Salisbury. The meeting was held in the police station and there were four of us there to hear what the general thought about the situation. The local member in charge, an army major operating on the other side of town, the district commissioner and myself made a pretty experienced bunch of men. We might have thought that Walls would lay his cards on the table, instead, he chose to prevaricate.

When it was my turn to report on operations, I told him that Bishop Muzorewa didn't stand a chance in the Wiltshire. Quite apart from his own ineptitude, the whole area had been thoroughly politicised by ZANU over the years and although a few locals might abstain from voting, I didn't think there would be one vote against Mugabe throughout the district. Both my uniformed colleagues confirmed this view and Walls frowned heavily. The DC immediately disagreed with my assessment, but Internal Affairs had lost touch with reality over the years and his scepticism didn't concern me.

Somewhat to my surprise, Walls supported the DC's view. He told us that although the Wiltshire was probably a borderline case, it could still be won. Meanwhile Muzorewa was gaining unprecedented support elsewhere in the country.

I listened to this drivel with mounting incredulity. This was the man leading the fighting forces of my country. This was a man I had admired — the man I was following and asking my own men to follow. This was a man I would have died for and he was lying through his teeth. I knew he was lying. We all knew he was lying and he must have known that we knew. His lies were totally pointless in the circumstances and he lost my respect at that moment.

Walls' talk left me more confused than ever and to this day, I have never been sure what he hoped to achieve by lying so blatantly to experienced men on the ground. As a nation we were in desperate trouble, but we were prepared to see things through, or we wouldn't have been there. Walls was the man responsible for the entire war effort and should have known everything that was going on, so he surely couldn't have believed his own words.

Throughout the country Muzorewa's support was almost non-existent and Walls would have gained more credence in my eyes, had he admitted the truth. That he chose — unsuccessfully — to con four experienced men into believing an obvious falsehood said little for him as man or as a military commander.

Less than a week before the meeting with Walls an incident took place that confirmed my own view that we had been on a loser from the start in the Wiltshire. A couple of hundred ZANLA members were being bussed through to Assembly Point Foxtrot on the other side of the TTL. The AP contained several thousand ZANLA and was in a perpetual state of simmering tension, so I was glad that Darryl Brent's Lima Company had been tasked with watching over the place. Darryl himself had been taken hostage at one stage and although that incident had been resolved, the camp had become a focal point for tension and racial hatred.

Three bus loads of former terrorists stopped off in Enkeldoorn on their way to the camp and as is the way with soldiers everywhere, they began causing problems in the town. The member in charge radioed for assistance and I sent a section down with instructions to 'get the bastards out of town with a minimum of fuss'.

But I had seriously underestimated the gravity of the situation and when the P/O in charge called up with a request for reinforcements, I took them in myself. In Enkeldoorn I quickly realised that we were in trouble. The dusty little farming town was overflowing with armed men, many of them drunk and most of them in ugly mood. As I drove through the shopping centre, ZANLA cadres shook their rifles in my direction and shouted abuse in both Chishona and English. At the police station three buses had been drawn up, but the passengers showed no inclination to board. Once again, we were subjected to screamed abuse and when they saw my fancy hat and the pips on my shoulders, I was singled out for particularly vituperative comment. It was rapidly developing into a terrifying situation.

Angry and frustrated, I marched in among the milling ZANLA men, shouting that I wanted them aboard the buses and away before there was trouble. This provoked a further torrent of profanity and my colour, my job and my antecedents were bandied about in graphically obscene detail. My own men formed up in a grim-faced line behind me and for a few moments, the gathering tension seemed set to explode into violence.

One man stood apart from the rest. He was dressed in denim overalls and watched the proceedings with a sardonic smile. At one stage I caught his eye and with an almost audible sigh, he stepped through the unruly throng and walked across to me.

'Do you want me to help, Mr Lemon?' he enquired mildly.

I took a long, hard look at him. Short and slender, he had a long thin face and tiny wisps of beard adhering to his chin. He carried an AKM across his shoulders and had about him that indefinable air of natural command that is recognisable in very few men.

'How the hell do you know my name?' I demanded angrily.

I was hot, sweaty and harassed, badly needing a focal point for my frustration.

His smile grew wider.

'I know a great deal about you', he explained.

There was a sudden silence around us as others paused to listen to the exchange.

'You were a policeman in Macheke and your home is now in Marandellas where your children go to school. You call yourself Charlie Nine and among your men, you are known as *Magirazi* — the one with spectacles.'

At last I was face to face with the elusive Sachiweshe. With the cease-fire there was no longer a price on his head, but in spite of all my research, he obviously knew a great deal more about me than I knew about him.

With the ZANLA leader's assistance, we had that unruly mob in the buses and away within a quarter of an hour. Sachiweshe and I shook hands before he joined them and as they drove off toward the distant assembly point, I couldn't help wishing that I'd had more time to talk with the man. Better still, would have been to have him on the same side and to me this really emphasised the tragedy of a civil war.

Sachiweshe and I were both Rhodesians. The country was home to each of us, yet our politics and our differing ideals meant that had we met a few weeks previously, one of us would surely have died.

Unfortunately I never saw or heard of Sachiweshe again. I presume he abandoned his *Chimurenga* name and went back to being an ordinary citizen. How I regret not spending more time with him that distant day in Enkeldoorn. There was so much I would have liked to know about life among the terrs. Even as he climbed into the bus, my mind crawled with questions I ought to have asked.

Did he feel as frightened as I did when bullets were flying? How did his men react to fireforce or the saturation bombing and terrifying firepower of the Hawker Hunters? Were they scared when the vicious little RLI troopies were closing in or when they saw those great, thundering jets streaking down on their positions? How did they collect their intelligence? Did they get R and R as we did? Did they miss their families and girlfriends? Did he ever feel like throwing it all up and going home to lead a normal life and what would he do now that the war was over? The questions remain unanswered but what an opportunity I missed.

I could have liked the man too. By stepping into a potentially nasty situation, Sachiweshe had helped me considerably and at the same time, shown why we had never been able to sort out the problems in the Wiltshire. I might not have approved of the methods used by his men, but I had to admit that the man known only as Sachiweshe was one hell of a leader.

British Bobbies had been brought in to supervise polling stations during the election and those in our area hailed from Nottingham. Cordial enough, they were obviously under orders not to fraternise and they took such matters seriously. I issued the routine invitations to visit our mess for dinner, but these were emphatically turned down so I left them alone as far as I could. In other areas, Bobbies enjoyed excellent relations with local people and many lasting friendships were begun, but my lot were an unfriendly bunch. Our only dialogue was in the nature of complaints regarding the Spartan nature of their quarters and the body odour of the voters — neither grumble likely to improve my opinion of Britons in general.

I kept armed patrols in operation throughout the election period and they reported many cases of harassment and coercion among those wavering in their support for Mugabe. This information was passed on to Comops but if anything was ever done about it, I didn't see the results.

On the second day of voting, Totohwiyo's section came across the residents of an entire village being herded by AK-wielding cadres toward the polling booth. When they reported this over the radio I ordered them to put a stop to it. Cease-fire or no cease-fire, a contact ensued and one of the guerrillas (as we had been instructed to call them) was killed. Loading the body into the back of my Land-Rover, I took it along to the nearest polling station and showed it to the bobby in control.

'Now tell me that there isn't any intimidation or coercion', I demanded after explaining what had happened. 'Now tell me that these elections are free and bloody fair!'

I produced the frightened villagers to emphasise the point but that particular policeman was more interested in photographing the dead man with his accoutrements than doing anything about the intimidation.

'My God!' He kept saying. 'That is a real terrorist. Look at his rifle. Look at that bloody bayonet. Wait till I show these photos back home. A real live terrorist indeed.'

Hardly 'live' but I took the point. For these British policemen, the war in Zimbabwe-Rhodesia was unreal. Most of them worked to the best of their ability on their monitoring chores, but they were from peaceful England and knew nothing of terror or the misery of a population under siege. Few of them made any real effort to understand the situation and most were merely in the country as paid tourists.

I didn't really blame them for their attitude. This wasn't their war and whatever they might have reported about the illegality of what was going on around them, would have been ignored and forgotten. Margaret Thatcher and Lord Carrington had determined to rid themselves of the Rhodesian problem and these elections were going to be deemed free and fair, no matter what skulduggery took place.

It was hardly the fault of the bobbies.

Although the election result was hardly unexpected, the scale of Mugabe's victory rocked most of us back on our heels. ZANU-PF won 57 of the 80 seats on offer, Nkomo took 20 and Muzorewa's UANC (United African National Council) won but three. Twenty seats had been reserved for white members while the new constitution was in force, but we all knew that Mugabe wouldn't tolerate that for long.

The announcement put me into a state of shock and it was difficult to appreciate the enormity of what had happened. In one fell swoop, black and white Rhodesians alike had lost everything they had been fighting for over eight long and bloody years. It seemed that all the terror, bloodshed and violent death had been for nothing. My own immediate worries were for the future of my family and I don't suppose I was alone in that. Black, white, pink or yellow, every family man who had taken up arms for the government was suddenly facing a very uncertain future. It was desperately depressing.

Most of my discussions on that grim day in March revolved around the contingency plan that was to save the nation from a Marxist future. My men were prepared for they knew not what and all commanders were confident in our allotted tasks. All day, we cleaned our weapons, tinkered with transport and waited for the code word *quartz* to be transmitted over the radio, but we waited in vain. The operation was never initiated and whether this was due to political expediency or fright at the magnitude of the proposed task, we shall never know. Whatever the case, that third day of March in 1980 was a bleak day indeed for Rhodesians.

Mind you, it wasn't only those of us in the Security Forces who had received a shock. Going in to Enkeldoorn at nine in the morning, I found the hotel bar crowded with farmers, all drinking heavily and most of them spoiling for a fight. At nine that evening, the bar was still crowded with farmers, still drinking heavily but quieter now and seemingly resigned to their fate in what was going to be the new Zimbabwe.

I was under orders to keep my entire company in camp until the situation had resolved itself and two days after the result was announced, we moved to another abandoned farm, ten kilometres south of town. For the next three weeks we sat around or conducted training exercises and once again I had general boredom to contend with. It added to my mounting depression and I took little part in company activities. Jonty Court had decided to resign ('I can't work under this lot') and I wasn't sure that I wanted to stay on, either in the Force or the country.

I longed to talk it out with Missy, but we were confined to camp while our new leaders sorted out their priorities. I don't know how real soldiers occupy themselves when there is nobody to fight, but if those few weeks outside Enkeldoorn were anything like the norm, I could only thank my stars that I hadn't joined the army. I was bored to distraction and so were my men. We wasted thousands of rounds of ammunition on the surrounding hills and practised 'buddy-buddy' drills till we could have done them sleepwalking. It all seemed such a waste of time too as the war was officially over and there was nobody left to fight.

Or so we thought at the time.

22

All change for peace

I think the men of Charlie Company breathed a collective sigh of relief when we were withdrawn from Enkeldoorn. It had been an unhappy area for us and a fair amount of our own blood had been spilled into the red dust of the Wiltshire. To add to the general delight was the fact that we were to operate in Salisbury. It was hardly inspiring work, but for everyone except me it meant being home every night and enjoying the fleshpots of the city. I moved back into Fife Hostel, where I kept myself to myself and tried to ignore the inanities of the young urban policemen.

Much of our duty time was spent on crowd control at Salisbury Airport as various dignitaries flew in for the Independence celebrations. Samora Machel received the most rapturous applause, but for me the fascination lay in seeing all these former enemies in the flesh. Most of them seemed terribly small and I found it surprising that they looked just like ordinary men and women. Where were the horns and forked tails dammit?! These people had spent years conducting a bloody war against my country and I found it difficult to reconcile their benign appearances with the dastardly deeds done in their name.

On two occasions I joined other policemen in Morris Depot, firstly to hear Ian Smith speak and then to be addressed by the ogre himself — Robert Gabriel Mugabe, premier-elect of the new Zimbabwe. Much as I admired Smithy, I couldn't help reflecting afterwards that Mugabe was the more impressive speaker. At times it was hard to believe I was listening to him in person. For years he had been the devil incarnate to Rhodesians. Now he was here before us — the faceless made flesh and holding us in thrall with the strength of his personality. He was another small man with a grating voice and a round face, half obscured by large spectacles.

Lounging as elegantly as possible in my uncomfortable chair, (losing side or not, I was still a Black Boot) I kept telling myself that here before me was an evil mass murderer, yet I couldn't help feeling a sneaking admiration for the man. By talking to us, he was entering the lions' den and I knew how nerve-wracking that could be. Yet Mugabe seemed perfectly at ease. He talked at length about reconciliation between black and white and between members of the Security Forces and the 'comrades.' I wanted to believe in what he said, but I was reluctant to put my faith in a man who had for so long been the most hated person in my life.

When asked whether the force would retain its name, Mugabe laughed.

'How can law and order in Zimbabwe be upheld by a police service that has the words 'South Africa' in its name?'

I suppose he had a point and it wasn't long before the 'Force in the Great Tradition' became the Zimbabwe Republic Police — just another cowboy outfit in Africa. Mugabe also promised integration in all the armed forces and that was worrying, but he advised us that the new Zimbabwe offered a chance of prosperity for everyone, no matter the faction they might have represented during the war.

The former terrorist leader was warmly applauded at the end of his address, but as I left the hall I couldn't help wondering how much of his talk had been mere empty rhetoric. Could we really trust a man with so much blood on his hands? Missy and I held long and anxious discussions as to what we should do and eventually agreed to give the new country five years before making a firm decision. We had invested too much of our lives into the place to just abandon everything and all three kids were doing well at school. The thought of starting again in a strange land was too daunting to contemplate.

Nevertheless, we hedged our bets by going to South Africa for a short holiday. While we were there, I studied the employment market and spoke to a few influential folk about the future. As far as I was concerned, it appeared pretty bleak. There were jobs available in the police and armed forces but the Republic was experiencing the same unrest that had presaged the beginning of our war and the outcome was bound to be similar. I saw no point in risking my life and the lives of my family for a land that wasn't our own.

The ethical considerations of remaining a copper in a country that now belonged to our enemies didn't pose a problem. As a policeman, I was apolitical, notwithstanding my reluctant efforts on behalf of Bishop Muzorewa. I had fought for Smith and fought for the Bishop. Would my task be any different fighting for Mugabe? I looked on him as a ruthless terrorist and responsible for a great deal of murder and mayhem, but my task as a Black Boot was to maintain peace in the country and that didn't depend on the man in ultimate power.

So it was that we returned from South Africa, happy to be home and determined to get through the next five years. By then Zimbabwe should have got over its inevitable teething troubles and be firmly back on the world stage. At least that was what we hoped.

My leave had lasted only four weeks, but I returned to find major changes in the world I knew best. Even our everyday uniform had changed. No longer were we glamorous fighting men in tailored camouflage. We were policemen again and our attire was grey shirts and long blue trousers, my own brittle and musty from years of disuse. Medal ribbons, colourful lanyards and *gondos* on the sleeve were still allowed, but the uniform smacked too much of the police reserve and seemed a terrible come down for fighting Black Boots. It would make us stand out like blisters on a baby's face should we be called on to operate in the bush conditions where we were normally at our best.

Other changes had been made to our military status. Companies were now knows as troops, troops as sections and sections as patrols. It was all very confusing. Daily routine remained the same, but back with my men I was immediately aware that much of the fighting pride had dissipated, to be replaced with a sense of apathy that was disturbing. Jonty Court had gone and been replaced by Mike Mukulunyelwa, one of the new breed of black officers who was being groomed to take over his own troop. My white staff had almost all resigned or been transferred so my immediate task was to learn about a whole new set of personalities.

The biggest change of all was in the emphasis of our duties. The war was over and it had been decreed that we would get back to policing and leave the mopping up of dissident elements to the army. The Selous Scouts, RLI and SAS had been disbanded, but the RAR continued as a fighting force although they were about to have their name changed.

Our job was to concentrate on stock theft, poaching and civil disturbance and to this end, even our training had changed. We still attended battle camp prior to deployment, but we no longer fought through jungle lanes or spent hours stripping and assembling weaponry, captured from the enemy. Instead, tracking skills were developed and — much to the disgust of all concerned — law and police lessons introduced.

Charlie Troop were already in the field when I returned from South Africa and I was told about the new regime when I motored out to join them with Badger Two. Superintendent Trigg was paying a routine visit to check on books, records and troop morale, but he didn't seem nearly as disturbed as I was by the change in everything I loved about the Unit.

A slight, intense man, Trigg was a fitness fanatic and an officer of proven bravery. Some years previously, he had been awarded the Police Medal for Gallantry after a gun battle with terrorists. Unmarried and solitary, he liked to do things by the book, but he was a good copper and when he was dismissed some time later, we all knew that the Support Unit had lost a fine officer.

But John Trigg's disgrace was well in the future when I arrived back in camp to the welcoming smiles of my men. Even on holiday, my thoughts had often strayed to their well-being and as I surveyed the entire troop, lined up for my inspection, I felt an enormous surge of pride in my chest. No matter what changes there might have been in the Force and the Unit, I was still Charlie Nine and these hard-headed cut throats were my extra family. Keeping my face impassive, I walked down the ranks, looking for imaginary specks of dust on pristine grey shirts and I couldn't help the occasional smile at being back among these marvellous fellows.

Stopping to chat with still-constable Totohwiyo, I commiserated with the fact that his promotion had not come through before the end of hostilities.

'You will have to study now, Totohs', I warned, but he just smiled his big, friendly smile.

'I will try', he promised, but we both knew that his chances of promotion had vanished forever. Augustine Totohwiyo wasn't the studying sort.

Sergeant Machisa was another one with rank problems. A small, intense tiger of a man, he had been a lance sergeant for two years, but his stripes would be withdrawn if he didn't sit a promotion examination. He had no hope of passing and he knew it. He smiled wolfishly when I reminded him of the need to study.

'I will be a constable if necessary, sir', he said. 'As long as I can stay with Charlie Troop.'

When Badger Two addressed the parade, cynical glances were cast in my direction and I couldn't help smiling.

'You have to remember that you are policemen, not soldiers', the superintendent thundered. 'You must uphold the law wherever you are and behave like worthy officers. No more stealing, drinking, fighting and whoring for you lot.'

How many times had I stood before these same men to remind them that they were soldiers, not policemen? Now I had to change my tune and they remembered and enjoyed my embarrassment.

So it was that our fighting life changed and we became upholders of the law that Black Boots traditionally ignored and were forgiven for ignoring. Life would never be the same again, but there was still a great deal of fighting to be done.

Assistant Commissioner Don Rowland had commanded the Unit with considerable aplomb throughout the last few years of war. A big man who rarely smiled, he was respected by the men and was always fair in his dealing with individuals. He was overdue for promotion when the war ended and we all assumed that the post would be upgraded and he would merely move another rung up the ladder.

But the faceless desk jockeys in PGHQ had other ideas. The post was indeed upgraded to senior assistant commissioner rank, but SAC Ian Hogg was brought in to supersede Badger. This meant that Rowlands would go down to being Badger One while Hogg would take over the top job. All the superintendents would see their Badger number increase by one, but I would still be Charlie Nine so it didn't affect me.

What did affect us all was the dismissal of John Trigg. It caused consternation among company commanders, but it was rumoured that he had been caught in *fragrante delicto* with a constable and if that was the case, then I suppose the powers-that-be had no choice.

Personally, I was sad to see him go. We had never got on particularly well, but whatever his sexual inclinations, he had brought considerable credit to the police force in general and to the Support Unit in particular. He lived for the job and led by example, never asking men to do what he wouldn't do himself. While I understood the reasons for his sacking, it seemed a terrible waste of a fine man.

The appointment of Ian Hogg was another matter. For a time he had been my Dispol in Lomagundi and I had worked with him at Kariba. A charismatic leader and vastly experienced policeman, he was a personal friend of Don Rowland and this undoubtedly alleviated what must have been a difficult position for them both. They went on to form a partnership that continued the proud tradition of the Support Unit and both men worked tirelessly for those of us under their command.

Personally I felt sorry for Rowland, but was pleased that 'Hoggie' had become one of us, particularly as his son was one of my new patrol officers in Charlie Troop. I had received an intake of four new P/Os shortly before Hogg senior's arrival and they quickly adapted to Unit ways. Direct entry officers, they had no Uniform Branch experience to colour their views and although they were very different personalities, they were great fun and came to epitomise the spirit of my troop.

Richard Hogg was a quietly efficient lad who found himself highly embarrassed at having his father posted to the top job at Chikurubi. Ron Jamieson was an ebullient young man, always laughing and with an answer for everything. So anxious was he to make his presence felt that I christened him 'General' for his habit of interrupting my briefings with suggestions of his own — many of them extremely pertinent to the situation.

Leon Oosthuizen and Peter Coventry were also quiet men, but a pleasure to have around. Leon was a farming boy from Headlands who gave his best in every situation and was known as 'Borse' by all and sundry. He was an incredible shot and very popular amongst the men. Peter came from a Rhodesian cricketing family, but was soon a valued member of Charlie Troop and also a pleasure to have around.

These four youngsters were to share many excitements with me and provide me with memories that will make me smile well into my dotage. They were wild and uninhibited, always looking for adventure or fun and possessed of that rare common sense that was typical of Rhodesian youth at the time.

Mind you 'Rhodesian youth' no longer existed. We were Zimbabweans now and it took a great deal of getting used to. The situation was put into perspective for me by an old friend who was wiser than I was.

'It will always be difficult for our generation', George Begg told me quietly. 'Brought up as Rhodesians, many will find it impossible to live with the changes. For our children, it will be different. They will grow up in a multiracial society and accept it as the norm. It is with the youngsters that the future of this country lies, not with the likes of you and I.'

It is always so and George was right. The young are more adaptable and my children are true Zimbabweans while their children will know nothing different. We fought for the Rhodesian ideal and suffered a great deal for our beliefs. As the years pass, acceptance becomes easier, but the change to Zimbabwe was a difficult one and even now, horrific memories of those violent days often make it difficult to forgive and forget.

For the record, Ron Jamieson and Richard Hogg eventually became successful businessmen in South Africa, Leon Oosthuizen was killed in a road accident in New Zealand and Peter Coventry became a pastor in Australia. They were fine young men and had we had more of their ilk earlier on, who knows, things might just have been different.

23

Travelling cop

For the rest of 1980, I was almost as much of a tourist as had been the British and Commonwealth Monitoring Force. There was hardly a corner of Zimbabwe that Charlie Troop didn't visit in the course of our duties. With time on my hands, I explored national parks, climbed rugged mountain ranges, saw sights seldom seen except by locals and made many friends in remote corners of the country.

There were new place names to accept as normal, but once I remembered that Hartley was Chegutu, Fort Victoria was Masvingo and dear old Enkeldoorn was Chivhu, I could almost find my way around. The other changes were minor although the expense involved must have been horrendous. I only hoped that with the lifting of sanctions, the international community was paying for all the changes.

In our new role as policemen, we chased stock thieves in Chipinge (formerly Chipinga) and poachers in Triangle, Chiredzi and Mwenezi. We looked for gold smugglers in Filabusi and illegal emerald traders in Sandawana and Belingwe. We curbed potential riots at Hwange and kept the peace when there was trouble at Silobela and Bikita. We removed squatters from farming lands, examined licenses and permits for a variety of activities and operated road blocks all over the country.

To be quite blunt, we were bored to tears. My only moment of excitement came in the farmlands outside Masvingo when a government minister had encouraged the people to take over farms that surrounded their TTL homes.

'The land is ours now', he thundered. 'The whites no longer hold claim to it.' Take it Comrades, cultivate it and make new homes for yourselves.'

So of course they did and the farmers were up in arms. The local police couldn't cope with 5 000 angry squatters, we were called in and I went down to see what was going on. For some reason, I was in a bad temper that morning and the situation was far worse than I had expected.

A vast sea of sullen humanity stretched over two fields, four five-ton trucks were drawn up to take them away. The people were determined not to go and uniformed policemen stood helplessly around. Nobody seemed willing to take the initiative and beyond the crowd, I could see other villagers settling down to their chores outside makeshift shelters. Of the farmers who had made the original complaint, there was no sign.

A coloured section officer approached me somewhat hesitantly. I wasn't carrying a rifle, but I had the heavy CZ in my belt and my leather swagger-stick in one hand.

'I have arrested the ringleaders, sir', the S/O pointed to a group of muttering men. 'There are about 200 of them but they refuse to move.'

The situation was at a stalemate, but someone had to do something. Judging from the way everyone was looking in my direction, that someone would have to be me. Slapping the cane against my leg I marched angrily across to the group who had been arrested and a low murmur from the crowd accompanied my advance. Suddenly my bad temper evaporated and I felt scared.

There was no longer the hot adrenalin rush of battle to bolster my confidence and my white skin was no protection. I was walking into a crowd of thousands and if they turned on me, I would be dead within seconds. Struggling to conceal my nervousness, I marched up to the group waiting beside the lorries.

'On!' I roared at an obvious elder wrapped in a red blanket.

I pointed my cane at the back of the lorry. I held my breath and for one long, pregnant second, everything went quiet.

'Yes, Boss', the old boy said quietly and climbed over the tailgate. He was followed by another and then another.

Ten minutes later, the lorries were loaded, the assembled coppers were open-mouthed at my success and to be honest, so was I. The bewildered crowd waited patiently for me to speak.

'Tell them', I said to Sergeant Mareve who was standing watchfully behind me, 'that these men will go before the government *dare* where the matter will be sorted out. Until the magistrate makes his decision, they can stay where they are, but I think they should prepare for a return to their homes.

One hundred and eighty seven recalcitrant squatters duly appeared before the court in Masvingo where they were fined a couple of dollars apiece and sent back to the TTLs from whence they came. None of them could understand what was going on and I felt desperate sympathy for their plight. Their mistake had been to put faith in a thoughtlessly racist politician, anxious only to make himself seem all powerful. I put in a report explaining what had happened and naming the minister involved, but nothing came of it and he went on to hold high cabinet rank.

In the context of the new Zimbabwe, it was a sad little episode, but for me it provided a moment of genuine fear and a tremendous boost to my reputation as a hard man amongst the Masvingo police. It was probably as well that nobody realised that it wasn't courage that drove me to face down that mob, but pig-headed bad temper. That wouldn't have been good for my newfound image.

There were a number of personnel changes in Charlie Troop during those first few months of Independence. The rank structure had changed and rapid promotions were taking place throughout the Force. Troop section officers had replaced company sergeant majors and most senior sergeants were studying for promotion to patrol officer.

CSM Lazarus left me at last and I can't say I was sorry to see him go. A good organiser and strict disciplinarian, he was inclined to be brutal at times and his drinking drove me to distraction. Even with the war behind us, I kept our camps dry but Lazarus was frequently smashed out of his mind. I blew my top with him on a number of occasions, but it was difficult to draw the line between disciplining the man and keeping his dignity intact as holder of the most important post in the troop.

Sergeant Molefe and my old friend Lance Sergeant Machisa went on transfer to other troops and among the constables I knew I would miss were Ndhlovu, Mangwanda, Dorowa and Sithole. All experienced Black Boots, they were replaced by raw recruits and with the general boredom of our existence, it was essential to get troop spirit running high again. There was no longer a kill table to measure our own worth against that of other troops, but competitions involving athletic events, shooting and tug of war were held in Chikurubi between patrols. We did well in these without ever claiming ultimate victory, but I wanted to win and whenever we had time on our hands I would put the men through gruelling training for the next round of events.

One way of promoting pride in the troop was the flying of our battle flag. There might no longer be battles to fight but our flag was a magnificent one and we were all proud of it. Missy had spent hours embroidering the huge, golden 'C' on a field of blue and our first task at the start of a deployment was to find a suitable flagpole. There were usually gum plantations about and a young tree was ideal, but occasionally more exotic poles were sported.

We were stationed outside Bulawayo at one stage and with the camp going up around me, I snapped instructions at my tame general.

'Find us a suitable flagpole please, Ron.'

Grinning at his fellow cut throats, Jamieson disappeared with a couple of constables and returned some hours later with a genuine flagpole, complete with ropes and pulleys. I didn't dare ask where it had come from, but we were less than 20 kilometres from the city and I avoided Brady Barracks and Government House for the remainder of our deployment. Both establishments ought to have been well guarded against such blatant theft, but Ron Jamieson was a resourceful little brute and I wouldn't have put anything past him.

Another tool I made shameless use of in efforts to raise morale was singing. Many of the men had magnificent voices and almost without exception, they loved to raise them in song. The morning run was a natural time for vocalising and on the rare occasions that we were based in civilisation, we made ourselves generally unpopular by running raucously through sleeping suburbs, well before the time that normal people rouse themselves from slumber. Punishment parades were another time when I insisted on the singing. It was cruel of me I suppose, but when a man is close to physical exhaustion, having to raise his voice in cheerful chorus adds considerably to the pain of tortured lungs.

For me, the most magical interludes of singing occurred during evenings in the bush. After stand-to, the men in camp would disperse for a quiet hour or two before bed.

Cooking fires twinkled into life as *sadza* was prepared and the camp would gradually subside into satisfied silence as darkness enveloped the countryside. Shadowy sentries could occasionally be seen prowling the camp perimeter and it was never long before someone started to sing quietly to himself.

Like the Welsh, Africans are natural harmonisers and within moments, their voices would fill the night and stir the hair on my arms. Their songs were the songs of soldiers everywhere, delivered with the deep throbbing rhythms of Africa. Songs of home like '*Amai na Baba*' — the story of a trooper dreaming of home and family. Songs of war and songs like the plaintive '*Saiwela*' — the sweetheart left to dream beside the Limpopo River. *Ishe Komberera Africa* was another favourite, later adopted by South Africa as *Nkosi sikeleli Afrika* — part of the national anthem for the new Rainbow Nation.

When the entire troop was in camp, music would saturate the darkness and even though it advertised our presence to anyone with hostile intent, it was therapeutic to overstretched nerves and I never bothered to stop it. These impromptu concerts always left me drained and full of emotion so that when I retired to my stretcher, I felt a deep sense of pride in my role as commander of these wonderful fighting men.

Another source of pride was the award of silver batons for courage, shown by Sergeant Mareve and Constable Majiga while we were in Filabusi. A school bus had been attempting to cross a flooded river when it was knocked sideways by the force of the water. As it teetered precariously on the edge of a flooded causeway, my two details, drove a crocodile mine protected personnel carrier into the flood water and gently transferred the terrified school children one at a time into the bigger vehicle. As the last child was lifted across, the bus went head over heels down the causeway to end up well downstream with the driver still aboard. He survived, but few of us had sympathy for his foolhardiness in risking the lives of his charges. I was pleased to recommend my two men for their bravery, however, and when the awards were announced, I relaxed my alcohol ban for an evening and we all celebrated to the full.

That was an isolated bit of excitement to our lives but to relieve the collective boredom, we were occasionally tasked to pursue groups of armed dissidents. Many of these had come out of Assembly Points as bored as we were and disillusioned with the slow pace of integration. One or more of them would lay waste to a patch of countryside, robbing, looting and pillaging with impunity. Most of the former combatants coming in at ceasefire had cached weaponry beforehand so they had no difficulty in equipping themselves for these forays and there were few parts of the country that were not affected by their depredations.

On these occasions, my briefings were carried out with more attention to detail and a greater sense of urgency. In spite of our new-found image as police officers, I kept up field training in weapon handling and bushcraft. When patrols went out on a dissident hunt, there was an air of suppressed excitement and enthusiasm about the men involved that indicated just how bored they were as patrolling coppers. I tried to nourish this with fighting talk, but we never had any success in our dissident hunts.

In the days before civil war ravaged the country, the Support Unit had been just another branch of the police force. Men were selected at random or because they dropped into trouble and postings to the Unit were made with little thought being given to a man's suitability for the role. With the advent of war this had changed. Since the mid seventies there had been direct entry and candidates were chosen more for their fitness, initiative and fighting potential than their ability to prepare a docket or direct traffic in downtown Bulawayo. Now these rough and ready fighting men were being asked to do a job for which they were neither suited nor trained and it wasn't working. They needed an enemy to fight and their natural aggressiveness was occasionally in evidence during tamer duties.

Roadblocks were a high-profile duty and my briefings contained repeated reference to politeness, turn out and the need to impress the public. On one occasion, a car full of overseas visitors was pulled up outside Bulawayo. A great, gangling Black Boot stuck his face through the driver's window.

'Where are you going, Fuckpig?' he enquired mildly.

When the horrified visitor reported the incident, my bloke couldn't understand what he had done wrong.

'I was polite, sir', he insisted. 'I didn't know his name. If I had, I wouldn't have called him 'Fuckpig'.

I didn't have the heart to discipline him.

On another occasion, one of my best sergeants asked for a driving licence and when the driver couldn't immediately produce it, insisted that the car be left at the roadblock until the document was found. The motorist's protestations that the licence was at his home, 80 kilometres away cut no ice with my sergeant.

'Bring it to me and you can have your car back. Fail to produce it and you cannot.'

That driver was an influential member of ZANU-PF and the repercussions took a long time to die down.

I tried to instil police values into my men by running classes to prepare for promotion, but only five of my hundred or so constables showed any aptitude for study. When they sat the written examination, Eddie Hove came first among Unit candidates and Mudakureva was only two places behind him. The other three were all in the top ten and at the end of that patrol, I joined in the celebrations with a will.

They were good days and hard days but they lacked something in the way of excitement. Once again, I should have been pleased that I was allowed to be a copper, but I didn't have the satisfaction of seeing cases through to a finish. Although I was still earning good money and seeing the country at government expense, I began to wonder about transferring back to regular police duties.

My sons were growing up and doing well on the sports field. Deborah was head girl at Godfrey Huggins junior school and was an excellent swimmer, but I rarely had a chance to see any of them in action. Missy was understandably fed up with my nomadic existence and our marriage was threatening to fall apart. Perhaps it was time to be an ordinary cop once more.

I was a chief inspector by that stage so I could probably find myself a comfortable number, running a large district station. We could settle down again as a family and I could play for the local cricket team, hack my way around a few golf courses and do all the things that officers in charge of large police stations did.

These and similar thoughts were ever more in my mind, but whenever I stepped on to the parade square of a morning, accepted the flashing salute of T/S/O Tamhla and looked at my assembled men, I felt such a surge of pride that I knew it could never be the same anywhere else. Charlie Troop was also my family and although no man is indispensable, these men needed me as much as I needed them.

And even while I gallivanted around the landscape with my wild and woolly Black Boots, the country was simmering again. Dissidents were running wild and as always it was the civilian population who suffered most. Murders became ever more frequent and were often horrific. Fathers were hacked to pieces in front of their families and mass rapes had become commonplace. Prime minister Mugabe called for calm among the people, but that is easy in a comfortable city office. In the remote kraals of Matabeleland and Manica, his pleas — if they were heard at all — were greeted with hollow laughter.

Officially, we were no longer at war but a deep feeling of unease pervaded the country. If the lid blew off, we would really be in trouble. Our crack fighting forces had been disbanded and many of our soldiers had decamped to new battlefields in other countries. Only the first battalion of the RAR and the Support Unit were left intact and morale in those integrated units was falling fast.

When the lid did blow off, it blew off in Bulawayo and Charlie Troop was 80 kilometres down the road.

24

Horror at Entumbane

A blow to morale throughout the Unit was the murder of Lance Inspector Billy Gloss. I was in Chikurubi when the call came through that inmates of Assembly Point Papa had shot him. Billy had been called in to sort out a quarrel between former combatants and taken two bullets in the stomach for his pains. By the time I got back to Matabeleland, he was dead and once again, angry hatred was building in my soul.

An unassuming young man, Billy Gloss had served as my deputy for a while and his enthusiasm for the job had been refreshing. I could remember his quiet pride at being given command of India Troop and knew that with his death, the Unit had lost a fine man.

Billy was the first Support Unit commander to be killed in action for a considerable time and his death came as a shock to us all. Badger called an immediate conference and reminded us that whatever the political situation, we were still at war.

'There are thousands of weapons out there', he waved his arm at the world outside the window. 'You guys are in the frontline and could find yourself in the same situation as Inspector Gloss at any time. You must remain alert for trouble and ensure that the message gets through to your men.'

I felt depressed on leaving that meeting. For the first time since joining the Unit, I was unsure of my role. I had 123 well-armed fighting men under my command, but was being asked to use them in a role they didn't understand. I could cope with that, but I had just been reminded that we were still at war. Reconciling the points of view enjoyed by ordinary coppers and fighting Black Boots was difficult. I struggled to cope with my own confusion.

The end result was that after that my men went out with strict instructions that if they saw an armed man outside an Assembly Point, they were to shoot first and ask questions afterwards. Hardly recognised police procedure perhaps, but my troopers were itching to get in on the action and we needed something to ease the boredom of our daily lives.

Nobody was ever prosecuted for Billy Gloss' murder, but that was par for the course in the new Zimbabwe. Former members of ZANLA and ZIPRA were apparently immune from prosecution, no matter how heinous their crimes. This led to bitterness amongst policemen and I wasn't the only officer who believed that we were heading for major trouble.

Other troops suffered casualties in this period of war that wasn't war. Two constables were bludgeoned to death by unidentified soldiers near Chikurubi and others fell to the fire of dissidents in various corners of the country. They had their successes too, while Charlie Troop somehow avoided the violence. It seemed we were stuck with our poachers, stock thieves and roadblocks, but I was envious when I listened to troop sitreps every morning. Well-trained and extremely fit fighting men are difficult to control at the best of times and when they are not allowed to fight, they tend to fret. I looked forward to action as much as they did.

Discipline was again causing a problem in the troop. I tried always to be hard but fair in disciplinary matters and the majority of offenders were summarily dealt with by the T/S/O and myself. Our punishments were brutal but effective, yet more and more men were flouting the rules. Entire patrols would sneak into beer halls or shebeens and return to base, hopelessly plastered. A trooper was arrested in Bulawayo for stealing from a roadside vendor and on two occasions, women were smuggled into camp. My patience was stretched to the limit and I resorted to ever-stricter methods of control.

In addition to military training, I introduced a vicious keep-fit programme, conducted boxing lessons in the afternoon and ensured that the football team had a continual succession of opponents. I also extended the morning run, ensuring that the runners were even more heavily laden. I suppose I was hoping that the men would be too tired to misbehave, but I don't know whether it did any good.

A different problem cropped up when Constable Tendere thought he was a leopard. It sounds harmless from this distance, but it was a serious matter. We were working in the Gona re Zhou National Park at the time so he was at least blending in with the surroundings, but it was frightening for all concerned. Tendere was a big man and an excellent worker in normal circumstances, but he attacked a number of colleagues with bared teeth and extended 'talons'.

When I arrived on the scene, Tendere was in a tree and the sounds emanating from the branches were the sounds of the great, spotted cat. Crackling snarls and deep rumbles of anger raised the hair on my neck and it took a long time to talk the man down from his perch. I had him shackled for the night, before driving him into town myself. Poor old Tendere was perfectly rational by then and seemed bewildered at the fuss. Medical staff at Chikurubi could find nothing amiss and a week later he was back with us, allegedly in full control of his faculties.

The T/S/O shook his head.

'These people are stupid, sir', he was referring to the medics. 'Tendere has been possessed by the spirits and ordinary *muti* can do nothing for him. He will soon go mad again.'

He did too. On the second occasion, Tendere ripped a colleague's arm to the bone with his teeth and it took four big men to subdue him. Back he went to Chikurubi and this time he spent time in a psychiatric unit, but was again returned to the field, allegedly cured of his ailment.

Tim Tamhla remained unconvinced.

'Tendere is cursed', he told me gravely. 'The medics cannot cure him.'

'So what can we do?' I asked somewhat plaintively. 'If we go on like this, he is going to kill someone.'

'He must see a spirit medium', S/O T told me seriously. 'Only traditional healing can help him now.'

On the third occasion that our resident *ingwe* ran amok, I had had enough. Using troop funds and some of my own money for medical fees, I sent Tendere with S/O T to see a *nganga* in the nearby tribal lands. Tim left him there and I don't know what that medicine man did to my would-be killer cat, but he rejoined us after a few days and never imagined himself a leopard again. Resuming his duties, Tendere proved himself an efficient copper and I considered his medical fees as money well spent.

Medical science has made incredible advances over the years but there are areas in which civilised mankind still has a great deal to learn. Supposedly enlightened folk tend to sneer at the traditional healing methods of Africa, but although they seem primitive to modern man, they are undoubtedly effective.

Almost a year into the new Zimbabwe, we were spending most of our time in Matabeleland. This was fascinating countryside with vast, scrubby plains to the south, Bulawayo and the Matopos hills in the middle and heavy forest spreading northwards to the Zambezi River and Victoria Falls. The entire province was starkly beautiful. Home to the traditional warrior tribe of Zimbabwe, it was all incredibly friendly and the hospitality we encountered from all sides was spectacular.

The weather was as varied as the landscape. Terribly hot during the day, the temperature plunged below freezing after dark and early mornings could be traumatic. During one particularly cold snap, I even considered doing away with morning PT for an extra hour in bed, but rejected the idea as being far too radical. I was supposed to be a hard man dammit!

There was frost on the ground when the orderly shook me from sleep. It was four in the morning and I was astonished to be told that Badger wanted me on the radio. Badger at this hour? Senior assistant commissioners were seldom seen before eight o'clock. Only we gofers in the field ever saw the early morning stars. Surely it couldn't be Badger? Shaking sleep from my eyes and vowing to strangle the orderly if he had roused me for nothing, I shivered my way across to the radio tent.

The orderly avoided strangulation as Badger was indeed about, in spite of the hour. Speaking quietly and without emotion, he told me that there was 'trouble in Bulawayo' and my troop was needed right away. I had one section at Filabusi, but the other two were with me at Gwanda, so rousing them out, I headed for Bulawayo, leaving my deputy to pack up and follow with the rest.

Dawn was breaking as I approached the city and the sky to the east was a spectacular display of fiery colour. I was hungry and had no particular feelings of anxiety or trepidation. Trouble in Bulawayo could mean anything from a municipal strike to a minor riot and Charlie Troop was capable of handling whatever was thrown at us. Whistling quietly to myself, I drove into town and straight into the most terrifying situation I had ever encountered.

The trouble had started with the extraordinary decision to set up four camps for former combatants in the Western area townships of Bulawayo. Presumably this had been done to relieve pressure on the overcrowded Assembly Point at Gwaai River, but it seemed incredible that hundreds of armed men should be brought right into town.

To make matters worse, they were segregated according to factions. In theory ZANLA and ZIPRA aspired to the same ideals but they were composed almost entirely of Shona and Matabele respectively. The two nations were traditional enemies and even when the liberation war was on, they had almost as many battles between themselves as they did with the Security Forces. The dopiest of administrators should surely have deemed it sensible to keep the factions a long way apart, but the camps were bundled cheek by jowl into the already crowded township of Entumbane. The inmates still had their weapons and drink was freely available, but nobody in authority seemed to have foreseen trouble.

It appeared the rioting had been sparked by comments made by a senior politician at a Bulawayo rally on Saturday 8 November 1980. Enos Nkala — himself a Matabele — had made disparaging remarks about ZAPU's Matabele leaders and the troubles escalated from there. Faction fighting once more became the order of the day and ordinary folk suffered for the crass stupidity of their political masters.

When it came, it quickly escalated into pitched battles between opposing factions and the situation was soon out of control. I arrived at Stops Police Camp in Bulawayo to see a military aircraft dropping bombs on one corner of town and the rattle of gunfire sounded horribly loud in the morning stillness. Reports of civilian casualties were flooding in to a hastily set up control room and already there was anarchy throughout the Western townships. The city centre had not been affected but radio warnings had gone out for everyone to stay at home. Few township residents ventured out of their houses and Zimbabwe's second city ground to an eerie standstill.

Bulawayo is one of the most pleasant urban centres in southern Africa. The buildings are old and shabbily genteel, while the streets are designed to allow a wagon and span, space to turn around. Originally the royal kraal of the Matabele nation — the name means 'place of killing'— and in 1981, that name once again assumed awful significance.

My initial briefing came from a uniformed superintendent who had obviously been up all night. Grey-faced and haggard he brought me up to date on the situation and explained what was being done to control it. The picture he painted wasn't a heartening one.

At that stage in the forces integration programme, only the RAR and ourselves could be relied on not to take sides in the conflict. Lima Troop were on their way to join us and 1 RAR were already in the thick of the action.

Many folk who are not involved look on recent conflicts in Africa as battles between black and white but this is seldom the case. In Bulawayo, one company of black soldiers and two Unit troops, almost entirely black brought the black rioters to heel. Apart from the three field commanders, there couldn't have been more than half a dozen white participants in the entire three days of fighting.

Early on that first morning, a white patrol officer from CID did venture into the townships and both he and his sergeant were dragged from their vehicle and killed by angry dissidents. We were not informed of this incident until nightfall, which was probably as well or we might have been tempted to get really stuck in. All over the world, policemen are notoriously sensitive to the killing of their own and we were no exception.

As it was, we were hamstrung from the start. My orders specifically instructed me to use firearms only when fired upon and when I queried this as unworkable, the superintendent shrugged.

'It comes from the top, I'm afraid. We must do as we are told.'

It probably sounds reasonable to those who have never been under fire, but it was an invitation to get ourselves killed. There were armed men roaming the townships, all of them spoiling for a fight. Our task was to herd them back into the camps, but without the threat of force to back us up, we were sitting ducks for anyone who felt like taking us on. We were as heavily armed as the rioters, but in that sort of situation, each contact lasts mere seconds and he who gets in the first shot holds all the aces.

I started out in my Land-Rover, but it had no doors and I felt totally exposed and vulnerable. As soon as I saw the bodies strewn about the streets, I returned to Stops Camp and waited for the back-up of my men and armoured transport. For the duration of the riots, my vehicle remained unused and I travelled in a high-sided mine protected hyena with an armoured mine protected crocodile troop carrier following close behind. These were two examples of the protected vehicles that had proliferated during the war and although they appeared cumbersome, they were effective indeed.

My first confrontation was with an arrogant young man from one of the ZIPRA camps. He carried an RPD light machine gun slung across his shoulders and was unimpressed with my polite request for him to return to his base.

'And get myself bombed by Mugabe's aircraft?' he sneered.

I could see the validity of his argument. Even as we spoke, there was the heavy crump of bombing in the distance and I cursed the lunatic who had ordered it. He was probably ensconced in a comfortable office while we had to cope with the consequences of his big ideas.

This young man was obviously hyped up to the eyeballs by the situation and I held his gaze. I could see the arrogant contempt in his eyes. As far as he was concerned, I was an agent of Mugabe, whose men were trying to kill him on the ground. By putting him back into a camp, I would be rendering him as cannon fodder for the aircraft.

It wasn't a pleasant situation and when he stuck the barrel of the machine gun under my nose, I was hard put not to flinch in startled surprise. In truth, I was more angry than afraid but it was a nasty moment. Trying to keep my voice calm, I explained that he wouldn't be hurt if he returned to base, but he wasn't having that. Spitting contemptuously at my feet, he turned and swaggered away, the RPD back across his shoulders. For a moment, blind rage burned in my chest and I was sorely tempted to gun him down, even though his back was to me. We were officially at peace but violent killing was taking place all around me and this villainous thug was part of it.

My finger caressed the trigger of my rifle but my senses cleared and I took a firm grip on my emotions. This wasn't the time for anger. I had to remain dispassionate or we were going to suffer casualties.

Throughout that morning I went from murder scene to murder scene and every one of the victims was a civilian. If the former guerrillas were killing each other, it wasn't readily apparent. As far as I could see, they were venting their frustrations on those who couldn't fight back and it was horrific. Men, women and children — their bodies were strewn around the streets, their twisted limbs and contorted faces testifying to the terrifying circumstances of their deaths.

This was hardly conflict. It was vicious, cold-blooded slaughter of innocents and did nothing for my confidence in the future of Zimbabwe. The bleak expressions of my companions showed that they shared my feelings of horror and revulsion.

One elderly couple had been on holiday from Mutare, visiting a son in Luveve Township. Puzzled and confused by evidence of a war they considered part of the past, they had been on their way to the bus station and a hurried return home when they were stopped by a group of ZANLA men. Party cards were demanded and when these couldn't be produced, the couple had been cut down along with two of their grandchildren. The bereaved son turned to me with tears in his eyes.

'The terrible thing is that they were paid up members of ZANU-PF', he told me sadly. 'It was only because they were coming to Matabeleland that they thought it better not to carry their party cards.'

By midday, city mortuaries were full and meat wagons, belonging to the Cold Storage Commission were being used as makeshift storage for bodies. There was an air of dulled horror about the city and everyone I could see — and there weren't many out of their homes — had the blank-eyed look I remembered from the war. Once again it was black killing black and civilians taking most of the flak. It was all very well for Mugabe to speak airily about reconciliation between black and white, but what was he doing about reconciling black with black and Matabele with Shona?

There was no answer to that question and I wondered whether the new country was about to explode into the anarchy, long predicted by embittered white Rhodesians.

The crackle of automatic gunfire cut into my gloomy musing and I hurried to investigate. Leaping from my ungainly staff car, I ran toward the sound of battle. Surrounded by carnage, my blood was running hot and I had no thoughts of danger in my mind. Besides, Augustine Totohwiyo was running behind me somewhere.

Another burst of automatic fire was followed by the shriek of rubber, a tumultuous crash and the sound of raucous laughter. Cocking my rifle as I ran, I rounded a corner and skidded to a halt. A big Ford stood with it front wheels in a ditch and the windscreen starred by bullets. Two black nurses were climbing from the wreckage and both of them were wailing in their terror. Away to my left, a group of armed men ran into the distance, their laughter drifting back through the dusty air. For a moment, I was tempted to fire into their midst. They were close together and a few heavy rounds from *Fabrique Nationale* would soon put a stop to their mirth.

The call of duty brought me back to reality and I turned to the nurses who had seen my uniform and were running towards me. One of them threw herself sobbing into my arms and the other put up a trembling hand to caress my neck. Embarrassed and unsure of myself, I patted the tearful one on the back and murmured what I hoped were comforting words. My erstwhile bodyguard Totohwiyo seemed to have disappeared.

Accompanied by great, gulping sobs the story came out. They had been on their way to work at Mpilo Hospital with their friend — himself a medical orderly. Yes, they had been warned to stay off the streets, but theirs was an essential occupation and people were dying. They had felt justified in taking the risk, but on their way to hospital they were fired on and the driver was hit in the head. The car ended up in the ditch and here they were, their friend dead and themselves stranded in the middle of a battlefield.

At that moment, the hyena rumbled around the corner and my men whooped with delight to see Charlie Nine entwined with two sobbing women. Two medics ran across to check out the dead driver, still slumped across the dashboard, his hair matted with blood.

'He is alive, sir', Constable Majiga called and this elicited squeals of joy from the nurses. Disentangling themselves from my uncomfortable embrace, they ran across the road, leaving me to gather my dignity together and get on with the war.

All three of those medical folk lived through the traumas of Entumbane. The driver had a scalp wound which knocked him out, but did no permanent damage and the girls soon recovered from their fright. For Charlie Troop the horrors were far from over.

Moving cautiously through a building where armed men had been reported, I edged through the back door and saw the familiar fountains of dust tacking towards me across an open yard. Milliseconds later, I heard the gunfire but by then, I was diving for cover behind a small wall, my anger threatening to erupt once more. The bastards were firing at me. Those rounds had been meant to kill me and very nearly succeeded. Didn't they know the war was over? Zimbabwe was at peace for God's sake!

All these thoughts and more flashed through my mind as I tried to make myself as small as possible behind flimsy brick but eventually the firing died away and I was able to move on. On this occasion I would have been perfectly justified in firing back, but I couldn't see a damned thing to shoot at. My position was surrounded by buildings and the enemy could have been in any one of them. Suddenly I felt enormous sympathy for soldiers in Northern Ireland and other war-torn European cities. My battles had been fought in the bush, usually in open countryside. They had been hard and frightening, but they had not had the cramped frustration of urban warfare, which I was now experiencing for the first time.

Throughout that long, hot afternoon, we came under continuous fire. Rockets and rifle grenades thundered from ambush positions and it seemed a miracle that nobody was hurt. We persuaded a few rioters to return to their bases, but the majority mocked our efforts to control the situation. On the radio I heard that Lima Troop was claiming a couple of kills and my blood really boiled. All we were doing was putting ourselves into ever increasing danger and getting nowhere. Lima Nine was far more experienced than I was and I wondered whether he was sticking to the rules. Somehow I doubted it.

But there was little else I could do and the crazy situation continued well into the night. We were based at a caravan park outside the city and after dark I allowed my men to rest in relays. The fighting died away around midnight, but for me there was little sleep. I sat in the control room through the wee small hours, listening to radio reports of sporadic violence and exchanging desultory conversation with another visitor to the room.

I have never held Joshua Nkomo in high esteem, but I have to admit that he was on hand throughout those initial riots at Entumbane. He managed less sleep than any of us and made repeated offers to go out and speak to his men. I was all for that, but those in overall command decided that as Minister of Justice, he couldn't be allowed to risk his life. This added to my frustration, as Josh was the one person apart from Mugabe who might have brought the killing to an end.

Shortly after daylight the situation worsened. Reports of further killings flooded in and there were numerous fire fights between opposing factions. Feeling very bitter and twisted, I went out again in the hyena, the crocodile lumbering in our wake.

I hadn't even had breakfast when I felt my stomach muscles clench in agonised fright at the dreadful, rushing whistle overhead. Almost simultaneously, we were deafened by a cataclysmic explosion and this was followed moments later by a lesser bang as the rocket exploded high in the sky beyond us. Further rockets and streams of tracer followed, but I was ready for it and the shock wasn't quite so great. As long as we kept our heads below the armour plating, we were safe from bullets. Rockets were another matter, but I pushed such worries from my mind.

Wally Johnson was a superintendent who had recently come over to us from the Uniform Branch. He didn't yet understand Black Boot ways and when he was sent down to take charge of Unit deployments in the Bulawayo fighting, he did things by the book. We were hammering through a particularly enthusiastic ambush when he called me on the radio. I barely heard him over the crackle of gunfire and repeated thunder of weaponry from the crocodile behind us. When he repeated the call, I grabbed irritably for the handset.

'What is your position?' he asked officiously.

'Under fire in cemetery road.'

I refrained from adding that I was trying desperately to keep my head below the armoured shield for fear of having it blown off.

'Confirm "under fire?"'

It was a long time since ordinary coppers had been involved in gun battles and he was obviously struggling to understand. My answer was even more succinct.

'Yes.'

'Charlie Nine, this is Badger Three.'

As if I didn't know! Scowling at the set, I asked God to protect me from over zealous superintendents who wouldn't let me get on with my job.

'Confirm how many details you have with you?'

'Oh, for Christ's sake, sir', I exploded as another howling rocket curdled my terrified insides. 'Will you get off the bloody air and leave us to it.'

My language was possibly a little more colourful than that, but in the interest of propriety, I have edited my expressions. Slamming the handset back into its cradle, I concentrated on getting out from the hail of death that shrieked, crackled and popped around us.

Fortunately Badger Three soon came around to the Unit way of thinking and nothing was ever said about my insubordination over the radio.

Ambush followed ambush with monotonous regularity and I knew it couldn't be long before one of us was killed or wounded. The former terrorists had had time to refine their tactics and wherever we went, it was the same. Luveve, Tshabalala, Ntabazinduna, Magwegwe — each township seemed to have its resident band of armed men shooting at Security Force vehicles, their original squabbles apparently forgotten. We were the enemy now. We couldn't hear how the army was doing as our radio frequencies were not compatible, but when Lima Troop reported two men seriously hurt, my patience finally snapped.

Moving slowly out of a devastated shopping centre where every store had been looted or burned, we approached a wide vlei. Open ground stretched for 500 metres to the next crop of houses and I don't think I was the only one in the vehicle who felt horribly exposed. One of my patrol officers was driving and he slammed the hyena to a halt at an urgent exclamation from Sergeant Major Chiromo.

'Look, sir.'

Chiromo was waiting on promotion to patrol officer and his eyes were alight with the prospect of battle.

'There — to the right of the road.'

I looked and anger flared in my brain. There were three of them lying on their bellies in the grass and waiting for us to come past. We were still 100 metres away, but I could see the bipod legs of an RPD machine gun and I suddenly lost patience with the whole crazy set up.

'Take them out', I grated.

There were four of us in the hyena and we were well protected by armour plating, so for once the odds were in our favour.

'Take them out. I will carry the responsibility.'

The ensuing fire fight was brief, bloody and shockingly noisy. Chiromo was firing an MAG beside me and the blattering roar was amplified by the armour plating. My eardrums ached with the onslaught of noise and at one point I was forced to sit down with my fingers in my ears to deaden the pain.

In their exposed position, the former terrorists didn't stand a chance. I suppose they hadn't expected us to take them on, but three minutes after I fired the initial shot, the battle — if such it can be described as such — was over. Quickly checking that everyone was okay, I ordered a 'debus' and we swept through the contact scene.

Three men in rice-fleck camouflage lay in the grass and their injuries were appalling. They had been cut to pieces by our sustained fire and I gazed grimly down at two of the bodies, lying sprawled across each other in the bloody communion of death.

My patrol officer called from away to the right.

'This guy is still alive, Boss. He's shot to shit, but there is a very faint pulse. What do we do with him?'

'Kill him', I said and another shot rang out.

In the years that have passed since Entumbane, I have often reflected on that incident. I fought a good war and a fair war. I played by the rules and ignored the fact that our enemy knew no rules. My conscience remained clear throughout and I could sleep soundly at night.

Yet on one hot afternoon in Matabeleland, I cold-bloodedly ordered the death of another man. Perhaps 'cold-bloodedly' is not apt because passions run high after a contact, but I deliberately gave the order and felt no remorse afterwards. As a police officer, I was responsible for upholding the law and according to the law that was murder, yet I felt no guilt for my crime.

In the frenzied hell of Entumbane, I was doing a copper's job, but as far as I was concerned I was once again a soldier at war. For two days I had gone from horror scene to horror scene. For two days I had been shot at, rocketed and mortared. I had endured insults, naked aggression, bullets and rifle grenades. I had picked up the bodies of innocents, savagely done to death by depraved killers and I had comforted grieving relatives. I had seen too much unnecessary death and destruction and I had finally had enough.

The dead man offered no threat at the time, but he was one of those responsible for the barbarity that surrounded me. As far as I was concerned, he was but a rabid dog that had to be dealt with before he caused others to die. He and his companions had settled down in that vlei with the specific intention of killing as many of us as they could. That they had miscalculated our capabilities was a basic hazard of the war they had initiated. As soon as they set up the ambush, they put their own lives on the line.

The level of firepower laid down by our vehicle was awe-inspiring and born of frustrated desperation. We were all fed up with being frightened and shocked by the horrors around us. We were fed up with being shot at by armed thugs from every street corner. We were fed up with flinching at the terrifying shriek of overhead rockets. We had fought a long, hard war and none of us wanted to be a casualty of the peace. I couldn't speak for the rest, but my nerves were stretched to breaking point and I was an angry man.

I had consciously made the decision to take the initiative and I had deliberately fired the first shot. When the contact was over, my blood was still hot but I knew exactly what I was saying when I gave the order for that man to die. At that moment I wasn't prepared to take any more nonsense, either from my superiors or from the mindless thugs terrorising Bulawayo. The situation was out of control and I was no longer willing to put my life and the lives of my men on the line. We had done our duty and more than that. Even had the wounded man not been 'shot to shit' like his colleagues, I am not sure that I wouldn't not have given exactly the same instruction.

It had become a question of kill or be killed and I was determined that Charlie Troop were not going to be the ones in the latter category.

I didn't inspect the third body, nor did the young patrol officer and I discuss the matter afterwards. As far as I was concerned, three terrorists had met their just deserts and I wasn't in any way sorry about it.

One of the most disturbing aspects of the Entumbane riots was the fact that local citizens didn't appreciate our efforts on their behalf. Wherever we went, we were subject to abuse from civilians and my blokes founds this difficult to understand. We were doing our job as agents of the government, but this was Matabeleland and the populace didn't believe that Mugabe and his men should be in power.

We were looked upon as enemies attempting to prevent their own boys from killing Shona dogs. Civilian themselves, they didn't seem to realise that those being killed were civilians and the original point of the argument — if an argument there ever was —had long been forgotten in the general orgy of killing. The irony of it was that in my troop, I had roughly equal numbers of Shona and Matabele.

Be that as it may, from the moment of that would-be ambush in the vlei, I adopted a far more aggressive attitude towards rioters at Entumbane. It was probably a question of being hung for a sheep etcetera, but it was perhaps significant that from that moment on, we began to get on top of the situation.

Towards evening of the second day, we were ambushed for the umpteenth time on a long, straight stretch of road. The attackers had positioned themselves in a line of houses and the firing seemed to go on for ages. Once again, nobody was hurt and we concentrated on getting out of that killing zone as quickly as possible. Pulling up half a kilometre beyond the ambush site, I spoke briefly to Sergeant Mataera who was driving the crocodile. When he heard what I wanted, the veteran sergeant rolled his eyes in horror.

'Ah, *Mambo*, we will all be killed for sure.'

'No, we won't', I told him briskly. 'We'll catch them by surprise.'

I was right. We drove straight back toward the ambush site and as we approached, our would-be killers were milling about in the road, no doubt congratulating themselves on putting the Black Boots to flight. Once again I fired the initial shot and this time we killed two, but the message must have got about that we were fighting back as ambushes abated and gradually — ever so gradually — the cadres drifted back into their camps.

When I returned to the control room that evening, I received another shock to my system. Badger was there to meet me and with him was the commissioner, Mr PK Allum. I thought I was in trouble, but Hoggie merely grinned at my worried face.

'Lead us back to your camp, Charlie Nine. We're staying the night.'

I was horrified. It was bad enough having an unannounced visit from Badger, but to have the Lord High Panjandrum as well — that was really stretching things.

Not that I was any longer a stranger to police commissioners. I had argued with Commissioner Sid Bristow at Marandellas (causing immediate panic among my superiors!) and his successor, Peter Sherren had been a not infrequent visitor to Macheke. I had never been overawed by rank, but my men were tired and didn't deserve to be subjected to the pomp and panoply of an official visit at that stage.

Fortunately Mr Allum wasn't looking for pomp or an official welcome. It turned out a very pleasant evening and although he frowned when I protested at the order to fire only when fired upon, he made no adverse comment about our activities. My only moment of real nervousness came when he produced a bottle of whisky after dinner. Scottish wine was a rarity in Zimbabwe, but my major problem lay in the face that we had no glasses.

'We don't mind drinking out of cups', Mr Allum conceded.

Badger tried to hide his smile. He understood my dilemma.

Daniel Machipisa had long since gone on his way and our cook was a Bulawayo lad with the improbable name of Melody Fair. Melody produced passable meals, but Hoggie had probably heard from his son about Melody's insanitary habits. Field kitchens were never pristine, but ours was a hygienist's nightmare. It was generally filthy and while stained crockery was of little import to busy fighting men, I wasn't sure how the commissioner would feel when he saw the bottom of his cup through the whisky.

In the event, nobody complained and we enjoyed a convivial evening. 'General' Jamieson was horrified the next morning when — unaware of our high-powered visitors — he went for his ablutions and found himself at a washbasin with the Commissioner of Police on one side and the man with overall command of the Support Unit on the other.

'I thought I was dead, Boss', he protested. 'There I was in heaven and the brass had come along to spoil it for me.'

That little meeting provoked more hilarious discussion than anything else that took place throughout the three nightmare days of Entumbane One.

If they did nothing else, the riots at Entumbane convinced our prime minister that integration of the Security Forces wasn't quite so immediate a task as he might have believed. The only troops who could have quelled the disturbances, because they were the only troops without personnel directly affected, were those that had not been integrated.

Shortly after Entumbane, we were assured by Mugabe himself that we in the Support Unit would be left as we were. It was a comforting thought for us all, but like so many political promises, it didn't mean a thing.

25

Back to Bulawayo

Middle Sabi was a hot, arid piece of countryside immediately below the mountains of Chipinge. In the early sixties the Rhodesian government had opened the place up to white settlement, selling off small tracts of land for ridiculously low prices and assisting the settlers with loans for irrigation equipment. The mighty Sabi River was the water source and the scheme proved so successful that although small by African standards, the farms could be worked the year round and yielded magnificent crops. The entire area was crisscrossed with irrigation canals and there was a small dam in the middle where hippopotami wallowed happily, oblivious to people and traffic.

Middle Sabi farmers were seriously rich people. Most of them flew their own aeroplanes and in many homesteads, front gates had been widened so that 'his' and 'her' aircraft could be kept in the garage. Less than five kilometres from all this luxury was Tongogara Camp, a spill over from Assembly Point Foxtrot. The camp contained former guerrillas who had already been accepted into the army and none of the farmers were happy when it was established on their doorstep. Tongogara was run on vaguely military lines and commanded by an impressive young man called Gumbo, who told me that he had spent considerable time in the Wiltshire during the war. It gave us a point of common interest, but we didn't really get on and treated each other with wary respect.

The farmers were understandably anxious at having two and a half thousand former enemies as their neighbours and the Unit were called in to keep the peace Gumbo ran a fairly tight camp so there was little trouble, but we had the occasional drunken flare up over weekends when the men were allowed out. These incidents were not difficult to deal with and my life was hardly stressful, although it had its moments. In between golf with the farmers and mountain walks around Chipinge, I had regular meetings with Gumbo and his officers, which could occasionally be tense. As former enemies, our arguments could be stormy and every time I entered the camp, I was subjected to a thorough search of my vehicle, my person and my equipment.

These searches were pointless as my truck was invariably piled high with ammunition, grenades or weapons of war and I was always allowed to continue without explanation. Nevertheless they were irritating, but we had been instructed to remain on good terms with former combatants — I still looked on them as terrorists — so I gritted my teeth and tried to be pleasant. But Middle Sabi is in the Zimbabwean lowveld and fiendishly hot. It is the sort of place where bad temper is never far from the surface and I am not known for my equanimity.

One afternoon I was on my way back to camp — hot sweaty and tired after a strenuous day of training. Gumbo had asked to borrow a book I was reading, so pulling in to Tongogara I stopped beside the entrance boom and waited while a bored sentry strolled across to check me over.

'Out!' he sneered, gesturing at me to debus.

'I'm in a hurry', I told him. 'I only want a quick word with Gumbo.'

'Out!' he repeated and I kept a tight rein on my temper.

'Listen', I soothed. 'This isn't an official visit. I'm merely bringing Gumbo something he wanted.'

'Out!'

It was too much. I was hot, sweaty, uncomfortable and tired. Gumbo had asked for the book so I was doing him a favour, yet this oaf expected me to waste time with a search, even though he knew full well who I was. My temper exploded and I threw a tantrum. Jumping from the cab, I tore into that unfortunate guard. Pushing my face into his, I berated him at the top of my voice for his stupidity, his crass lack of manners and his ancestry. My language was colourfully military and very descriptive. Spittle flew and I could see him wilting visibly under my attack, while nervous faces peered from the guardhouse.

I was probably taking a considerable risk. My rifle was in the Land-Rover and he held his AK nervously across his chest as he backed away from me. I didn't care a jot. My blood was up and I was determined to have my say. In that frame of mind, I would have shouted down the entire ZANLA army.

Ending my tirade with a petulant stamp in the dust, I climbed back into the cab, started the engine and drove for the boom. It rose abruptly and as my temper faded, I couldn't help smiling at the thought that Africa had changed little since colonial days. When the white man shouted, the black man still jumped. It was blatantly racist and hardly fair in the circumstances, but it cheered me up at the time.

Not surprisingly, I was never asked to stop at the Tongogara gate again.

But tragedy wasn't far away for Charlie Troop and inevitably it occurred in the local beer hall. I was on occasional leave at the time, but my presence wouldn't have made any difference.

It was a Sunday afternoon and the men from Tongogara were celebrating. A number were drunk and a fight started with locals. One man was badly beaten and the incident was reported to our camp on Middle Sabi airfield.

Sergeant Kandeke, an enthusiastic young man who had only been with us a few weeks, led the reaction patrol. Taking his men into the beer hall, he arrested two of Gumbo's men and put them into the back of a troop carrier. The patrol climbed aboard with them and as the sergeant turned to shut the armoured doors, a rescue attempt was mounted from within the beer hall. Shots crackled through the sultry air and the young sergeant fell dead on the dusty ground.

The person who fired the shots was never identified and the murder enquiry was quickly dropped. Kandeke was buried with full military honours and his death hit the troop harder than many other deaths, suffered during the war. I suppose that was because we were supposed to be at peace, although it wasn't only at Middle Sabi that the word had a hollow ring to it.

In Matabeleland the army were on the rampage and innocent civilians were dying. Charlie Troop was about to become closely involved in yet more horror.

After our efforts at Entumbane, we seemed to have been designated a Matabeleland troop and it wasn't long before we found ourselves back in that fascinating province. This time, however, everything had changed. From Lupane in the north to Beit Bridge on the South African border, we had to clean up the aftermath of killing and a deep sense of self-revulsion rose in my soul. I was working for a government, obviously intent on wiping out the Matabele people and I felt deeply ashamed.

Shortly after Independence, a new brigade had been formed in the National Army and they seemed to have been designed to act as Mugabe's Praetorian Guard. Trained by North Korean instructors, the Fifth Brigade were allegedly tasked with sorting out the dissident problem in Matabeleland, but their reputation for dark and dastardly deeds soon began to spread. The Matabele leaders must have been worrying Robert Mugabe, because these viciously evil soldiers soon embarked on a campaign of systematic murder throughout the province. This was to be known as *Gukurahundi* — loosely translated as 'the washing of the land' and once again, Charlie Troop was employed in a civil police role.

We attended scene after scene of murder, rape and arson, our only real task being to clean up the mess. Entire kraals were wiped out, their inhabitants gunned down and their possessions put to the torch. Herds of cattle were hamstrung and left to die, while men, women and children were shot or taken away, never to be seen again.

Women of all ages and their children were raped and mutilated before they died and hardened though they were to the horrors of war, my men were sickened by the carnage. I had thought of myself as immune to horror by that stage, but I took to wearing dark glasses, if only to hide the sickness in my eyes.

An atmosphere of fear and suffering hung over Matabeleland and people became sullen and uncooperative. Wherever we went, we were greeted with blank eyes and hostile silence — not what we were accustomed to in that huge, generous province. We wanted to help but entire communal lands (the former TTLs) were frozen and we were never allowed to stay in an area for long. Requests for information on the whereabouts of army platoons were curtly dismissed and once again my frustration was mounting.

I found it particularly curious that the international media, so vociferous when Rhodesians had been in power, seemed oblivious to the atrocities in Matabeleland. Local newspapers were notoriously sycophantic toward the government but I listened to the BBC World Service and was dismayed to hear no mention of the dark deeds taking place around me. Matabeleland was the forgotten province and this a forgotten war.

Mind you, it could hardly be called war. It was too one-sided for that. We attended seven scenes of mass murder in one five-week stint but were never allowed to do more than guard the immediate area. Army patrols were called in to follow up on the killers, yet from my questioning of survivors, I was convinced that the army were responsible for the atrocities. All too often, descriptions were specific and those who dared to speak were dismissive when I suggested that the killers might be dissidents from the camps.

'They were *masojers* [soldiers]', was the emphatic reply on almost every occasion. My bitterly worded reports on the matter disappeared into the system and when I queried this with the Officer Commanding Matabeleland Province, I was told to 'wind my neck in.' It seemed that as mere policemen, we were powerless to do anything about the escalating carnage and my bitterness mounted by the day.

I was perhaps fortunate (hardly a suitable word in those circumstances) that I was only in Matabeleland at the start of *Gukuruhunde*. It was to continue for two years after I left the Unit and I missed most of the killing. The world remained silent throughout the carnage, but Amnesty International finally managed to publicise the activities of Fifth Brigade and perhaps coincidentally, the murders and other atrocities began to diminish. It was surely not coincidental that Amnesty was promptly banished from the country.

For the Matabele people, it was too late. Thousands had died and their young fighting men had been subdued by the terror. Those who remained belligerent were killed or imprisoned on trumped up charges.

One evening I was approached by Sergeant Dube — he with the divided family loyalties.

'I can do no more, sir', he told me sadly. 'I have been a policeman for eight years and have always been loyal to the government. I fought for Ian Smith and in Bulawayo I fought for Mugabe. Now I'm not allowed to fight against the jackals who are slaughtering my people. You know as I do that these killers come from the government we serve, so how can I continue to fight?'

There was no answer to that. Whether with the tacit support of Mugabe or not, army details were running amok in the province and we were helpless to control it. Our job was to collect bodies, clean up devastated villages and cry hot tears with the few survivors. We were witnessing the death of a proud nation and my heart went out to Dube and the other Matabeles in my troop.

'What will you do?' I asked when he handed me his resignation form.

'Become a dissident', he told me flatly. 'I will join those in the hills and together we will fight Mugabe and his men.'

I don't know whether Dube became a dissident, but I couldn't have blamed him if he had. The cheerful spirit of Charlie Troop had been destroyed by the killings that we were so helpless to prevent and I was experiencing increasing problems with morale. An entire nation was being slaughtered around us and there was absolutely nothing we could do about it. Such a situation hardly made for contentment in the ranks.

My own sense of pride in being part of a fighting elite had long since dissipated. I took to driving around aimlessly in my new Nissan Patrol and the clear, Matabeleland evenings seemed to act as a minor panacea for my troubled spirit, but there were times when I wondered what I was doing. I was a footloose soldier-cop fighting a war that didn't officially exist and when I saw distant lights, I pictured family men relaxing with their wives and children. My own family were far away and I missed them desperately, while camp routine and a cramped caravan (I had graduated from a tent) made me restless and ill at ease.

The men looked to me for inspiration, but I was sick to death of the endless cycle of murder and mayhem that was our daily routine. I seriously considered leaving — not only the Unit — but the police force and probably the country itself. The politicians were not interested in what was happening in Matabeleland and although for a while I had almost come to admire Mugabe for his statesman-like attitude toward national reconciliation, I couldn't help feeling that he had to be condoning the slaughter. He controlled the army and they were the ones who were doing the killing.

I told Badger of my feelings and he was sympathetic, but could offer no assistance.

'It goes higher up the scale than mere soldiers', he told me. 'Some very big names are involved, but there is nothing you or I can do except make our feelings known.'

There I had to leave it but as 1980 drew to a close, I was disillusioned and bitter, while morale in the Troop was at an all time low. In such circumstances, it was probably inevitable that we would be flung back into the firing line and perhaps equally inevitable that the trouble when it came would be in the western townships of Bulawayo. Entumbane was to be the scene for yet more needless slaughter of innocents and if I had known what was to come, I might well have joined sergeant Dube in his new life as a dissident civilian.

On the first day of fighting on 11 February 1981 Eland 90 armoured cars, manned by white soldiers of the former Rhodesian Army, knocked out four of ZIPRA's ex-Soviet BTR152 armoured personnel carriers on the main road into Bulawayo, one outside the Holiday Inn in Selborne Avenue. We passed the wreckage on our way into Bulawayo. Later in the day I watched in horrified amazement as soldiers and policemen removed charred bodies and bits of charred bodies from the still hot wreckage outside the Holiday Inn.

Darryl Brent and his Lima Troop were away chasing dissidents at this time so we were the only Black Boots involved in the fighting. At that stage, Darryl was the only troop commander who had been with the same troop longer than I had been with Charlie. Barry Woan — a former Charlie Nine — had more experience than either of us, but Charlie had been my family for three long years. Darryl had been with Lima for seven years and they were a highly efficient outfit, so we would miss their help.

For three days we chased dissidents around the streets of the western townships, while the army collected loot and prisoners from Nkomo's many properties. There were fewer civilian casualties this time and nor were we subject to the same volume of ambushes and personal attacks, but it was still a hair-raising experience. I spent a great deal of time on foot with my patrols and it was while we were investigating a sighting of armed men in a long row of houses that disaster struck with a vengeance.

Our quarry had disappeared into a particular building and I charged toward the door, my rifle cocked and adrenaline surging through my system. This was battle once again and I was on a high. For months I had been forced to act as mute witness to atrocity, but now I was taking the initiative and it felt good. As I moved to kick the door of that house open (the time for finesse was long past) Constable Totohwiyo shouldered past me. He had long since abandoned hope of becoming a sergeant, but I gave him what responsibility I could and at that stage he was in charge of my personal back-up.

'Let me do it, sir', he advised quietly. 'It will be better that way.'

I suppose he had a point. In those troubled and confusing times, nobody was sure who was fighting who and my white face probably marked me down as the enemy to both factions. The occupants of the house were Matabele and Totohs was a Shona, but he was black and his tribal affinities wouldn't be immediately obvious. In fact, he was so large and fearsome that either side would willingly claim him as their own.

One savage smash with his heel on the doorjamb and the flimsy wood flew open. Augustine Totohwiyo took a step through the opening and the world fell apart. The detonation seemed to batter my eardrums and almost absently I heard shrapnel whine past my head. Instinctively I flung myself to the floor and was vaguely aware of my colleagues doing the same. Totohs was already down and through billowing smoke I could see the shape of an armed man behind him. I couldn't see what he was doing and nor did I care. He was the enemy and my options were limited.

Firing coldly and deliberately with bitter hate fuelling my actions, I emptied a magazine into the man and continued firing long after he had gone down. At each two-ton impact of an FN bullet, his body jumped and twitched, but I didn't care. I wanted to kill him and I was going to make good and sure that I did.

Augustine Totohwiyo was still alive but deeply unconscious. He had taken the full blast of the grenade and the front of his body was shredded. Blood oozed over my hands as I held him and screamed for assistance. Constable Sibanda had been trained as a medic, but Totoh's injuries were far worse than any he had yet been called upon to deal with. He worked in grim silence while someone else radioed for a casevac.

While the everyday chaos of warfare went on around me, I sat with the big fellow's head in my lap, tears running down my face and hate in my heart. I don't think I have ever felt as bitterly angry as I did at that moment. Not only had Totohwiyo been injured by him taking my place, but the whole ridiculous situation had been initiated by the callous ranting of idiot politicians.

I had always been a loyal copper, serving the government of the day no matter what policies they espoused, yet at that moment I was a dissident at heart. I could easily have gone to war on my own account and for some time afterwards, I seriously considered it.

Just before cease-fire when it was obvious that the Rhodesian cause was lost, there had been a great deal of talk about a scorched earth policy from emigrating whites. It was said that vital installations would be razed and even the dam wall at Kariba would be blown up by departing Selous Scouts. A few folk did burn their farms rather than leave them for the new government, but most of the talk proved similar to *Operation Quartz* — just so much hot air and a focus for frustration.

Yet for a few days after Entumbane Two, one troubled Support Unit commander seriously considered going on the rampage. I knew I could inflict a great deal of damage before inevitably being captured or killed. I had the weaponry and the expertise. My uniform allowed me into places where the average gunman couldn't go. It might have worked and for a while I was grimly determined that a number of smug politicians were going to suffer if my friend Totohwiyo died.

I was saved from my own foolishness by the big fellow himself. He had taken the full force of a Chinese stick grenade in his body and didn't have a hope of surviving, but such was his strength that he hung on for days. By the time he died, my rage had cooled and I had started to consider matters like my future and my family. The kids were at a government school and besides, they needed a father. My plans — if such they could be considered — were impractical and I had no desire to throw my life away for Mugabe's Zimbabwe.

Although it was inevitable, Augustine Totohwiyo's death hit me very hard. All along he had been a favourite among my troopers. How well I remembered that day when he had looked down on me — a brand new Black Boot, yet to prove myself — with an expression of amused tolerance and wry good humour. I had eventually earned his respect and as much as it can be so in a military situation, I had looked on him as a friend. He had given his life for me and that was something I could never forget. I should have been the one shredded by that grenade and that I wasn't was entirely due to Augustine Totohwiyo's sense of what was proper. Although he led from the front himself, he didn't consider it right that his Troop Commander should be ahead of him when the bullets were flying.

The Matabele always looked upon the Shona as cowardly agriculturists and clerks, but Augustine Totohwiyo was a great fighting man. He might not have been an intellectual heavyweight, but he had a heart as big as Africa and in any man's language, he was a warrior to the core.

I was going to miss him.

Entumbane Two was a personal disaster for Joshua Nkomo and on a personal note, the start of my total disillusionment with the system I served. The battle on the ground was as shambolic as it had been the first time and although we no longer had the 'no shooting till you are shot at' rule, some desk-bound genius had decreed that we should 'keep a low profile.' He had obviously never been in Bulawayo when the comrades were on the rampage.

In February 1982 Soviet-built armoured fighting vehicles, and large quantities of ammunition and heavy weaponry were discovered on isolated farms and other properties belonging to Nkomo and these were ferried through to Harare where they sat in storage waiting to be used on someone else. I couldn't help remembering the charred remains of people, livestock and kraals I had wandered through over the previous months and wondered when all that hardware would be brought into action against the very people it was originally designed to help.

With Totohwiyo's death, my passion for the Support Unit had ended. I soldiered on for a while, but when — in spite of Mugabe's promises — it was announced that the Unit was to be integrated. I applied for a transfer to Uniform Branch. The post of officer in charge at Marondera was vacant and my home was still there so it seemed the obvious place to go. Badger backed my application, but he was on his way in any case, as was Don Rowland and most of the Unit hierarchy. We had been fighting ZANLA and ZIPRA for many years and we had witnessed too many atrocities to be comfortable with them in our ranks. It was desperately sad, but inevitable in the circumstances.

My young white patrol officers were also leaving the Unit. Peter Coventry had already gone and Ron Jamieson announced that he was going to become a professional student. Richard Hogg left for South Africa with his family and Leon Oosthuizen went off to farm at Macheke. Their departure was a bitter blow to everyone who knew them and there was a general sense of despondency in Charlie Troop. It was the end of an exciting chapter in all our lives and when it was announced that my place was to be taken by Inspector Tegere, my troopers were really worried.

'How can a black man command Charlie Troop, sir?' Sergeant Mataera asked when the news came through. 'Charlie Nine has always been a *marungu*.'

I found that somewhat ironic in the new Zimbabwe, but I just hoped they would be okay.

The farewell party for what might have been called the 'old' Support Unit was held at Chikurubi and it was a spectacular affair. The Unit band played throughout and magnificently uniformed waiters scurried around with drinks and snacks. The new black OC made only a brief appearance, but there were other black faces amongst the white. Sam Chikovore was now a superintendent and Mike Mukulunyelwa had his own troop. Inspector Tembo, who had long been the Unit Sergeant Major, looked resplendent in his new uniform and black wives giggled girlishly with their white counterparts. Troubles were forgotten. Don Rowland made an emotional speech and the festivities went on for a long time.

The Unit as we knew it was going out in style. We had been through a great deal together in the years of war and peace. We had coped with it all and in the process, learned much about ourselves and our fellow men. So many of our own had paid the ultimate price and I am sure I wasn't the only one who wondered whether it had been worth it. Pride had always run high in the soul of a Black Boot and it was only the possibility of losing that sense of pride that was driving us into different lives. As the dawn sky brightened over the barracks and sleepy waiters began repairing the ravages of the night, there was a deep feeling of loss in the morning air.

Don Rowland summed it up for all of us. Suavely dignified in a beer-stained suit, he gave us our last team talk and it was probably his best.

'Wherever you go, chaps, and whatever you do, you will never forget your days in the Support Unit. You have all done incredibly well in almost impossible circumstances and like the rest of you, I am proud to have been a Black Boot.'

His words brought tears to my eyes and I wasn't the only one.

26

The end of the road

With the coming of Independence, Marandellas was one of the towns to undergo an immediate name change. The original chief in the area had been Marondera and he was a hero of the first *Chimurenga*, so it was inevitable that the little farming town should take his name. For most of us it meant nothing. The country we had been so proud to call Rhodesia was now Zimbabwe and if we could accept that, we could take a minor change like Marandellas to Marondera.

This was my third stint in the town, so I knew exactly what I was coming to and this time I was the boss. Like any new officer in charge, I made changes in station procedure, but they were cosmetic and didn't achieve a great deal. I was to be a full time copper again and the prospect filled me with horror. I no longer wanted to be a policeman. Me — the cocky young bobby who had refused in this very station to become involved in the war on the grounds that I was only a cop!

The killings were increasing in both frequency and horror in Matabeleland and a dissident, known as the Lone Ranger was enjoying a reign of terror in the north-east, but these were not my problems. I was a desk jockey now, not a Black Boot and I didn't enjoy the feeling. My life had been changed by Support Unit service and I missed the hard-bitten, troublesome, lovely men of Charlie Troop. I also missed the disciplined excitement of life at the sharp end.

It was nice to be back with my family, but even that had changed. Missy and I had grown ever further apart during my years in the Unit and her friends were no longer mine. I was subject to moods of deep depression and while these might be recognised as symptoms of stress in this more enlightened age, they merely convinced her that I was fed up with my marriage.

It wasn't true, but I was bored both at work and at home. My job was a question of supervision and public relations, while none of my family could understand my restlessness. I couldn't blame them, but I had nothing to vent my frustration on. The police reserve was still in existence, but their role had changed and I found the concept valueless. I had many old friends in the farming community and I spent much of my time visiting and setting the world to rights over copious quantities of beer. Missy lectured me on my drinking habits and she was undoubtedly right to do so, but I felt I could cope if only I had something worthwhile to do.

Dispol went on three months leave and there was nobody to take his place, so I was made acting chief superintendent. For two months it was great fun and I made earth-shattering decisions like authorising a new stereo set for the station pub. I drove out to Mrewa, Mtoko, Wedza and Nyamapanda again and enjoyed the familiar countryside, but the standard of paper work in these outlying stations made my hair curl. Even my Black Boots could have produced work of a higher standard and I wondered how magistrates and prosecutors coped when dockets came to court.

Integration with ZANLA and ZIPRA had taken place throughout the Force and although many of the newcomers claimed to have undergone training in Russia or Romania, their work was of a standard far below that to which our Force was accustomed. As many of them came in relatively high up the rank structure, it was a recipe for chaos. I couldn't blame the individuals involved, but it was a stupid move on the part of a government, afraid of offending its followers by giving them additional training.

I have always believed that policemen should remain apolitical, but that wasn't to be the case in the new Zimbabwe. Political indoctrination classes were held openly in police stations and the carrying of party cards was commonplace. Any adverse comment from me was regarded as subversive and I soon realised that if I tried to maintain normal standards of policing, I would end up doing even more damage to the entire rickety system. I was forced to accept the politics as well as substandard work and that added to my sense of bitter dissatisfaction.

I had two inspectors on my staff, one white and one black. Robbie Robertson was my deputy and Abel Bhunu ran the enquiry section, which I had managed all those years previously. I sympathised with Abel's problems in dealing with written work that was often gibberish and we had long talks on how best to resolve the situation. There was no simple solution. Standards were plummeting throughout the Force and many senior officers were resigning in disgust. Others were hanging on for their pensions, content to get through each day with little or no attention to the job for which they were being paid. Law and order was rapidly breaking down.

A farming friend from Wedza put the situation into perspective for me. Having heard about my mounting dissatisfaction, he urged me to think hard before making any irrevocable decision.

'The more decent men leave the force, the quicker it will disintegrate', was his argument and I could see the logic behind that, but he didn't have to put up with the day-to-day hassles of coping with illiterate and inefficient policemen.

The last straw for me was when a new officer was posted to Marondera as a replacement for Dispol. A big, slow speaking man, Mr Dingiswayo was pleasant enough, but he didn't have a clue. He had been promoted from sergeant major to chief superintendent and was completely out of his depth. My brief was to teach him how to command the district and in a state of considerable ire, I telephoned the Officer Commanding Mashonaland Province — Propol.

'How can a chief inspector', I protested, 'teach a chief superintendent to do a job that he — the chief inspector — is not supposed to understand?'

It was a ridiculous situation, but one that was symptomatic of a countrywide problem. What irked me most was that Dingiswayo earned considerably more than I did, yet I was supposed to teach him his job.

Standing in winter sunshine outside my office one afternoon, I pondered my situation. I was dressed in tunic, shorts and blue-topped socks. My shoes were brilliantly shined, but they were brown, as was my heavy belt. I couldn't help but smile as I remembered the carefully tailored shirts, the magnificent blue and gold lanyard and the martial eagle emblem that had been part of my regalia in the Unit.

And of course, the shoes and belt had been in deep, shiny black. How I missed being a Black Boot.

That very afternoon, the new promotion list was announced and my name wasn't on it. Abel Bhunu's was. I immediately submitted my resignation to Chief Superintendent Dingiswayo and returned to my brooding.

I was finished. Black Boot or Brown Boot, I no longer wanted to be part of the Zimbabwe Republic Police. I was unlikely to go any further up the promotional ladder and in any case, I wasn't enjoying my work. It was time to take early retirement.

'What are you going to do?'

Abel Bhunu now outranked me, but he was obviously concerned for my welfare.

'I will go and write stories of the bush', I told him airily. 'I'll take a farm cottage somewhere and settle down to write.'

Which is exactly what I did having put my life as a policeman behind me on 4 September 1982.

27

Never quite a soldier

A quarter of a century has passed since the Rhodesian war officially ended and the entire episode has been consigned to history as just another nasty little conflict in the long tale of man's inhumanity to man. Other wars have come and gone. Other terrorists have hugged the limelight before being forgotten as media attention switches to other parts of the world where people are dying.

Almost 28 000 people died in the war for Zimbabwe and many more were killed in its terrible aftermath. Most were civilians and most were black. The conflict is generally looked upon as a 'liberation crusade' by so-called free thinkers in the West, but it seems that the only way modern 'freedom fighters' can liberate a country is to maim, terrorise and kill as many as possible of that country's innocents.

Terrorism is an abomination wherever it occurs and whatever the cause espoused. Why should ordinary people be killed and brutalised for somebody else's ideal? It is high time that a proper stand was taken, but all too often terrorist campaigns are given spurious respectability by being labelled 'revolutionary' or part of an 'armed struggle.' Is Osama Bin Laden a worse man than Robert Mugabe because he hates America rather than white Rhodesians? Both men are terrorists, yet all too often former terrorists with the congealing blood of innocents on their hands are acclaimed as statesmen, while smirking killers are released from jail to resume their briefly interrupted campaigns of mayhem and murder. As these men take up their arms once more, politicians glibly assure bewildered victims that their tormentors are being freed to kill again because 'that is the way forward.' The politicians do not have to live with the results of their own crass stupidity, but the ordinary people do.

I was never quite a soldier but I was a copper in the front line of a particularly brutal war. In Rhodesia, I fought for Ian Smith and the perpetuation of white rule in my country. I ended up on the losing side because no small nation can afford to go against the wishes of the international community and friendless Rhodesia didn't really stand a chance.

In Zimbabwe-Rhodesia, I fought for Bishop Muzorewa and again I ended up on the losing side. Britain and her politicians were determined that the land should be given to Mugabe and Nkomo, so once again we didn't stand a chance.

In Zimbabwe I fought for Robert Mugabe and almost ended up as another military statistic in Bulawayo. I was nominally a peacekeeper. But I was also part of a murderous government scheme to quell any opposition. I witnessed the start of a genocidal campaign and to my shame, I did nothing to stop it. At the time I consoled myself with the thought that the opinion of a lowly chief inspector couldn't make a difference, but I was putting career before principle and that can never be justified.

For a man who wanted only to be a policeman, I almost enjoyed my war. Life was lived on a higher plane than normal and I found myself adapting to circumstances in a way that amazed even me. I wasn't alone in this. Throughout the country, ordinary policemen were called upon to perform Herculean tasks for which they were neither trained nor suited We all acted as we saw fit at the time and if some of those actions appear ill-considered, brutal or illegal when set down in cold print, these considerations should be balanced against the times we lived in. Violence begets violence and for all its horrifying brutality, war is an exciting experience. Blood runs hot in the veins and the meekest of men finds themselves capable of cruel depravity while under the frenetic spell of conflict.

I came through the war and its aftermath without a scratch, but emotionally badly scarred. With my life restored to normality, I craved excitement and the inevitable break up of my marriage added to my restlessness. I adopted the role of travelling scribbler, but even though I wandered the highways and byways of Africa in search of excitement, there was always something missing. Perhaps it was the feeling of companionship that is peculiar to fighting men in a hostile environment. I needed something different, but apart from being arrested twice in Tanzania — that is another story — excitement was in short supply.

All too often my thoughts turned to those who had died and all too often I asked myself what they had died for. Although the new nation of Zimbabwe started well, the rot has well and truly set in. After decimating the Matabele Nation in *Gukurahundi*, Mugabe concentrated on appeasing the white farmers. Without them the economy couldn't survive and he did well for a while although his true feelings have now made themselves felt. Corruption has become endemic in my country and many thousands of Zimbabweans are destitute and hungry. As in so many African dictatorships — and Western leaders are at last accepting that Mugabe is a dictator — our politicians grow fat on the sweat of the people. While they bolster their overseas bank accounts, the general populace face acute food shortages, mass unemployment and ultimate starvation — for once without the phlegmatic acceptance that is so basic a part of African culture.

The economy of Zimbabwe slithered into chaos faster than that of any other African state and when the new millennium dawned, the people had had enough. It was a trade union leader, Morgan Tsvangirai who started up the first effective opposition to Mugabe's policies. Tsvangirai's Movement for Democratic Change stirred the nation into action, but laudable thought its aims undoubtedly were, that led to yet more violence. Mugabe is an evil man and a pathological killer. To divert attention from his own incompetence and corruption, he orchestrated another campaign of intimidation and murder. With the occupation by ZANU-PF thugs of white-owned farms, the country descended into a state of near anarchy and the slaughter started again.

Those brave and headstrong farmers of Virginia were the first to suffer directly from the violence. Many of them were forced to flee their homes and Dave Stephens — he was a young manager in my day — was the first white farmer to be murdered by Mugabe's so-called war veterans. Before being shot, he was badly beaten and made to drink diesel oil in front of a laughing throng. Further murders followed and throughout the country, civilians again found themselves living in fear as they had lived in fear through those terrible years of war.

As they have always done when it comes to Africa, Western politicians condemned the mounting savagery without doing anything to stop it. 'We want free and fair elections', was their cry, but any elections held in Zimbabwe will be as free and fair as they were in Rhodesia in 1980. Commonwealth observers made no difference then, made no difference in all the elections held since 2000 and will make no difference in any future elections. Robert Mugabe has lived by the gun for 35 years and he will be the judge of what is free and what is fair.

In spite of massive intimidation the MDC did surprisingly well in 2000 and although their results have slipped since then, Tsvangirai would easily have won the presidential election had the entire system not been hopelessly rigged. Mugabe has consolidated his hold on power till 2008 and although the economy of his country is at rock bottom and millions of people are hungry, he is the Big Man and he will concentrate on staying that way, no matter what the cost to his people might be.

There are barely a hundred commercial farmers still working the land in Zimbabwe and all of them are struggling under huge government restrictions. The rest have gone. Some have started farming again in neighbouring countries who welcomed them with open arms, but others have settled in Britain, America, Australia and anywhere else where the capacity for hard work is appreciated. Those farms from which they once fed much of central Africa now lie untended and forgotten.

The emigration rate among Zimbabweans in 2005 was higher than ever it was during the terrible years of war. They had a police force to look after them then. They also had an army, but it seems that neither the ZRP (Zimbabwe Republic Police) nor the Zimbabwe National Army will do anything to assist the present day victims of violence. As he did in Matabeleland all those years ago, Mugabe allows his killers free rein and as they did with Matabeleland all those years ago, the rest of the world sits back with wringing hands but without any real interest in the ultimate fate of my country.

Yet for all its problems, my children still refer to Zimbabwe as home and to their children, Rhodesia will be but a name in the history books. That is as it ought to be. My generation did what we thought was right, but now it is time for the young ones to do things their way. When I was a boy, my favourite game was 'cowboys and Indians.' My sons played 'terrorists and soldiers'. My grandchildren played 'war vets and farmers'. It seems that the fashions of time are mirrored by kiddies' games and perhaps it is in these games that hope for the future lies. Zimbabwean children come in all colours and a white skin is no guarantee that its owner will be designated a farmer in the next game. He or she could as easily be caste in the role of villainous 'war veteran'.

I was proud to be a Rhodesian, but nowadays I call myself Zimbabwean and love that country with a passion that borders on the fanatical. I fought an honourable war for white rule, but that war was lost and life went on. The world had its way so why on earth are my countrymen still being allowed to suffer?

That seems an unanswerable question in this hypocritical age, but I pray that the fighting spirit of a great little nation will eventually ensure that there is a future for everyone in the land that was once Rhodesia.

Glossary

AK 47 — Kalashnikov assault rifle, used by guerrillas worldwide.
AKM — later AK47.
APR — African Police Reserve.

B
BSAP — British South Africa Police

C
Call sign — radio call sign, often used to denote a section of men in the field.
Casevac — casualty evacuation
Chimurenga — Chishona word for liberation war
Comops — Combined Operations
Contact — engagement with the enemy
Dare — tribal court, usually presided over by a chief. Office at police station for junior ranks
Fireforce — reaction force, airlifted to a contact scene usually with air support
FRELIMO — Front for the Liberation of Mozambique
FROLIZI — Front for the Liberation of Zimbabwe
GMO — Government medical officer
G-car — troop-carrying helicopter
Gondo — Chishona for eagle. The martial eagle emblem of the Support Unit
Gook — slang for terrorist believed to have originated during the Korean War

Ground Coverage — police intelligence gathering operation
Hondo — Chishona for war.
Int — Intelligence
Internal Affairs — formally Native Department.
JOC — joint operational command centre, staffed by all services and responsible for local operations
K-car — helicopter gunship
MAG — medium automatic gun/general purpose machine gun
Mujonnie — Zulu for soldier. White police officer in Rhodesia
Mantle — Support Unit
Mambo — Shona for chief or sir
Marungu — white man. Plural warungu.
Mombe — Chishona for cow
Mujiba — civilian young male scout used by ZANLA forces
Muti — African medicine
Nganga — traditional healer
Nkosi — chief in Sindebele, frequently used in Shona
Nkosi Mukulu — big chief
PGHQ — Police General Headquarters
Panga — wide-bladed knife
PATU — police anti-terrorist unit
P/O — patrol officer
Pole & dagga — traditional building materials
PRAW — Police Reserve Air Wing
Pungwe — ZANLA political indoctrination meeting
R and R — rest and recuperation

RAR — Rhodesian African Rifles
Ratpak — ration pack
RLI — Rhodesian Light Infantry
RPD — Russian-made light machine gun
Rooibos — South African herbal tea
SAC — senior assistant commissioner
SB — Special Branch
Sadza — maize meal cooked into a stiff porridge
Sitrep — situation report
Situpa — personal registration certificate for black males
Skelm — Afrikaans for criminal
S/O — section officer
Stick — 4-8 man security force section men
T & S — travelling and subsistence allowance
TTL — tribal trust land
Terr — Rhodesian. Colloquial word for terrorist
Tsotsi — Zulu for criminal. Widely used in other African languages
Vakomana — Chishona. 'Boys from the bush', used by locals to describe guerrilla forces
WFR — Women's Field Reserve
ZANLA — Zimbabwe African National Liberation Army
ZANU — Zimbabwe African National Union
ZAPU — Zimbabwe African People's Union
ZIPRA — Zimbabwe People's Revolutionary Army.

Index

2-Independent Company, Kariba, 66

A
Agric-alert, 81, 85, 96, 113, 147
Air Rhodesia Viscount 'Hunyani' was shot down, 149
Air Rhodesia Viscount 'Umniati' shot down, 150
Aitken, Chris, PO, 49
Allum, Peter K Commissioner BSAP, 240, 241
Altena Farm, attack, 46, 204
Andrews, Frank, Kariba Lake Captain, 61
Arnold, Toc Macheke farmer, 118
Assembly Point Foxtrot, 213, 215, 242
Assembly Point, Gwaai River, 233
Assembly Point Papa, 205, 230
Assembly Point Romeo, 205

B
Baisley, Keith, PATU, attacked, 84, 115
Barnard, Roy, PO, 48
Bate, Major Ian, 60
Battle of Marandellas, 165
Begg, George, 223
Beit Bridge, 244
Beit, Alfred, 16
Bellingham, Peter, C/Supt, 124, 125, 137, 155, 156
Beveridge, S/O Duncan, 52
Bhunu, Insp Abel, ZRP, 251, 252
Bikita, 224
Black Boots (see Support Unit BSAP)
Black Watch, PATU, 91
Blair, Chief Supt 'Yogi', 56, 57
Blake-White, Chief Constable Gloucestershire, 18
Botswana, 90
Bradshaw, David Scott, PO 125-129, 148
Brent, Darryl, Lima Company, Support Unit, 215, 246
Bristow, Sid, Commissioner BSAP, 240
British and Commonwealth monitors, 204
British South Africa Company, 20
Britter, Roger, farm attacked three times, 115
Brown, Athol, PATU, 84, 137
BSA Company Police, 20
Bulawayo, 226, 228, 229, 232, 233, 237, 239, 253
Bullen, S/O Mike, Support Unit, 143, 146
Bumi Hills Safari Lodge, 62, 65, 66, 69

C
Caetano, Marcello, Portuguese premier, ousted, 58
Callaghan, James, British premier, 75
Capco — Central African Power Corporation, 73-75
Carey, Dave, Field Reservist, KIA, 77
Carrington, Lord Peter, 201, 217
Carroll, Chris, PO, 135, 138, 139
Carson, Matt, Hotel, 79, 138, 139
Carter, Jimmy, US President, 165
Central Intelligence Organisation (CIO), 76
Chademana, John, 75, 150
Chakaipa, Patrick, RC Archbishop of Salisbury, 147
Chalk, Ian, BSAP, 23
Charlie Nine, 167, 200, 249
Chenjeke, Sergeant Major, BSAP, 26, 28
Chibvongodze, Const, Support Unit, 167-169
Chiduku TTL, 137
Chikovore, Sam, CSM to Supt, Support Unit, 163, 249
Chikurubi, 135, 162, 171, 197, 200, 213
Chimurenga War, 250
Chiota TTL, 31, 36, 43
Chipinge (formerly Chipinga), 224, 242
Chiredzi, 224
Chiromo, Sgt Major, Support Unit, 238
Chirundu, 66, 208
Chitepo, Herbert, 76
Clark, Andrew, Macheke farmer, 113, 148

259

Clements, Pete, Selous Scout, 61
Collet, Dale, Selous Scout, 60
Collings, Ashley, Special Branch, 62
Combined Operations (Comops), 95, 163, 211, 213, 217
Court, Jonty, Support Unit, 218, 221
Coventry, Peter, Support Unit, 223, 249
Crombie, Mr, farmer murdered by ZANLA, 146, 147
Crombie, Mrs, Macheke farmer's wife, 145
Crossley, Ant, Special Branch Aide, 65
Cullingworth, Brian, 67

D
Da Costa, John, Angical Dean of Salisbury, 149
Dart, DSO Neil, 120, 12, 127
De Borchgrave, Marc, 46
Department of Internal Affairs, 152, 224
Dingiswayo, Chief Supt, ZRP, 251, 252
Dombo Tombo Township, Marandellas, 27, 29, 32, 34
Du Pont, Clifford, President, 77
Du Preez, Daphne, WFR, 84
Du Preez, Tony, PATU, 84, 91
Dube, Sgt, Support Unit, 198, 199, 245
Dzorwa, Sgt, 40, 126

E
Elim Mission, ZANLA massacre of missionaries, 136
Enkeldoorn, 49, 163, 199, 205, 214-216, 218, 219, 224
Entumbane, 233, 236, 237, 239-241, 244, 248
Farrar, Ewan, Macheke farmer and PATU, 84, 137
Farrell, Mike, C/Insp, 158
Farrington, Dave, PO, 78, 260,
Featherstone, 197
Ferguson, Alex, S/O, 44, 45
Fifth Brigade ZNA, 244
Filabusi, 224, 227, 232
Fort Victoria, 163, 224
Franklin, Alan 'Stretch', Selous Scout, 60
Fuel storage depot in Salisbury rocketed, 151

G
Gamela the Silent, ZANLA terrorist, 142, 144, 145, 155
Geneva Conference, 83
George, Dave, Supt, SB, 69
Gloss, Billy, Lance Inspector, murdered, 230
Gloucestershire Constabulary, 15, 16
Gona re Zhou National Park, 231
Goromonzi, 44, 45
Gorumatanga, Ishe, FROLIZI political commissar, 47, 49
Gray, Andy, Bravo company commander Support Unit, 207
Gukuruhundi, 244, 254
Gumbo, ZANLA commander, 242, 243
Gundani, Sgt TV, 116-120, 124, 129, 134, 140, 143, 145, 146, 156, 157, 161
Gwanda, 232

H
Harris, Kinsley, killed by terrorists, 196
Hartley, 224
Harvey, Harry, Major, 60
Hawkins, Roger, Minister of Defence, 95
Headlands, 80, 87, 223
Hill, John, BSAP, 22, 23
Hitch, Bob, 20, 22
Hodgson, Ted, farm attacked, 115
Hogg, Richard, PO, Support Unit, 223, 249
Hogg, Ian, SAC, 222, 240
Home, Sir Alec Douglas, 44
Hove, Eddie, Support Unit, 213, 228
Hozheri, Mike, Const, 140
Hustler, Rusty, Chief Instructor Support Unit, 164
Hwange, 224

I
Internal Settlement, 165
Inyanga, 51, 80

Inyazura, 139

J
Jamieson, Ron, Support Unit, 223, 226, 249
Jeffries, murdered by ZANLA, 153-155
JOC Hurricane, 46
JOC Mtoko, 87
Johnson, Wally, Supt, Support Unit, 237
Jordan, Barbara, police wife, 118
Jordan, Jannie, PO, 117
Joubert, Andries, Wedza farmer murdered, 47-49

K
Kamasukiri, Const, Support Unit, 195
Kandeke, Sgt, Support Unit, murdered by ZANLA, 243, 244
Kariba, 57, 59, 60, 62, 65, 69, 73-78, 208, 222
Katete Anchorage, Kariba, 67, 69, 70
Kaunda, Kenneth, 42, 58, 66, 76
Kinch, Tommy, PATU, 79, 84
Kok, Martinus 'Bushpig', Selous Scout, 60
Krynauw, Danie, PATU, 84
Kwande, Const, KIA, 53, 54, 64

L
Lafferty, Jimmy, Selous Scout, 60
Lamont, Donal, RC Archbishop of Umtali, 144
Lancaster House Conference, 94, 200, 204
Lazarus, CSM, Support Unit, 13, 226
LDF (Macheke Local Defence Force), 124, 125, 127, 131, 143, 145, 146, 155, 157, 159-161
Leask, James, PATU and LDF, 84, 85, 92, 93, 124, 128, 143, 148, 157, 159
Lebish, Roger, C/Insp, BSAP, 160
Lee, Dr Kevin, Govt pathologist, 119
Lemon, Brian Douglas, 16, 71, 116, 135, 141, 195
Lemon, Deborah, 32, 37, 61, 141, 228
Lemon, Graeme, 16, 135, 195, 233, 236, 238, 246
Local Defence Force (see LDF)
Lupane, 244
Luveve Township, 235, 238

M
Macheke, 25, 46, 78, 79, 81, 85, 91, 92, 94, 95, 114-117, 120, 124, 127, 130, 133-138, 140, 141, 147, 156, 157, 159, 160, 216
Macheke Local Defence Force (see LDF)
Machel, Samora, Mozambican president, 75, 219
Mackay, Duncan, S/O, murdered by terrorists, 49, 50
Mackay, Sackie, Supt, 163
Maclaren, Archie, Air Vice Marshall, 77, 95
Madziwa, Nebbie, Station Sergeant, 73, 150
Magwegwe, 238
Mahombekombe Township, Kariba, 74
Majiga, Const, Support Unit, 227, 236
Makanda, Const, Support Unit, 200
Makuti, 209
Mandiwa, Sgt, dies in landmine blast, 195
Mangwende TTL, 50, 51, 80, 81, 88, 91, 95, 130-132, 155, 156
Mangwende, Chief, 82
Manicaland, 79
Marandellas, 24-27, 30-32, 34, 35, 40, 42, 46, 49, 54, 56, 64, 85, 93, 114, 117, 120, 124, 135, 142, 147, 148, 151, 158, 165, 196, 197, 200, 213, 216, 240, 250
Mareve, Sgt, Support Unit, 200, 213, 225, 227
Marondera (was Marandellas), 249-251
Mason, Fred, C/Supt, BSAP, 163, 210
Masvingo (was Fort Victoria), 225
Mataera, Sgt, Support Unit, 213, 240, 249
Matambashora, Const, Support Unit, 200

261

Matusadona National Park, 59, 71
McGuinness, Supt Mac, 61
Merris, Tony, Charlie Company, Support Unit, 163, 166
Mhora, Govati, 31, 150
Mola, Chief, and people, abducted, 65, 66
Molefe, Sgt, Support Unit, 226
Mondoro TTL, 166, 170, 175, 176, 202
Monte Cassino Mission, Macheke, 141-145, 147
Moore, Cpl, KIA, 46
Morris Training Depot, 20, 35, 219
Mostert, Johan, farmer attacked, 115
Mount Bogota, contact at, 127
Mount Darwin, 46
Movement for Democratic Change, 254
Mozambique, 69, 75, 127, 132, 196
Mrewa, 25, 44, 45, 50, 51, 81, 84, 88, 91, 117, 132, 251
Mtoko, 25, 45, 79, 81, 82, 84, 87, 91, 120, 125, 137, 251
Mudakureva, Support Unit, 228
Mudzimurema, Chief, 43
Mugabe, Robert, ZANLA leader to premier, 58, 75, 78, 165, 166, 174, 196, 201, 210, 213, 214, 219, 244, 253

Mujibas, 202, 204, 208
Mukulunyelwa, Mike, Support Unit, 221, 249
Muller, Dr Hildegard, South African Foreign Minister, 83
Mupepe, Sgt, abducted by terrorists, escaped, 65, 66
Mutare (was Umtali), 235
Muzorewa, Abel, Bishop, premier Zimbabwe-Rhodesia, 131, 165, 210, 212-214, 220, 253
Mwenezi (was Nuanetsi), 224
Myerscough, Father Dunstan, massacre survivor, 95
Ncube, Const, Support Unit, 200
Ndhliwayo, Const, murdered by terrorists, 195
Nduna, Sgt, 88, 89, 94
Ngarwe TTL, 51
Nkala, Enos, ZANU-PF, 233
Nkomo, Joshua, ZAPU president, 59, 78, 149, 165, 166, 201, 210, 217, 237, 246, 248, 253
North Korean, instructors trained 5-Brigade, 244
Ntabazinduna, 238
Nyakasoro TTL, 51-56, 55
Nyamapanda, 25, 54-56, 81, 125, 251
Nzou, Const, wounded in action, 195

O
Omayi TTL, 65

Oosthuizen, Leon, Support Unit, 223, 249
Operation Detonate, 66-69, 72, 75
Operation Hurricane, 137
Operation Quartz, 213, 247
Operation Repulse, 75
Operation Tangent, 75
Operation Thrasher, 75, 84, 137
Owen, David, 116

P
Paradise Island, Kariba, 67, 71, 72
Parker, Jack, 37, 40, 46, 52
Patriotic Front, 78, 165
Pattison, John, 40
PATU (Police Anti-terrorist Unit), 38, 46, 51, 84, 90-92, 124, 143, 211
Pearce Commission, 44-46
Peech, Michelea, 87
Peech, Timothy Michael Steele, 87, 88, 91, 124, 125, 127, 131-133, 137, 148
Pephanis, Gerry, farm attacked, 115
Pepukayi, Sgt, 153
Pfumo re Vanhu — Spear of the People, 198, 199
Placidis, Sister i/c Monte Cassino Mission, 142, 144, 145, 147
Platen, Fred, PATU, 84, 92, 93
Police Reserve Air Wing, 66, 205, 208
Police Reserve Air Wing (PRAW), 208
Ponderosa Farm,

Marandellas, 40
PRAW (see Police Reserve Air Wing)
Pym, Det C/Insp Brian, CID, 139, 140, 142, 143

Q, R

Rabie, Andre, shot by own forces, 95
Raminore, Const, wounded in action, 195
RAR (Rhodesian African Rifles), 221, 229, 233
Rayne, Mike, Det Insp, SB, 131, 131
Reid Daly, Major Ron, 60, 61, 203
Rekommetjie Research Station, 205, 208, 209
Rens, Paul, BSAP, 68, 71
Rhodes, Cecil John, 16, 20, 43
Rhodesian Air Force, 60, 151
Rhodesian Defence Regiment, 211
Rhodesian Front party, 29
Rhodesian Light Infantry (see RLI)
Richard, Ivor, British negotiator, 91, 116
Ritson, Detective S/O, 31
Rixon, Duncan, attacked, 115
RLI (Rhodesian Light Infantry), 21, 66, 67, 173, 221
Robart-Morgan, Peter, Macheke farmer, 148
Robertson, Insp Robbie, ZRP, 251
Rose, Mick, Macheke farmer, 148
Ross, Angus, Supt, CID, 48
Rowland, Don, Assist Comm, 166, 171, 222, 249
Royal Visit Farm Macheke, 85, 87, 94, 113, 114

S

SAAF (see South African Air Force), 66, 83
Sachiweshe, ZANLA commander, 196, 198, 203, 216
Sadza Township, Wedza, 212
Salama Farm, Macheke, 87, 124-126, 130, 133, 137-139
Sanyati Gorge, Kariba, 71
SAP (South African Police), 164
SAS (Rhodesian), 68, 69, 71, 127, 139, 213, 221
Saul, Eric, SAC BSAP, 160
Savory, Alan, 130, 151
Schlachter, Sister Jenny, 88-90, 114, 115, 147, 148
Schmidt, Adolf, Catholic Bishop of Bulwayo, murdered, 83
Selous Scouts, 60, 69, 127, 221, 247
Sengwa Basin, Kariba, 67
Shamva, 164
Sibanda, Const, Support Unit, 247
Sibilobilo Lagoon, Kariba, 62
Silobela, 224
Simons, Jack, Special Branch Liaison Officer, 166-169
Sinoia, 79, 83, 207, 208
Sipolilo, 163
Sithole, Constable Ignatius, abducted by terrorists, 65
Sithole, Ndabaningi, ZANU leader, 58, 198
Smith, Ian Douglas, Rhodesian premier, 15, 16, 19, 44, 59, 76, 122, 166, 219, 220, 245, 253
Soames, Lord, S Rhodesia governor, 204
Soswe TTL, 152
South African Air Force (see SAAF)
South African policemen, murdered, 59
South African tourists killed, 75
Spurwing Farm, 176, 194, 197, 198
St Paul's Mission at Musami, missionaries murdered, 95
Stanton, Pete, DSO, SB, 63, 64, 120
Stenner, Ray, Assist Comm, BSAP, 76
Stephens, Dave, murdered by war veterans, 254
Stops Police Camp in Bulawayo, 233, 234
Support Unit, 13, 14, 52, 53, 135, 143, 147, 151, 161-164, 166, 172, 173, 176, 197, 198, 205, 207, 209, 211, 213, 219-222, 226, 228-230, 240, 241, 245, 248, 249

Support Unit Alpha

Company, 163
Support Unit Bravo Company, 207
Support Unit, Charlie Company, 13, 14, 166, 170, 172, 174, 176, 194, 196, 197, 200, 202, 203, 205, 210, 213, 219
Support Unit, Charlie Troop, 221-225, 229, 231, 232, 236, 239, 243, 244, 249
Support Unit, Echo Company, 163
Support Unit, India Company, 163
Support Unit, India Troop, 230
Support Unit, Lima Troop
Sutton Pryce, Lawford, RBC, 91, 96

T
Tamhla, TSO, Support
Tasker, Rob, Squadron Leader, Rhod Air Force, 60
Tegere, Inspector, Support Unit, 249
Tendere, Const, Support Unit, 231
Thatcher, Margaret, British premier, 65, 165, 201, 217
Thorpe, PO Simon, Support Unit, 135, 139, 141
Todd, Judith, 42, 43
Todd, Sir Garfield, 42
Tomlinson AP Depot, 53
Tongogara Camp, 242, 343 Const, Support Unit, 13, 14, 170, 199, 200, 206, 207, 217, 221, 235, 247,
248
Transitional Government, 151
Triangle, 224
Trigg, Supt, 221, 222
Tshabalala Township, 238
Tsvangirai, Morgan, 255

U
UANC, 217
UDI (Unilateral Declaration of Independence), 15, 16, 18, 28

V
Van Aardt family, 85, 86, 96
Van der Byl, PK, Defence Minister PK, 75, 95
Victoria Falls, 59, 232
Virginia, 82, 91, 121, 136, 148, 160, 254
Vorster, John, Prime Minister RSA, 58
Vuti African Purchase Area, 149

W
Wallace, Patrol Officer, 35
Walls, Peter, Lt Gen, 77, 95, 214, 215
Walters, John, murdered by terrorists, 64
Ward, Ken, BSAP, 54
Weare, Raymond, C/Insp,26, 30, 35, 38, 46
Weather Island, Kariba, 67, 69
Wedza, 25, 32, 47, 49, 60, 117, 211, 212, 251
Weya TTL, 85, 91, 137
WFR (Women's Field Reserve), 84, 92, 96, 175, 176
Whistlefield Farm, Centenary, attack on, 46
White, Ant, Selous Scout, 60
Wilson, Harold, British premier, 16, 17, 58, 65, 75
Wiltshire TTL, 176, 195, 197, 201, 203, 205, 210-212, 214-216, 219
Woan, Barry, Support Unit, 210, 246
Women's Field Reserve (see WFR)
Woolworths, Manica Road, Salisbury, terrorist blast at, 123

XYZ
Zambia, 66, 69, 127, 165
ZANLA, 68, 75, 95, 126, 127, 134, 142, 145, 156, 175, 196, 198, 203, 205, 208, 215, 230, 233, 235, 243, 251
ZANU (Zimbabwe African National Union), 76, 123, 217, 235
ZAPU (Zimbabwe African People's Union), 123
Zimbabwe Republic Police (ZRP), 220, 255
Zimbabwe-Rhodesia, 201, 204, 213, 253
ZIPRA (Zimbabwe People's Revolutionary Army), 68, 149, 208, 209, 230, 233, 234, 251
Zwimba TTL, 210